HEREDITARY

HEREDITARY

The Persistence of
Biological Theories
of Crime

JULIEN LARREGUE

Translated by
PETER KEATING

STANFORD UNIVERSITY PRESS
Stanford, California

Stanford University Press
Stanford, California

Hereditary: The Persistence of Biological Theories of Crime was originally published in French in 2020 under the title *Héréditaire: L'éternel retour des théories biologiques du crime* © Éditions du Seuil, 2020.

Printed in the United States of America on acid-free, archival-quality paper

Library of Congress Cataloging-in-Publication Data
Names: Larregue, Julien, author.
Title: Hereditary : the persistence of biological theories of crime / Julien Larregue ; [translated by] Peter Keating.
Other titles: Héréditaire. English
Description: Stanford, California : Stanford University Press, 2024. | Originally published in French under the title: Héréditaire : L'éternel retour des théories biologiques du crime. | Includes bibliographical references and index.
Identifiers: LCCN 2023027953 (print) | LCCN 2023027954 (ebook) | ISBN 9781503636439 (cloth) | ISBN 9781503637764 (paperback) | ISBN 9781503637771 (ebook)
Subjects: LCSH: Criminal behavior—Genetic aspects. | Criminal Behavior—Psychological aspects. | Criminology—Philosophy. | Sociobiology.
Classification: LCC HV6018 .L37 2020 (print) | LCC HV6018 (ebook) | DDC 364—dc23/eng/20230718
LC record available at https://lccn.loc.gov/2023027953
LC ebook record available at https://lccn.loc.gov/2023027954]

Cover design: Daniel Benneworth-Gray
Cover art: Alphonse Bertillon, *Tableau synoptique des traits physionomiques pour servir à l'étude du "portrait parlé"* (ca. 1909), gelatin silver print, Twentieth-Century Photography Fund, 2009, The Metropolitan Museum of Art, New York

CONTENTS

ACKNOWLEDGMENTS

This book owes much to the generosity of friends and colleagues. First, I would like to express my gratitude to my dissertation advisers, Muriel Giacopelli and Sacha Raoult. The time spent in the United States from December 2014 to September 2015 was also of paramount importance. At the University of Chicago, I wish to thank Andrew Abbott, as well as James Evans and the entire Knowledge Lab team, whose weekly seminars have been a valuable source of inspiration and motivation. In California, I thank Jonathan Simon, Johann Koehler, Carroll Seron, and Charis Kubrin for having welcomed me so warmly at the University of California Berkeley and the University of California Irvine.

My research has benefited from the careful reading and thoughtful advice of Andrew Abbott, Warren Azoulay, Jérôme Bourdieu, Gaëlle Chartier, Julie Clarini, Michel Dubois, James Evans, Yves Gingras, Johan Heilbron, Mahdi Khelfaoui, Johann Koehler, Marc Joly, Sylvain Laurens, Séverine Louvel, Laurent Mucchielli, Xavier Pin, Pierrette Poncela, Sacha Raoult, Oliver Rollins, Pierre Roubertoux, Arnaud Saint-Martin, Loïc Wacquant, William Wannyn, and two anonymous reviewers from Stanford University Press.

Although this book originally appeared in French, translations are also occasions to revise, amend, strengthen, and clarify the original text. I would like to thank Peter Keating for his fantastic translation, as well as Camille Lévesque and Leo Gosselin-Mercure for their wonderful assistance in the last effort. This publication would not have been possible without the funding support of Presses de l'Université Laval (PUL), the Faculté des sciences sociales at Université Laval, and the Centre interuniversitaire de recherche sur la science et la technologie (CIRST). I am very grateful to Marcela Cristina Maxfield from Stanford University Press, who enthusiastically supported my project from the outset, as well as to Oliver Rollins, whose generosity simply cannot be overstated.

Finally, I would like to thank the criminologists who spoke with me at length and whose experiences have been an invaluable source of knowledge for this book.

INTRODUCTION
THE REVIVAL OF BIOCRIMINOLOGY

IN SEPTEMBER OF 2009 at the Court of Appeal in Trieste in Northeast Italy, Abdelmalek Bayout, an Algerian citizen who had been living in the country since 1993, went on trial for murder.[1] Two years earlier, in 2007, while in Udine, he had been attacked by a group of young men who made fun of the eye makeup he wore for religious reasons, taunted him with being a homosexual, and eventually knocked him about. To avenge this humiliation, he returned a few hours later and killed one of his assailants with a knife.

In his defense, Bayout's lawyer asked the court to consider her client's mental state at the time of the commission of the crime. The trial judge granted her request and ordered a psychiatric examination of the accused. The three reports submitted to the court convinced the judge that Bayout's mental state did indeed constitute a mitigating factor. The exams had portrayed him as "suffering from a serious psychiatric and psychotic disorder and, in particular, a psychotic delusional disorder accompanied by impulsive-antisocial traits and cognitive-intellectual capacities below normal limits."[2] Nevertheless, the court sentenced Bayout to nine years and two months in prison.

On appeal, during a preparatory hearing held in May of 2009, the appellate judge, Pier Valerio Reinotti, ordered a new psychiatric examination of the convict. Pietro Pietrini, a professor of molecular biology at the University of Pisa, and Giuseppe Sartori, a neuroscientist at the University of Padua, were appointed experts. They conducted a series of tests, including a brain scan and an analysis of genes[3] that had been associated with greater aggressiveness in the scientific literature (*MAOA*, *COMT*, *SCL64*, and *DRD4*). In their report, Pietrini and Sartori stated that they had identified abnormalities in Bayout's brain imaging as well as in several genes. Their report relied on a study published in the prestigious journal *Science* in 2002, which had concluded that there was a correlation between a polymorphism of the *MAOA* gene and the subsequent appearance of antisocial behavior among maltreated children.[4] According to the experts, the accused bore a version of the *MAOA* gene that predisposed its carriers to violence. At the hearing, Pietrini explained that "there is a growing body of scientific evidence that certain genes, when associated with a particular adverse environment, may predispose people to certain behaviors."[5] Pietrini went to emphasize that genes associated with violence produce their deleterious effects only when the individual's environment is also unfavorable. In other words, the occurrence of antisocial behavior, although linked to the biology of individuals, was not inevitable but statistically probable. On September 18, 2009, the Court of Appeal of Trieste upheld Bayout's conviction for murder. On the basis of the experts' reports and the genetic anomaly attributed to the accused, however, the sentence was reduced by one year.

The Trieste case is not an isolated event. It must be understood in a more global context in which crime is biologized, both within the legal sphere and in scientific research. Since the 1950s, the number of scientific publications on the biological factors of crime has grown steadily in criminology, psychology, and behavior genetics. While this revival of the biological conceptualizations of crime has its roots in the second half of the twentieth century, the 2000s have seen the emergence of an unending stream of research devoted to the study of the interactions between biological and environmental factors in the development of criminal behavior. Generally referred to as biosocial criminology, this branch of criminology "incorporates the effects of genetics, physiological and neurological factors, as well as influences of society and family in the causes of antisocial behavior"[6] (box 1). Since 2000, dozens of articles in biosocial criminology have been published on the influence that genes, alleles, hormones, heart rate, or neurons might have on deviant conduct. The development of this research movement is such that the historian and criminologist Nicole Rafter has written that "biosociality is likely to become the leading model in 21st-century criminology."[7]

As the Bayout trial shows, biosocial criminology has gone beyond the borders of science. Since the 1990s, criminal courts have increasingly resorted to a range of expert assessments based on behavior genetics and neuroscience, the primary aim of which has been to evaluate the criminological dangerousness of offenders in order to assess their chances of reoffending. The importance of this movement is demonstrated by the fact that legal scholars have created a new area of law, sometimes referred to as "neurolaw," to govern the use of genetic and neurological evidence in criminal proceedings.[9] While mainly confined to English-speaking countries, particularly the United States[10] and the United Kingdom,[11] other legal systems have begun to follow this trend as well: Italy,[12] Canada,[13] the Netherlands,[14] and France,[15] which was the first country in the world to pass a bioethics law on this issue.[16] Contrary to what one might think, the use of biosocial criminology in courtrooms has not just been initiated by repressive judges. In the United States, defense lawyers have been very actively resorting to neuroscientific and behavior genetic expertise in an attempt to reduce their clients' criminal responsibility and to avoid the death penalty.[17] The results are staggering: in a single decade (2005–15), more than 2,800 judicial opinions discussed neuroscientific evidence in the context of U.S. criminal justice cases.[18]

Whether repressive or humanistic, the use, actual or potential, of this type of legal expertise raises several questions insofar as biosocial criminology is a recent, still uncertain undertaking. As we shall see, research in this field remains subjected to intense controversies within the scientific community. By examining the historical formation of

BOX 1. THE FIVE BRANCHES OF BIOSOCIAL CRIMINOLOGY

Quantitative genetics: Quantitative genetics studies the influence of genetic and environmental factors on human behavior. It includes twin and adoption studies. Research in this area estimates the relative importance of these two factors without, however, identifying the specific genes or environmental conditions involved in the phenomenon under study.

Molecular genetics: Molecular genetics identifies specific genes that are correlated with given behaviors. For example, much research has been carried out on the influence of the *MAOA* gene mentioned in the Bayout case, including the classic study by Avshalom Caspi and colleagues.[8] Other genes that have been associated with criminal behavior in biosocial research include *DRD2* and *DRD4*, *DAT1*, and *5HTT*. The idea of biosocial criminologists is not to identify the "crime gene" per se but to identify risk factors that increase the chances of developing antisocial behavior. These different genes are sometimes grouped together to create a genetic risk index.

Neurocriminology: Neurocriminology aims to identify the neuropsychological factors that favor delinquency. Researchers have examined the correlation between criminal behavior and prenatal and perinatal risk factors such as a mother's smoking habits, the relationship between the frontal cortex and the caudate nucleus, and the mechanism of self-control.

Biological criminology: Biological criminology is concerned with the role of human physiology in the development of criminal behavior. This branch of research has focused on three main themes: hormones and pubertal development, heart rate rhythms, and blood lead levels.

Evolutionary psychology: Evolutionary psychology applies the Darwinian principle of natural selection to criminal behavior. By tracing human evolution, it seeks to understand the ultimate causes of criminal behavior and answer the more fundamental question of "why."

this criminological specialty and providing a sociological analysis of its scientific results, this book is aimed at providing a critical, reflexive understanding of the stakes at play, both within and beyond the scientific field's boundaries. How does one proceed to investigate the biological factors of crime? What led to this steady revival of biocriminology, after decades of symbolic discredit? And perhaps more importantly, what credibility can biosocial criminologists justly claim in the face of criticism and skepticism?

Addressing these questions is especially imperative at a time when we are increasingly exposed to a biological culture that purports to discriminate between normal and pathological personhoods.[19] Hence, the news of Judge Reinotti's decision in the Bayout case spread quickly around the world, a fact that can surely be better explained by its sensational appeal and alignment with the bio(ideo)logical framework than by the institutional prestige of the Trieste Court of Appeal. In France, the left-leaning *Libération* dramatically announced, "An Italian judge discovers the gene for murder";[20] in Great Britain, *The Times* compared the *MAOA* gene to a "get out of jail free gene";[21] opting for a somewhat more sober formulation, the *Chicago Tribune* simply ran the headline "Exploring links between genes, violence, environment."[22]

It would be presumptuous, however, to assume that the potential uses of biosocial criminology are strictly limited to the field of criminal justice. In the mid-2000s, an expert group put together by the French National Institute for Health and Medical Research (INSERM) vaunted the reliability of the biosocial approach for the prevention and "treatment" of antisocial behaviors among children and adolescents.[23] The publication of the ensuing report gave rise to an intense public controversy.[24] An online petition denounced their intervention as an "attempt to instrumentalize care practices in the field of child psychiatry for the purposes of security and public order,"[25] while others wondered if scientists promoting genetic screening ran the risk of turning into "police auxiliaries."[26] Aside from the controversies it generated, the INSERM report is also interesting insofar as the proposed prevention program implicated educational personnel and not simply legal institutions. In fact, one of the main recommendations of the expert group was "to improve the current experiments in the prevention of aggressive, antisocial, and delinquent behavior developed in France by adding prevention methods that have been validated at the international level. Following pilot experiments, it [the group of experts] recommends generalizing interventions within existing educational structures (PMI [mother and infant protection], day care centers, schools . . .) by training educational personnel in these prevention methods (nursery nurses, educators, teachers . . .)."[27]

The renewed interest in the biological dimension of delinquent behaviors thus follows a more global movement where numerous social problems are redefined as individual pathologies falling within the purview of a broadly conceived biomedical expertise (cognitive psychology, behavioral genetics, neuroscience, etc.).[28] This means that analyzing the development of biosocial criminology entails much more than the single question of delinquency and its management by the criminal justice system. It engages the restructuring of expertise in contemporary societies and the territorial struggles that different professions have engaged in for the monopoly of diagnosis, handling, and treatment of personal problems.[29] Indeed, the emergence of biosocial criminology interrogates the division of labor between law and medicine (especially psychiatry) for the control of at-risk populations, an issue that has existed since the nineteenth century.[30] As in many professional struggles, scientists, because of their ability to establish on-the-ground realities, that is to impose their own definition (sociological, psychological, biological, etc.) of the nature of a given problem, play a predominant role in this process. For if, as biosocial criminologists suggest, crime is a biological as well as a social problem, then it might demand medical as well as legal solutions, thus putting legal practitioners at risk of losing all or some of their clientele to the health sector.[31]

BIOCRIMINOLOGY AND THE EARLY HISTORY OF SOCIOLOGY

Historical precedents might provide some perspective and clues on the issues at stake, for the temptation to see crime as a biological deficiency is hardly new. In the nineteenth century, when contemporary criminology was just in its first years of existence, the Italian physician and anthropologist Cesare Lombroso developed an approach that tainted the future history of his discipline: according to his theory of the "born criminal," criminals were biologically inferior beings akin to the "colored man."[32] In a context deeply structured by racial hierarchies, colonization, and the domination of the North over the South (not only in Italy, but also more broadly at the international level), and inspired by the theory of evolution that Darwin had just formulated,[33] Lombroso was convinced that criminals, like "savages," exhibited atavistic traits.[34] Criminals could thus be placed on an evolutionary scale[35] that ran from the "savage" or the "man of color" at the bottom, closer to a white child, a backward adult, or even an ape,[36] to the criminal, whose traits were reminiscent of those of inferior species, and finally on to the white man, who functioned as a normative reference and model throughout the demonstration. Lombroso also believed that criminals bore the physical traces of this atavism and that they could be identified by various physiognomic and bodily stigmas (shape of the skull, length of the limbs, facial features, etc.).

The skull that supposedly inspired this criminological theory, that of the Calabrian, dark-skinned "brigand" Villella, had already been subjected to inquiry in Lombroso's racist treatise *L'uomo bianco e l'uomo di colore*. In a comprehensive sociogenetic investigation, historian Renzo Villa has demonstrated that Lombroso's descriptions of Villella and his skull had actually changed over time, which would indicate that his so-called revelation was more a myth than an actual scientific breakthrough.[37] The focus on Villella, however, was not a mere coincidence. Born in Verona in northern Italy, Lombroso probably "deemed Villella racially inferior (and hence criminalistic) partly because he came from southern Italy."[38] Lombroso kept this skull on his desk throughout his career, making it a "'totem' of his new school of criminal anthropology."[39] The racist dimension of this symbol remains a cause for concern. In 2009, the opening of a museum dedicated to Lombroso in Turin gave rise to a wave of protests and a demand for the removal of Villella's skull by Neo-Bourbon associations.[40]

Although it was quickly refuted on a scientific level,[41] the Lombrosian theory acted as an intellectual facilitator for Italian fascism from the 1920s onwards.[42] To be clear, the promotion of Lombroso and his work began before Mussolini came to power on October 29, 1921. A statue in his honor had, for instance, already been erected in Verona, his birthplace, on September 25, 1921.[43] The ceremony was then attended by representatives of the entire political spectrum: socialists, Christian democrats, liberals, and fascists.[44] Nonetheless, Lombroso's theses gained even greater influence in the Mussolini era, particularly through the new generation of criminologists—Enrico Ferri, Raffaele Garofalo, Alfredo Niceforo, Salvatore Ottolenghi, and Scipio Sighele—many of whom would join the Fascist party.[45]

In Germany, the influence of the Italian criminologist began to be felt during the Weimar Republic (1919–33). His theory of the born criminal became the principal source of inspiration for German criminology at the time.[46] But the Nazi regime took the Lombrosian ideas of social defense and the exclusion of incorrigibles to a new extreme. The Nazis used Lombroso's theories to present political opponents as criminals with physical stigmas,[47] and biocriminology provided scientific support for the confinement and extermination of groups as diverse as Jews, prostitutes, homosexuals, alcoholics, Jehovah's Witnesses, and the indolent.[48] In sum, "criminal anthropology nourished Nazi biocriminology and was in turn amplified by it and carried to its own worst possible conclusions."[49] The scientific racism of the Italian doctor fit perfectly into the program of biological purification pursued under the Third Reich.[50]

On the other side of the Atlantic, the biocriminological program initiated by Lombroso also gained some traction.[51] The key writings of the Italian positivist school were translated into English and published by the Bostonian Little, Brown and Company in the 1910s (Lombroso in 1911, Garofalo in 1914, and Ferri in 1917). At the time, key figures of the social sciences seemed to be attracted by the eugenics movement and social Darwinism.[52] Hence, as late as 1921, celebrated Chicago sociologists Robert E. Park and Ernest Burgess were reprinting an article by Francis Galton ("Eugenics as a Science of Progress") in what can certainly be regarded as the "first highly visible textbook of American sociology,"[53] *Introduction to the Science of Sociology*. Although Galton's ideas about nature and culture are not explicitly referred to anymore, we will see that they keep exerting a strong influence on the way some social scientists try to decipher the respective impact of genetic and environmental factors on human behaviors.[54]

It is unquestionably the case that when it came to the study of crime, social scientists offered a credible scientific alternative to Lombroso's theories by developing a sociological approach based on the careful collection of empirical data. As early as 1900, following in the footsteps of the method that his mentor W. E. B. Du Bois had put into practice (notably in *The Philadelphia Negro*),[55] Monroe N. Work published an article in the *American Journal of Sociology* in which he attributed African Americans' "excess of crime" in Chicago to the transition in economic state that this group was undergoing.[56] Deploying a strictly sociographic approach, Work not only made no mention whatsoever of Lombroso's ideas or biological factors but also put into doubt Frederick L. Hoffman's atavistic-like argument that African American crime could be attributed to this racial group's "retrograding."[57]

Edwin H. Sutherland, a sociologist trained at the University of Chicago, would be the one dealing the final blow to biocriminology. By the early 1920s, he had established a scientific program that would "set the tone"[58] for decades to come in the study of crime, namely the three-part study of the production of norms, the transgression of norms, and the reaction to the transgression of norms.[59] While imposing this newly defined scientific program, Sutherland also fiercely attacked what he perceived as the last vestiges of the Lombrosian paradigm, including the multifactorial approach to crime developed by the Harvard criminologists Sheldon and Eleanor Glueck.[60]

WHAT DO WE KNOW ABOUT THE REVIVAL OF BIOCRIMINOLOGY?

Past forms of the biocriminological tradition—those that pre-
date the biosocial criminology of the 1960s based on genetics and
neuroscience—have been the subject of thorough sociohistorical analyses.[61] Although such investigations constitute an excellent starting
point, the conclusions that specialists of early biocriminology arrived
at cannot be easily transferred to more recent developments in biosocial criminology. Indeed, this literature contains little or no discussion
of the contemporary biosocial criminology movement, and the few
historians who have compared past and present forms of biocriminology have consistently identified important differences between them.[62]
Put differently, it cannot be assumed that biosocial criminology is little
more than an attempt to update Lombroso's work by replacing the Italian criminologist's crude anthropometric measures with state-of-the-
art genetic and neuroscientific technologies. The relationship between
"old" and "new" biological investigations of crime is more complex and
ambiguous than simple comparisons might suggest.[63]

Part of this uncertainty lies in the fact that a good deal of contemporary research on the biology of criminal behaviors is conducted
outside of criminology, by people who sometimes do not even claim
to study crime per se. Thus, in *Conviction*, Oliver Rollins offers a rich
and thought-provoking analysis on the way the brain is constructed
in certain scientific programs as "violent." Yet most of these neuroscientists and psychologists "do not have criminological training or see
themselves first as researchers of crime."[64] Their situation is thus quite
different from that of biosocial criminologists, who, on their part, are
predominantly active in what I shall call the criminological field. To
be sure, some contacts do exist between neuroscientists and criminologists, but these remain secondary and do not seem to reshape the
broader social dynamics that we can observe on both sides.

If we try to restrict the scope of analysis by directing our attention
to criminologists, it appears that contemporary biocriminology has to
date been studied along three main lines. A first approach takes biosocial criminology as a new stage in the long history of biological theories

of crime, highlighting contrasts and affinities, breaks, and continuities. A second approach, which draws primarily on the sociology of science, has focused on some of the more high-profile research generally associated with biosocial criminology. The third approach is less thematically oriented and more centered on issues of biologization: it interprets the revival of biocriminology as just one example among many of the tendency to think of human behavior in biological terms.

The work conducted by the historian of criminology Nicole Rafter, notably in *The Criminal Brain*, constitutes a point of reference for the first approach.[65] The aim of her book is to trace the history of biocriminology, from psychiatry and phrenology in the eighteenth century to the most recent developments based on the methods and data of genetics and neuroscience, via Lombroso's anthropometry and other now-discredited research on the physical constitution of criminals. Rafter's book has the merit of addressing the factors that may have allowed the biocriminological tradition to reemerge in the second half of the twentieth century. As she explains, the study of crime as a biological phenomenon was long discredited by criminologists, who preferred to focus on social and nonindividual factors. Thus sociology dominated the study of crime in the United States throughout the second half of the twentieth century. How then should we interpret the return of the biocriminological tradition? According to Rafter,

Two factors in the late 20th-century social context were particularly important in this change of direction: the emergence of a culture pervaded by assumptions about the biological roots of human behavior, on the one hand, and, on the other, a burgeoning interest in the prevention of harms of all types, from cancer to terrorism to criminality. These two factors—a profound cultural involvement with and investment in human biology, including massive funding for genetics research, and an equally profound determination to prevent harms and minimize risks—have persisted into the 21st century and promise to drive the development of biocriminology for decades to come.[66]

In contrast to this *longue durée* perspective, a second approach grounded in science and technology studies has studied biosocial criminology by selectively focusing on a few prominent works. Borrowing the ideas of actor-network theory developed by Bruno Latour, Michel Callon, and John Law, Canadian criminologist Martin Dufresne has analyzed the development of contemporary biocriminology as a "translation" operation: that is, as a social process through which a scientific proposal is progressively elaborated and solidified.[67] From this perspective, the primary objective is not to analyze the validity of biosocial criminology's scientific results but to understand "'science in action' as a process that evolves from controversy to general acceptance (black boxing), where propositions are presented, agreed upon, contested, carried on, or simply discarded."[68] As a case study, Dufresne chose a central article published in 2002 in the prestigious journal *Science*, which was also used by the Italian experts as an anchor point in the Bayout case.[69]

A final approach takes a more global perspective, situating the revival of biocriminology in a social context where human actions have been increasingly depicted in biological terms as the disciplines of genetics and neuroscience were developing.[70] Far from being exceptions or anomalies, biological studies of violence and crime are just one example of the increasing role assigned to naturalistic frameworks in Western societies, particularly since the launch of the Human Genome Project at the turn of the 1990s, a period that also happened to be the "decade of the brain."[71] In the United States, for instance, a country where racialized structures and inequalities remain deeply entrenched, sociologist Troy Duster has unpacked the intimate relationship connecting the genetic study of violence and the social reproduction of inequalities between racial groups, with science coming to legitimize policing and legal discrimination against African Americans.[72]

Another example is the growing importance of biology in mainstream culture, which has been particularly well documented by Dorothy Nelkin and Susan Lindee in their now-classic *The DNA Mystique*. In this book, the two authors trace the reception of genetic knowledge in popular culture, showing how DNA has acquired a "cultural meaning independent of its precise biological properties."[73] Not just a sequence of deoxyribonucleic acid, DNA has become a signifier that is capable of accounting for a person's behavior but also, more curiously, for the character and distinctiveness of nonhuman entities. A company, a football club, or a radio station can now refer to their DNA without raising eyebrows. This appropriation is particularly visible when it comes to the topic of crime, where a wide range of cultural productions (advertisements, novels, TV shows, films, etc.) have been propagating the idea that the criminal is biologically distinctive from the well-behaved, average citizen.

BRINGING THE SCIENTIFIC FIELD BACK INTO FOCUS

Although undeniably enlightening, these complementary takes on the contemporary manifestations of the far-from-new idea that crime is somehow linked to biology do not fully explain the revival of biocriminology in the second half of the twentieth century. Thus, while the micro-level approach adopted by Dufresne[74] allows him to propose an in-depth analysis of a major publication in contemporary biocriminology, this strength also constitutes the greatest weakness of his study, for we learn very little about the social profile of biosocial criminologists and their position within the scientific field. Furthermore, it is hard to discern whether the research dissected by Dufresne is representative of biosocial criminology in general. At no point do the authors of the article claim to be doing "biosocial criminology." In fact, the term *biosocial* does not appear once in their publication.[75] The fact that they did not contribute to a collective textbook on biosocial criminology only adds uncertainty regarding their centrality within this movement.[76] Put differently, Dufresne's work tends to ignore the heterogeneity that lies behind the all-encompassing term *biosocial criminology*, a weakness that is not uncommon in actor-network approaches.[77]

Similarly, Rafter's historical analysis focuses primarily on the content and epistemology of biocriminological research.[78] However, very little is learned about the surrounding institutional context. It resembles more a history of criminological ideas than a history of biosocial criminology as a social movement. Rafter does address several scientific disciplines in her analysis, but without really paying attention to their structural and cultural specificities. One immediate consequence of this lack of attention manifests itself in the explanation that Rafter proposes for the revival of the biocriminological tradition. According to her, two main factors are at play in this process: the biologization of human actions on the one hand, and the development of a culture of control on the other. Although it is certainly possible that these factors played a role in the emergence of biosocial criminology, they do not constitute a sufficient explanation, as they disregard the autonomy and singularity—however relative—of the scientific field. Indeed, biosocial criminologists would have had to have drawn on structural resources to put their research program into practice, to obtain funding, to train doctoral students, and so on. Rafter does not address these questions, which is obviously problematic when we know from decades of empirical research that "the birth and development of science depend closely on particular institutional configurations."[79]

Rather than focusing solely on the specific situation of a few individuals and publications, however notable they might be, this book shifts the focus to the institutional and configurational factors that can at once account for the sociohistorical development of biosocial criminology, its organization and internal dynamics, the nature of its scientific program, and the type of controversies that this program gave rise to. We will see, for example, that it is no coincidence that it was not until the mid-2000s that the movement consolidated and was able to reproduce itself via the training of a new generation of criminologists. Nor is the precedence given to genetics over neuroscience in biosocial criminology articles the product of an accident. Pierre Bourdieu's theorization of scientific activities[80] offers various conceptual and methodological tools that are particularly well suited to the examination of the sociogenesis and transformation of disciplines and research programs across time. The concept of field, in particular, makes it possible to empirically grasp what may be defined as a network, or a configuration, of objective relations between positions. These positions are objectively defined, in their existence and in the determinations they impose upon their occupants, agents or institutions, by their present and potential situation (situs) in the structure of the distribution of species of power (or capital) whose possession commands access to the specific profits that are at stake in the field, as well as by their objective relation to other positions (domination, subordination, homology, etc.).[81]

What can field theory bring to the sociological study of science? For one thing, paying attention to the structure of the scientific field makes it possible "to grasp the work of a researcher or a laboratory as the product of a particular position within a space with its own logic,"[82] which is precisely what Dufresne and Rafter failed to do in their analyses of the revival of the biocriminological tradition. It is in this regard crucial to take into account that the scientific field itself is subdivided into relatively autonomous spaces. Despite the constant calls for interdisciplinarity, disciplines remain the fundamental organizational structures for the conduct of scientific activities.[83]

Another merit of the concept of field is to draw attention to the hierarchical and unequal dynamics that take place in science. This influences not only the production of scientific knowledge but also the distribution of scientific rewards and merit among researchers.[84] Importantly, academics who have less symbolic capital might try to "articulate an alternative view of the field and their position within it."[85] In short, they could attempt to subvert the rules of the game and thus hierarchies of their field. One way dominated scholars can achieve this is through the guise of scientific controversies, which, from their first appearance to their stabilization, are "opportunities for social actors to question certain power relationships and certain beliefs that have been instilled up to now, to redistribute 'magnitudes' and positions of power among themselves, and to invent new organizational and technical devices that are called upon to constrain their future relations differently."[86]

Finally, it is important to emphasize that social hierarchies are the product of historical struggles and have no absolute value. Since fields cannot be something else than relational spaces, the value of different types of capital—cultural, social, economic, and symbolic—might vary greatly not only across time but also from one subspace of the scientific field to another. As Bourdieu put it, "One person's pedigree can become another's mark of infamy, one's coat of arms another's insult, and vice versa."[87] This has immediate methodological consequences, for it is impossible to determine a priori a given field's social hierarchies. Only empirical analysis can show that historians dominate sociologists in the field of science studies,[88] or that in behavior genetics it is more valued to work on humans than on animals.[89]

THE FIELD OF CRIMINOLOGY IN THE UNITED STATES

The criminological field can be defined as the relatively autonomous subspace of the scientific field that takes the study of crime and penal institutions as the primary object of its research. The historically evolving boundaries of the criminological field are determined by what Neil Fligstein and Doug McAdam call "internal governance units," that is, those institutions that "are charged with overseeing compliance with field rules and, in general, facilitating the smooth functioning and reproduction of the system."[90] The primary internal governance unit of the U.S. criminological field is the American Society of Criminology, an academic association with approximately four thousand members. Other important governance units of the criminological field are the departments of criminology and sociology, which are responsible for the training of criminologists, and criminology scientific journals, which are responsible for the control and dissemination of knowledge about crime.

The mention of sociology departments might seem surprising. After all, sociology itself can be defined as an autonomous disciplinary field. Why, then, make it a part of the criminological field if the latter is indeed autonomous? As we shall see, criminology has long been thought of as a specialty of sociology, and this discipline remains fundamentally important in the study of crime. This means that the autonomy of the American criminological field, although increasingly asserted, is relative and limited since it still depends on the internal governance units of a neighboring field, namely sociology.

Biosocial criminology has thus developed within this relatively autonomous field of American criminology. Biosocial criminology is not itself a field, however, at least not in the sociological sense of the term. Indeed, if one leaves aside the Biosocial Criminology Association, which was founded in 2014, there are no institutions of biosocial criminology that act as "legitimacy-giving authorities"[91] and that have acquired an autonomy—even a relative one—with respect to neighboring disciplines. We should therefore speak of biosocial criminology as a specialty within the field of criminology or, better still, as a scientific movement[92] whose members, who belong to adjacent disciplines (sociology, criminology, psychology, or behavior genetics), act primarily within the field of criminology. This makes it comparable to other neighboring movements, including neurocriminology.[93] Far from stopping at the borders of the scientific field, the biosocial criminology movement has also found outlets in other professional areas such as law, as illustrated by the Bayout case.

The empirical material that was necessary to understand the revival of biocriminology has been drawn from various sources. In addition to documentary and oral publications and archives on the history of criminology in the United States, I have compiled a corpus of 188 biosocial criminology articles published in peer-reviewed journals.[94] These articles were subjected to a variety of qualitative and quantitative analyses. Biographical data on the authors of these 188 biosocial criminology articles were also collected, which made it possible to situate these researchers within the scientific field in general and the criminological field in particular. Finally, the analyses presented in this book are based on twenty-two semistructured interviews with biosocial criminologists and their critics.

Intervening in heated controversies "as a sociologist carries the temptation of claiming for oneself the role of the neutral arbiter, of the judge, to distribute rights and wrongs."[95] This temptation is even greater when sociology's scientific authority is directly at stake. As we shall see, some biosocial criminologists hurl some harsh words at sociology, presenting it as a pseudoscience whose main goal is not to produce knowledge about the world but to promote and impose progressive ideologies. Subscribing to the methodological principle of impartiality that is fundamental to the study of any controversy[96] constitutes, in my view, the best way to demonstrate sociology's rigor and raison d'être, even when its contributions and, possibly, its existence as a legitimate scientific activity are under threat.

As a result, the purpose of this book is not to "criticize" biosocial criminology in the traditional sense, nor to comment on the quality of the research that has emerged from it. Nor is it to separate the "true" from the "false," to settle past or ongoing controversies, or to propose an alternative conception of biosocial criminology. Instead, critiques will be treated as an integral part of the scientific corpus to be studied, since the opposition to biosocial criminology calls for the same kind of sociological explanation used to understand the historical development of this movement.

Another clarification is needed before presenting the layout of the book. Readers should not expect to find a comprehensive review or summary of the literature on the biological factors of crime. The book's primary focus on the U.S. criminological field largely excludes research produced and disseminated outside of criminology journals, associations, and departments, as it falls outside the scope of this study. Yet while this book is primarily concerned with the field of criminology, it does not completely ignore what might have happened outside of it. For example, biosocial criminologists have greatly benefited from the development of behavior genetics, which has led to the appropriation of data and methods from this proximate field. This phenomenon must be addressed if we are to understand the revival of biocriminology.

Now that the methodological and conceptual framework has been clarified, a few words about the national focus of this book must be offered. In a context of internationalization of scientific research,[97] restricting this study to the American scientific field as if it were isolated from the rest of the world might seem problematic. Indeed, several

THE REVIVAL OF BIOCRIMINOLOGY 19

factors relativize "the influence of national borders on the dynamics of the scientific field:"[98] the circulation of researchers, the internationalization of funding sources, linguistic homogenization, and so on. Yet the dynamics of the scientific field still frequently intersect, at least partly, with geographical borders,[99] if only because of the national differences that exist between knowledge production systems. The importance of national specificities and local power struggles explains why many historians and sociologists of science still investigate national objects. The decision to focus on a particular geographical area finds even greater justification in the case of criminology. Like economics,[100] criminology takes on strikingly different forms from one country to another. In fact, the singularities of the U.S. criminological field might explain why the revival of biocriminology is observed almost only in this country.

ORGANIZATION OF THE BOOK

Chapter 1 analyzes the genesis of the American criminological field beginning in the 1940s. The creation of the American Society of Criminology (ASC) in 1941 at the initiative of police officers, followed a decade later by the opening of a school of criminology on the campus of the prestigious University of California Berkeley, constituted important steps for the autonomization of criminology vis-à-vis sociology. Nevertheless, the internal governance units regulating this field were quickly taken over and controlled by sociologists, thus further extending sociology's domination over the study of crime. The police professionals who had been at the origin of the creation of the ASC were removed from its main committees, which led to the creation of a new organization in 1971, the Academy of Criminal Justice Sciences. The Academy, however, suffered the same fate as the ASC: academics took over and gave it a scientific rather than a practical vocation.

Chapter 2 begins in the 1960s, a period that marked the return of biological theories of crime. Within the American criminological field, this return took two main forms. The first, which was compatible with sociological theories of crime, was developed primarily by sociologist

Marvin Wolfgang. Wolfgang's idea was to use biological data to improve culturalist theories of crime. The second approach, much more subversive of sociological domination, was developed by a former student of Sutherland, Clarence Jeffery. The first to speak of a "biosocial criminology," Jeffery mustered knowledge developed in behavior genetics to question the relevance of sociological theories of crime. Although Wolfgang and Jeffery succeeded in training a few doctoral students, their dependence on geneticists, particularly for data access, prevented them from developing their movement further. Above all, the domination of sociologists within criminological organizations was such that biosocial criminology became structurally suffocated and had difficulty reproducing itself. The newly created autonomous departments of criminology were few and insufficient to tip the balance in favor of biosocial criminology. This situation persisted until the end of the 1990s. Throughout this period, biological knowledge on crime was mainly produced by psychologists and behavior geneticists who were not very active in the criminological field.

Chapter 3 focuses on the factors that have enabled biosocial criminology to achieve its contemporary revival. The 2000s marked a turning point in several respects. Within the field of criminology, autonomous criminology departments multiplied over the years, resulting in a cohort of PhDs in criminology who needed to establish their legitimacy vis-à-vis other social scientists. Although it persists, the domination of sociologists eroded as autonomous criminology was expanding. The development of biosocial criminology thus parallels the emancipation of criminology from the sociological field. Beyond the field of criminology, the development of genetics, marked by the completion of the Human Genome Project in the early 2000s, fostered easier access to genetic data and methods.

Chapter 4 discusses the heterogeneity of the biosocial line of work and the division of labor between different subcommunities. Biosocial criminology is generally identified with a small group of criminology graduates who seek to subvert the domination of sociology in the field. Two other groups can be added to this main group. First, we find psychologists who come from the field of behavior genetics and who share with criminologists an idea of what biosocial criminology should be. But there is also a group of sociologists, more prominent than the psychologists in the criminological field, who see genetics as a means to refine sociological theories of crime. These groups have led to different conceptualizations of the respective roles of genetic and environmental factors. While criminologists and psychologists emphasize genetics to challenge the relevance of sociology, sociologists prefer to emphasize the influence of environmental factors on gene expression.

The purpose of chapter 5 is to show that these different orientations have had the effect of resurrecting the nature-culture debate within a movement that claims to go past it. This was made apparent in a scientific controversy displayed in *Criminology*, the leading journal of the American criminological field. Beyond differences of opinion with regard to the relevance of behavior genetic methods, this controversy clearly betrayed the various scientific and academic interests of the participants. The controversy was primarily devoted to questioning the appropriateness of the research methods employed by criminology graduates, and the reliability of twin studies in particular. Twin studies use samples of homozygotic and dizygotic twins to quantify the respective share of genetic and environmental factors in the explanation of various human behaviors (intelligence, drug use, violence, etc.). Discussion of the validity of these results, which often point to the heritable character of criminal behavior, raised the question of the continuation or subversion of sociologists' domination within the criminological field.

Chapter 6 examines the strategies deployed by subversive biosocial criminologists. One might think that they would seek to quell controversy and convince fellow criminologists of the quality of their work. Instead, biosocial criminologists have adopted a combative and polemical attitude, which has allowed them to gain considerable visibility within the criminological field. Rather than explaining how genetics could help improve sociological theories, biosocial criminologists have attacked sociology as pseudoscientific and ideological. In addition to these criticisms of sociology, they have done everything possible to appear heretical according to the dominant criteria of legitimacy. Not only do some scholars present themselves as conservative criminologists in a social universe dominated by progressives, but they have also exhumed a classic but widely mocked figure of nineteenth-century biocriminology, the Italian anthropologist Cesare Lombroso. The sociologists who dominate the criminological field have remained largely silent in the face of these provocations, which may be explained by their position of power and the confidence they display in their explanations of criminal phenomena.

Chapter 7 addresses the feasibility and credibility of the biosocial research agenda, specifically the constraints involved in accessing data and methods from genetics and neuroscience. Unlike Jeffery and Wolfgang, biosocial criminologists in the 2000s can now generate biological knowledge about crime using databases developed in other fields. The advantages of mobilizing genetic knowledge explain their heavy investment in this branch of biosocial criminology, particularly at the expense of neuroscience, which requires the use of expensive brain imaging technologies. Biosocial criminologists cannot just practice any type of behavior genetics, however. Genome-wide association studies remain inaccessible to them, so they are forced to resort to methods that are gradually being abandoned by geneticists because of their lack of reliability, namely candidate gene studies.

The Conclusion offers a reflection on the development and diffusion of the biosocial lingua franca in contemporary societies. Not only are the social effects of biosocial criminology already noticeable, especially in the legal context, but the social imaginary advanced by some of its main proponents promotes public policies that would give pride of place to medical, preventive solutions for criminality. This social imaginary, which is not strictly limited to the issue of crime, is to a large extent based on neuroscience: the brain has become a privileged site of action for the resolution of a wide range of social problems (such as school failure, delinquency, and drug use).

1 THE BIRTH AND SOCIOLOGICAL DOMINATION OF CRIMINOLOGY IN THE UNITED STATES

SCIENTIFIC FIELDS ARE GROUNDED ON a shared set of more or less explicit norms and values that allow their members to practice science without having to continually question the very foundations of their enterprise. Whether these rules concern the type of data used, the favored methods, the preferred concepts, or the theories deployed, together they grease the wheels of scientific creation, facilitate exchanges among peers, and organize the distribution of the symbolic capital of recognition. This set of rules, and the social sanctions without which they would be rendered ineffective, are simultaneously defined and imposed by the institutions that produce and disseminate scientific knowledge: academic associations, research prizes and awards, the university system, and scientific journals.

It follows that these institutions play a leading role in the struggle for the control of a given scientific field. As the sociologists Scott Frickel and Neil Gross have pointed out, the success of a scientific movement largely depends on its ability to mobilize institutional resources.[1] Conversely, the scarcity of resources helps to explain why some scientific movements take time to consolidate, even though the scientific knowledge needed to sustain the movement is available from the outset.[2] In this regard, Frickel and Gross have isolated three factors that determine the success or failure of a scientific movement. First, the members of a movement must have access to employment in the academic and scientific world. Second, success predominantly relies on the intellectual prestige of members. Finally, the organizational resources that members can mobilize—associations, research networks, journals, and so on—are decisive.[3]

As we shall see, the importance of institutional factors was readily apparent in the fate of the first generation of biosocial criminologists (1960s–1990s). Although this innovative current of thought saw itself as an alternative to mainstream criminology, sociologists' scientific and academic domination stifled the criticisms voiced by this heterodox branch of criminology. The structure of the American criminological field supported this marginalization well into the end of the twentieth century.

THE DEVELOPMENT OF A RELATIVELY INDEPENDENT FIELD OF CRIMINOLOGY

Several disciplines contributed to the production and transmission of knowledge about crime in the United States. From Earnest A. Hooton's biology to Gary Becker's economic models and Edwin H. Sutherland's sociology, criminology has been nourished by a variety of methods and theses. Prior to the development of independent criminological structures, the organization of the study of crime was left to the discretion of each disciplinary community. There was, in other words, no such thing as a criminological field, and to invest in crime research meant investing in one's own discipline (sociology, psychology, law, etc.). Although this investment occasionally led to flexible forms of institutionalization such as the creation of the criminology section of the American Sociological Association in 1943, there was no space dedicated to interdisciplinary exchange or institutions bearing the imprimatur of "criminology." Academic and scientific relations between members of different disciplines were guided primarily by personal initiatives and relationships, as well as by public controversies, as can be illustrated by the theoretical and disciplinary debate that pitted

Sutherland against Sheldon and Eleanor Glueck between 1920 and 1950.[4]

A relatively autonomous field dedicated to criminology emerged slowly during the twentieth century (box 2).[5] As Alberto Cambrosio and Peter Keating have pointed out with regard to chronobiology, the transition from a space integrated into each discipline (sociology, psychology, etc.) to one that is autonomous entails more than a change of names.[6] Practical consequences flowed from the formation of a criminological field: the creation of professional associations, departments and doctorates in criminology that were independent from the traditional disciplines,[7] specialized criminological journals, and research prizes for criminologists, including the recent Stockholm Prize in Criminology (created in 2005), which, like the economics prize "in memory of Alfred Nobel,"[8] imitates the Nobel Prize to benefit from its cachet.[9]

Criminology nevertheless offers an atypical case study for the sociologist of science since the development of the field of criminology was initiated not by academics but by police officers and professionals from the paralegal field. The latter saw criminology as a means to provide police officers with higher education and thus enhance the social prestige of their profession. Their efforts took two main forms: the creation of an organization now known as the American Society of Criminology[10] and the emergence of autonomous departments of criminology, independent from the traditional disciplines, in American universities.

From the 1950s to the mid-1970s, the most iconic criminology department resided on the campus of the prestigious University of California Berkeley.[11] While it was not the only institution of higher learning with criminology courses,[12] it is well established that "Berkeley remained the Mecca for police education."[13] The history of the Berkeley School of Criminology is symptomatic of the status of criminology in American universities. Opened in 1950, the School was regularly challenged and criticized, so much so that it shut down in 1976. The fact that the School was founded by police agents also weighed on its reputation. Its directors had difficulty legitimizing the presence

1941   Founding of the American Society of Criminology (ASC)

1950   Opening of the School of Criminology at the University of California Berkeley

1958   First doctoral program in criminology established at Florida State University

1963   First issue of *Criminology,* the official journal of the ASC, published

1963   First Edwin H. Sutherland Award given by the ASC to the sociologist Walter Reckless

1964   Election of sociologist Walter Reckless as president of the ASC, marking the beginning of the association's academicization and the marginalization of professionals

1964   First issue of *the Journal of Research in Crime and Delinquency* published

1969   Law Enforcement Education Program scholarships established

1971   Founding of the Academy of Criminal Justice Sciences (ACJS)

1973   First issue of the *Journal of Criminal Justice* published

1974   First issue of *Criminal Justice and Behavior* published

1976   Closing of the School of Criminology at the University of California Berkeley

1976   First Bruce Smith Sr. Award given by ACJS to the legal scholar Leon Radzinowicz

1984   First issue of *Justice Quarterly,* official journal of ACJS, published

1985   First issue of *Quantitative Criminology* published

of a professionalizing structure on the campus of an elite university devoted to fundamental scientific research. Lying somewhere between a scientific discipline and a profession, criminology has had difficulty gaining recognition from the most prestigious academic institutions. Unsurprisingly, most of the autonomous criminology departments that have developed since the Berkeley episode are in local institutions of lesser prestige. This is not to say that prestigious universities are not interested in crime as an object of study. Rather, elite universities produce knowledge about crime and the criminal justice system through more established disciplines, particularly sociology.

At the scientific level, many people questioned the usefulness of the School of Criminology. Given that Berkeley had a very active sociology department when it came to issues of deviance and crime, the added value of the School seemed unclear to university administrators. For example, while the School was open, Berkeley's sociology department included such luminaries as Erving Goffman and David Matza, both authors of classic works on deviance. In fact, when the Berkeley School of Criminology offered Matza a professorship in 1961, his colleagues in the Sociology Department advised him to decline (which he did). The decision to institutionalize criminology and separate it from the traditional disciplines garnered little consensus among sociologists, an element that gained significance when the same sociologists subsequently began to control the newly created criminological institutions.

If the Berkeley experience can be seen as a failure, this missed opportunity nevertheless furthered the tendency to develop departments of criminology that were statutorily autonomous from the traditional disciplines. During this movement, the universities benefited greatly from the financial support of the federal government. In 1967, the Presidential Commission on Law Enforcement and the Administration of Justice, established by President Lyndon Johnson as part of his "war on crime," observed:

> The independent research which has been done in the past has been centered in law schools and sociology departments of universities. Much of it has been the work of professors working alone or with one

or a few graduate students. This form of research has produced significant contributions to our learning and will continue to be a major
source of new data and new ideas, but there are large areas where it
is inadequate. Since the complexities of crime cut across many disciplines, and many projects require a group of people working together,
it is important that there be some collaborative, organized research
projects and centers.[14]

Two years later, the federal government followed up on these recommendations and set up a vast funding program for students wish-
ing to pursue a career in law enforcement and the judiciary: the Law
Enforcement Education Program. The idea was simple: students who
graduated from criminology would have their tuition covered by the
program if they worked for a federal agency for a specified period.[15]
The program was a success: "Between 1969 and 1975, LEEP grants grew
from $6.5 million for 485 funded institutions to $40 million for 1,065
colleges. Thousands of police officers returned to school for college
education and degrees in law enforcement programs."[16] Hence, these
independent criminology programs came to be seen by university administrators as a veritable cash cow.[17] By the mid-1960s, 152 institutions
of higher learning offered degrees in criminology and/or criminal justice. In 1958, the first stand-alone doctoral program in criminology
was established at Florida State University. Ten years later, there were
729 criminal justice programs, including six doctoral programs and
121 master's level programs.[18] By 1990, more than 1,000 universities
and institutions of higher learning offered a degree in criminology or
criminal justice,[19] including 13 at the doctoral level.[20]

SOCIOLOGISTS' DOMINATION OF THE CRIMINOLOGICAL FIELD

Despite being a police initiative, the American Society of Criminology
was quickly taken over by academics, which led to the marginalization
of its creators and other affiliated professionals. This marginalization
in turn generated the creation of a new association dedicated to professionals, namely the Academy of Criminal Justice Sciences,[21] which

would meet the same fate as the ASC. Since the police and other justice professionals did not have any legitimacy within the scientific field, and because it was impossible to rely on PhDs from the departments of criminology that had only just been created, the autonomization of the criminological field raised a crucial question: Which discipline would control the newly created institutions?

Extending their scientific domination, the sociologists ultimately took advantage of these new resources. The period from the 1930s to the 1960s is generally referred to as the "golden age of criminology."[22] From Edwin H. Sutherland to Marvin Wolfgang, Clifford Shaw, Henry McKay, Thorsten Sellin, Robert K. Merton, and Howard Becker, some of the most respected sociologists were drawn to the question of crime and deviance. For example, when the sociologist Albert Cohen was interviewed by the criminologist John Laub in the 1980s, he explained that

> all of the better graduate students [in sociology] were in criminology. They were all studying with Sutherland. There was a sense that the department of sociology at that particular time was really the breeding ground of theory. You were there at the source. The most exciting things in criminological theory were happening right there and they all somehow had to do with differential association [a theory developed by Sutherland]. Differential association was theoretically the end of the world.[23]

Hence, the autonomization of the criminological field provided an opportunity for sociologists to solidify their scientific domination in institutional terms and to impose themselves on other disciplines that shared an interest in crime (psychology, law, etc.). This domination expressed itself through the distribution of prestige and the hierarchies observed within this field.[24] The distribution of academic capital within the U.S. criminological field can be seen primarily in the disciplinary training of the elected presidents of the American Society of Criminology[25] and the faculty employed in independent criminology schools. Although the presidents of the Academy of Criminal Justice Sciences are less central to the U.S. criminological field, they also provide convincing evidence of sociologists' domination.

The provenance of the presidents of the American Society of Criminology during the period of 1980–99 clearly betrays the academic domination of sociologists over researchers from criminology and criminal justice departments. Indeed, of the ten presidents who served between 1980 and 1989, nine were sociologists. While this centrality diminished somewhat thereafter, sociologists remained the primary representatives of U.S. criminology, with seven of the ten ASC presidents during the 1990–99 period holding a doctorate in this discipline. Given the history of the creation of the Academy of Criminal Justice Sciences, it follows that greater importance was given to researchers from criminology departments. Nonetheless, following an initial period marked by a vision of criminology as an applied science, the 1990s saw a growing importance of sociologists within the association, with half of the elected presidents (five) coming from this discipline. The different orientations of the ASC and the ACJS are also reflected in the types of individuals who were drawn to these associations in the last part of the twentieth century. While ASC members were mostly sociologists from research institutions who devoted a significant portion of their time to scientific research, ACJS members mainly came from the legal and paralegal environment, an experience that they passed on within institutions geared toward teaching and professional training rather than scientific research.[26] The growing presence of sociologists within the ACJS is therefore all the more notable since few of its members were initially trained in this discipline.

The domination of sociologists can also be seen in departments of criminology. Indeed, as soon as they were created in the 1950s, the question was raised as to where the faculty should be drawn from. Although the disciplinary training of the professors employed in these academic units was much more varied and interdisciplinary than that of the presidents of the ASC and the ACJS, sociologists' experience in the field allowed them to impose themselves as the most natural candidates. At that time, criminology had been taught in American sociology departments for several decades.[27] The first recorded course can be traced back to 1902; in the 1939–41 period, criminology was the fifth-most-taught course in American sociology departments, ahead of social psychology, anthropology, and urban sociology.[28] Sociologists would thus naturally join the newly created departments of criminology. By the early 1980s, 40.2 percent of the professoriate was trained in sociology, followed by political science (9.8 percent) and psychology (9.4 percent).[29] Professors actually trained in criminology departments were thus less numerous than sociologists, political scientists, and psychologists: criminal justice graduates represented 6.8 percent of criminology professors, while criminology graduates represented only 4.9 percent. This marginality can be explained in part by the demographic dependence of criminology. Although PhD programs in criminology and criminal justice were progressively established from the late 1950s, the number of doctors was still insufficient in the early 2000s to meet the field's need for professors and researchers.[30]

The scientific domination of social scientists is even more pronounced than their academic domination. The ASC and the ACJS annually reward researchers who have advanced the understanding of crime and criminal behaviors, so much so that analyzing the disciplinary origins of the awardees provides an objective indicator of the distribution of scientific capital in the criminological field. During the period of 1980–99, nineteen of the twenty recipients of the ASC's Edwin H. Sutherland Awards were sociologists. Even the ACJS, which might have been more reluctant to accept the domination of sociologists, awarded most of its prizes to researchers trained in sociology (twelve out of nineteen).[31] Conversely, researchers from criminology or criminal justice departments remained in a particularly precarious scientific position. In fact, over the period of 1980–99, not a single researcher with a PhD in criminology or criminal justice received an Edwin H. Sutherland or a Bruce Smith Sr. Award.

This polarized distribution of scientific capital can be collated with an analysis of the doctoral discipline of the researchers most cited in scientific journals. While the awarding of prizes is partially dependent on the distribution of academic capital, and thus ultimately on the extensive representation of sociologists in the committees of the associations that distribute them, bibliometric indicators are less exposed to the influence of academic power. Nevertheless, the scientific centrality of sociologists remains evident during the period of 1945–72: in August and September 1974, the sociologist Marvin Wolfgang and two of his colleagues asked a sample of five hundred American criminologists to nominate the ten best works in criminology. The domination of the view of crime as a social problem was readily apparent in the ranking of the most popular articles. Research conducted in psychology or biocriminology did not figure among the most frequently mentioned articles, and the list of authors reiterated the list of the most prominent sociologists of the time, including Edwin H. Sutherland, Richard Cloward, Howard Becker, David Matza, and Marvin Wolfgang himself.[32]

Similarly, the ranking of the most-cited researchers in *Criminology* and *Justice Quarterly* both confirms and adds nuance to the scientific domination of sociologists in the production of criminological knowledge (table 1.1). More than half of the most-cited researchers in *Criminology* and *Justice Quarterly* during the period of 1986–2000 held

TABLE 1.1

Doctoral discipline of the most-cited researchers in Criminology (CR) and Justice Quarterly (JQ), 1986–2000

	1986–90		1991–95		1996–2000	
Doctoral discipline	**CR**	**JQ**	**CR**	**JQ**	**CR**	**JQ**
Sociology	62%	61%	60%	47%	60%	54%
Criminal justice	4%	4%	6%	12%	6%	8%
Criminology	6%	4%	6%	7%	6%	6%
Criminology, law, and society	0%	2%	0%	2%	0%	2%
Psychology	15%	8%	15%	12%	13%	10%
Other	13%	20%	13%	21%	15%	21%

Sources: Cohn and Farrington, "Who Are the Most-Cited Scholars"; Cohn and Farrington, "Changes in the Most-Cited Scholars"; Cohn and Farrington, "Changes in Scholarly Influence."

Note: CR, *Criminology*: 1986–90, n = 47; 1991–95, n = 47; 1996–2000, n = 47. JQ, *Justice Quarterly*: 1986–90, n = 49; 1991–95, n = 43; 1996–2000, n= 48.

a doctorate in sociology. At the same time, this ranking clarifies the interdisciplinary nature of the study of crime. Although it scored much lower than sociology, psychology still ranked among the most prominent disciplines. Comparatively, researchers from departments of criminology and criminal justice ranked low, although they became increasingly visible as we approached the twenty-first century. This can be explained by the increase in the number of doctoral programs in criminology and the subsequent growth of this social group in the field.

In sum, all the available indicators point to one simple fact: from the beginning of its autonomy in the 1950s–1960s until the 2000s, criminology was dominated by sociologists. This domination was important not only in its objectified state. Bourdieu has clearly shown that any objective state of domination is always accompanied by an incorporation of this domination, which is expressed "in the form of scientific habitus, systems of generative schemes of perception, appreciation and action, produced by a specific form of educative action, which make possible the choice of objects, the solution of problems, and the evaluation of solutions."[33] The integration of sociological domination played a special role in the independent departments of criminology. Indeed, the leading role that sociologists were called upon to play in those newly established structures helped to reinforce this domination within spaces that had been thought of as interdisciplinary and autonomous. Unsurprisingly, a report published in 1970 showed that the so-called criminal justice programs were in fact increasingly oriented toward the social sciences and even humanities.[34] In the short and medium term, the creation of autonomous departments of criminology had the paradoxical result of reinforcing and reproducing the sociological conception of criminal phenomena. Since the education of criminology PhDs had been entrusted primarily to sociologists, the former adopted the same scientific reflexes as the latter—so much so that the creation of doctorates in criminology and criminal justice from the end of the 1950s did not prevent "sociological explanations of crime" from "dominating theoretical work for the rest of the 20th century."[35]

Despite this overwhelming domination, the question of what

criminology should be continued to be debated among scholars. For some, criminology had acquired the status of an autonomous discipline; for others, it remained a field of research within the traditional disciplines.[36] These debates can be seen as further evidence of the domination of sociologists in the field. Sociologists' denial of the criminological field's autonomy allowed them to legitimize their overrepresentation in the newly created institutions. As "any exercise of force is accompanied by a discourse aimed at legitimizing the force of the person exercising it,"[37] this naturalization process is a normal characteristic of any social field.[38] Thus, even when the attachment of criminology to sociology was questioned, the underlying idea of an attachment to a dominant discipline remained. The naturalization of criminology's attachment to the field of sociology was clearly illustrated by Sutherland's view of criminology as a subfield of sociology, not as an independent discipline or even as an interdisciplinary field that would be nourished by contributions from different disciplines.[39] A few decades later, Ronald Akers, also a sociologist and president of the ASC in 1979, similarly reinforced this position when, in an article entitled "Relating Sociology to Its Specialties: The Case of Criminology," he asserted that "sociology remains the intellectual 'center of gravity' for criminology."[40] Indeed, he continued: "Among the mix of disciplines found on criminology faculties and in articles published in the major criminology journals, sociology remains a strong theoretical and methodological force. While this is viewed by some criminologists as an undue and detrimental influence of one discipline, I believe sociology has been and will continue to be of immense benefit to criminology."[41] At the same time, the successful attempt to create autonomous criminological institutions raised the "disciplinary stakes":[42] academic associations were created, specialized journals began to be published, and teaching and research positions were created in the new departments of criminology. All these resources had to be distributed and shared within the scientific field. Thus, although opposed to disciplinarization, many sociologists invested in the field of criminology and made it their "second nationality,"[43] that is, an activity that was complementary to their main identity as sociologists. The criminological field thus offered them a respite from the competition of the sociological field,[44] while capital accumulated in the criminological field (publications, citations, prizes, etc.) could be reimported and invested in their field of origin.

———

This chapter traced the genesis of the field of criminology in the United States. From the creation of the short-lived Berkeley School of Criminology to the rise of the American Society of Criminology, the role played by sociologists has been central in the emergence of an autonomous space dedicated to the study of crime. This is somewhat paradoxical given that the aim of its initial promoters, police officers by training, was to collaborate with academics while maintaining control over professional associations essentially intended to train men and women in the field. The skills that sociologists had acquired in the scientific understanding of deviance, however, thwarted the plans of practitioners: not only were professional associations progressively placed under the umbrella of sociology, but the newly created departments of criminology also came to rely on professors trained in sociology to fulfill their functions. Thus the genesis of the field of criminology, rather than relativizing the role of sociologists in the study and understanding of crime, provided them a new opportunity to exert their domination.

2 THE STRUCTURAL SUFFOCATION
OF THE FIRST GENERATION
OF BIOSOCIAL CRIMINOLOGISTS

THE SOCIOLOGISTS Marvin Wolfgang and Clarence R. Jeffery articulated the initial formulation of biosocial criminology at a time when sociologists dominated the field. The stance they adopted can be understood only within the social, political, cultural, and scientific context of the time. To begin with, "The 1970s were marked by a strong resurgence of theories on aggressiveness and human violence."[1] In the 1960s and 1970s, a flurry of bestsellers on human biology appeared,[2] including Richard Dawkins's *The Selfish Gene* (1976) and Edward Wilson's controversial *Sociobiology* (1975). This wave of publications was preceded by the publication of *Crime and Personality* by the British psychologist Hans Eysenck in 1964, which signaled the revival of biocriminology.[3]

Despite this favorable cultural climate, the state of criminology constituted a major obstacle to the development of biosocial criminology. Yet notwithstanding this and other obstacles, the kind of biosocial criminology produced during the period of 1960–90 prefigured later developments. To understand how, it is important to underline that references to biology in criminology can be deployed in two ways: to either reinforce or challenge sociological theories of crime. In this regard, the first wave of biosocial criminology mainly constituted an attempt to subvert the dominant theories of crime. Then, like the second generation of biosocial criminology that developed from the 2000s onwards, the first generation attached itself to the autonomization of the criminological field. The maneuver failed to gain traction, however, as departments of criminology were still in the early stages of development. Furthermore, the first wave of biosocial criminology depended too heavily on resources from outside the field of criminology, namely the data and methods of behavior genetics.

REINFORCING OR REPLACING SOCIOLOGICAL THEORIES?

Implicating biology in the explanation of criminal phenomena does not automatically call into question the sociological definition of crime. Indeed, biological theorizations of social problems can be placed on a scale running from "strong biologism" to "weak biologism,"[4] depending on how much room they leave for environmental explanations. These two poles were clearly in place in the first generation of biosocial criminology, which was divided into two main branches: the first used biology to refine existing sociological theories, whereas the second branch used biology to challenge these theories. In Bourdieusian terminology, we can say that there was a conservative and a subversive branch. Whereas the conservatives did not seek to replace existing sociological theories, the subversives attacked the majority view of crime and thus attacked the domination of sociologists within the criminological field.

The most orthodox (i.e., sociological) approach to biosocial criminology appeared in the writings of the American sociologist Marvin Wolfgang. In his well-known *The Subculture of Violence*, first published in 1967, Wolfgang proposed a theory of violent crime that integrated data from sociology, psychology, psychiatry, and biology.[5] As Wolfgang was unfamiliar with the psychological and biological literature, he sought the assistance of a coauthor, the Italian physician-psychologist

Franco Ferracuti, to write the chapter on individual factors in crime. This lack of familiarity with the nonsociological literature on crime is not surprising. Wolfgang received his doctorate in sociology in 1955 from the University of Pennsylvania, where he remained for the rest of his career. His dissertation was supervised by Thorsten Sellin, who was mostly known for having put forth an explanation of criminal behaviors rooted in the idea of culture conflict.[6] The culturalist explanation of African American violence that Wolfgang deployed in *The Subculture of Violence* was thus a product of this sociological tradition, a matter made clear by the fact that almost all subsequent empirical tests of his subcultural approach were written by sociologists and published in general sociology journals.[7] Wolfgang himself never went further than a simple synthesis of biological theories of crime, and we find no concrete applications of biosocial criminology in his writings.

Wolfgang integrated biology, limited though it was, into his theory only after having undertaken an epistemological reflection on the status of criminology. In a field dominated by sociology, any recourse to individual explanations—whether biological or even psychological—had to be justified. Thus the first part of his book on the criminal subculture was entirely devoted to the definition of criminology.[8] According to Wolfgang,

> Criminology should be considered as an autonomous, separate discipline of knowledge because it has accumulated its own set of organized data and theoretical conceptualisms that use the scientific method, approach to understanding, and attitude in research. . . . Thus, sociology, psychology, psychiatry, the law, history, and biology, with such allied fields as endocrinology, may individually or collectively make substantial contributions to criminology without detracting from the idiosyncratic significance of criminology as an independent subject matter of scientific investigation and concern.[9]

While this conception of criminological research had the effect of denaturalizing and problematizing the domination of sociologists within the criminological field, Wolfgang himself continued to work from a sociological perspective. Here was a tension between his habitus as a sociologist and his growing investment in the field of criminology, especially after his election as head of the American Society of Criminology in 1964. In brief, combining violent subculture theory with biological factors amounted to producing a biosocial theory of crime. But Wolfgang did not make a break with mainstream criminological knowledge. In a sense, one could say that Wolfgang reinforced rather than challenged the sociological domination within the U.S. criminological field. Indeed, by extending the scope of sociological theories to psychological and biological data, Wolfgang not only emphasized the primacy of the sociological paradigm but also showed that the individualistic approaches that had to date been excluded by his predecessors could be subsumed under existing sociological theories.

In contrast to Wolfgang's approach, Jeffery's was more critical of the role sociology played in explaining criminal phenomena. This subversive turn came rather late in his career. Following a dissertation completed under the supervision of sociologist Edwin H. Sutherland— who, interestingly, was also one of the principal actors of the sociology/biocriminology controversy of the first half of the twentieth century[10]—Jeffery received a doctorate in sociology at Indiana University in 1954. In keeping with the sociological tradition, his early research was devoted to the influence of social structure on crime and to the question of the legal definition of crime.[11] Jeffery thus remained faithful to his tradition, writing, for example, in 1965 that "criminal behavior is learned" and that "Sutherland's theory of differential association is basically correct."[12]

Jeffery's turn to biosocial criminology proceeded as he slowly turned toward the behavioral sciences. This can be seen in the first edition of his major work, *Crime Prevention through Environmental Design*. In the 1971 edition, Jeffery mentioned the importance of biology and the brain in understanding human behavior. But he left it at that and advanced no further into the analysis of these factors.[13] But Jeffery's scientific orientation took a more decisive turn when he became a professor in the School of Criminology and Criminal Justice at Florida State University in 1977. That same year, the second edition of his *Crime Prevention* was published. Unlike the first edition, which had remained elusive as to the exact nature of the biological factors that were to play a role in criminal behavior, the second edition devoted considerable space to research in behavior genetics.[14] Retrospectively, Jeffery himself acknowledged the change in perspective between the two editions of his book.[15]

Jeffrey completed his biocriminological turn in 1978 with the publication of an article in the leading journal of the field, *Criminology*, in which he called for a "new criminology," a "biosocial criminology" that he described as "a merging of biology, psychology, and sociology" that would come to "reflect the hierarchy of sciences as found in systems analysis."[16] Whereas Wolfgang saw biology as a means of complementing culturalist theories of crime, Jeffery went so far as to assert that "there is no such thing as a social variable; there are only biosocial variables."[17] The following year, he edited a book entitled *Biology and Crime*, which drew together contributions from geneticists, psychiatrists, and psychologists, in short, researchers who were neither sociologists nor active in the field of criminology.[18] In the introduction, provocatively titled "Biology and Crime: The New Neo-Lombrosians," Jeffery argued that criminology was an "interdisciplinary field" that had had the "historic misfortune" of having been "captured" by sociology.[19] Drawing on the work of the historian of science Thomas Kuhn,[20] Jeffery called for a paradigm shift,[21] a challenge to the domination of sociologists within the American field of criminology. His marginalization and the resistance of sociologists, however, prevented him from realizing his project.

CONTROVERSIES AND MARGINALITY: THE RECEPTION OF THE BIOLOGICAL APPROACH IN THE CRIMINOLOGICAL FIELD

Jeffery's change of convictions came at a time when he had finally secured a comfortable position in the field of American criminology. As a result of his academic rise, Jeffery was elected president of the American Society of Criminology in 1977 for the year of 1978. Although now established, his position was nonetheless atypical. Florida State University had been the first American university to offer a doctoral program in nonsociological criminology (starting in 1958). However, in the early 1960s, "To be a criminologist meant to be a sociologist,"[22] and independent criminology departments had very limited scientific legitimacy. As late as the early 1970s, the ASC lived in the shadow of the criminology section of the American Sociological Association. Jeffery's academic position was nevertheless symptomatic of the affinity between biosocial criminology and criminology departments. His proposed biosocial paradigm was liberating for the discipline of criminology in that the domination of sociologists might seem less natural and might even be challenged with his new pyramid of sciences, where sociology no longer stood at the summit of crime knowledge.[23]

Whereas Wolfgang had invested in criminology while maintaining a comfortable position as a professor of sociology at the prestigious University of Pennsylvania, Jeffery's ties to sociology were almost nonexistent. Indeed, before becoming a professor in the Criminology Department at Florida State University in 1977, Jeffery had been unable to obtain a permanent position in his field of training. He accumulated temporary contracts in institutions that were inconspicuous in the field of criminology in the United States: first at the University of Chicago Law School, then at the Washington School of Psychiatry. In this regard, his investment in the field of criminology, rather than the second nationality that it represented for most sociologists, resembled more closely a change of nationality. Jeffery abandoned the sociological approach to crime at the same time as he left sociology, and his investment in the process of creating a criminological discipline was accompanied by a new theoretical perspective that challenged the traditional Durkheimian vision of crime.

But Jeffery did not have the institutional resources that would have allowed him to garner acceptance for his biosocial criminology. The balance of power was too lopsided for criminologists to stand up to sociologists. As the criminologist Arnold Binder wryly wrote in the late 1980s, "The accomplishment of interdisciplinarity in criminology . . . implies that a group that does not contain the leading scholars in a field, does not control the major avenues of publication, and does not have influence over the brightest students and future scholars (who, presumably, choose the major research universities for their graduate study), can have a revolutionary influence in the field."[24]

When Jeffery proposed his biosocial model, criminological organizations that were independent of the traditional disciplines had been in existence for only a few years. Above all, this autonomy was only statutory: sociologists controlled the ASC and its flagship journal, they were influential in criminology departments, and they defined what counted as legitimate criminology. In short, Jeffery's academic capital was insufficient to compensate for his lack of scientific centrality. Even his presidency at the head of the main academic organization of the American criminological field did not enable him to impose his vision of crime and his biosocial paradigm. A fitting illustration of his marginality took place during the annual meeting of the ASC in Dallas in 1978, where approximately six hundred people were present. According to his own account, Jeffery, then president of the ASC, was taxed as a "neo-Lombrosian" after presenting a paper on the genetics of crime.[25] When Nils Christie was awarded the Sellin-Glueck Prize, the Norwegian sociologist took the opportunity to denounce what he saw as an attempt to revive Lombroso's ideas. Jeffery revisited this event with a certain bitterness during an interview conducted in March 1996 by his former doctoral student Diana Fishbein:

> In 1977 I was president of ASC in Dallas, where I was raked over the coals for being a neo-Lombrosian. . . . I was ridiculed from the floor while I was president and I was very upset by the whole thing, and . . . one of the people, I can't remember his name, it was a Swede [it was in fact the Norwegian sociologist Nils Christie] who got the Glueck-Sellin Award for an outstanding European scholar, I remember making the comment from the podium, "Sheldon Glueck must be turning over in his grave now because he is so interdisciplinary and so interested in getting away from the confines of either law or sociology."[26]

Similarly, in an article from 1979, the Marxist criminologists Tony Platt and Paul Takagi were highly critical of Jeffery's biosocial program, which they presented as a "new conservative trend" and a reaction to radical social science and Marxism in particular.[27] They went on to argue that "Jeffery demonstrates that a little knowledge can be irresponsible as well as dangerous"[28] and that he was yet another example of researchers who had ventured beyond their field of expertise, joining, for example, William Shockley and Arthur Jensen, who had presented controversial views on the genetic transmission of intelligence. Although Jeffery did not respond publicly to Platt and Takagi, the publication of his book *Biology and Crime* in 1979—based on presentations made at the 1978 ASC annual meeting—provided him with an opportunity to position himself politically in relation to criminological trends. Interestingly, although Platt and Takagi accused him of conservatism, Jeffery saw his work as an alternative to conservative criminology. He did not believe that offenders merited harsh treatment or that the ultimate recourse was the death penalty.[29] Jeffrey, in other words, provides yet another illustration of the political malleability of biology.[30]

Jeffery's failure was not absolute, however. Despite the domination of sociologists in the field of criminology, his position in the Criminology Department of Florida State University allowed him contact with doctoral students. This led him to train Lee Ellis, who in turn became one of the foremost promoters of the biosocial paradigm and created a bridge with the second generation that emerged in the 2000s. Ellis's doctoral dissertation, which he defended in 1983, was entitled "Androgens, the Nervous System and Criminal Behavior." His research was based mainly on work conducted in behavior genetics and evolutionary psychology, an orientation that was clearly apparent in an article he had published a year before his dissertation defense,[31] as well as in a second one published a few years later.[32]

Ellis was not the only doctoral student to be trained in biosocial criminology by Jeffery. Diana Fishbein wrote her dissertation on the impact of refined carbohydrate consumption on deviant behavior[33] under the direction of Jeffery and psychobiologist Karen Glendenning. But the list ends there, reflecting the difficulties Jeffery encountered when he tried to propagate the biosocial approach in his own department. According to one of them, it was only Jeffery's major role in creating the doctoral program in criminology at Florida State University that enabled him to override his colleagues' initial refusal and train his two doctoral students in biosocial criminology: "Jeff [Jeffery's nickname] was helpful in terms of getting us admitted to a PhD program in criminology. You know, in other words . . . PhD programs weren't looking for people that were thinking biologically. So Jeffery, since he was there and, you know, helped to establish the PhD program at Florida State, he kind of . . . he kind of bent the rules or bent the criteria for admission."[34]

Although Jeffery and then Ellis initiated the biosocial trend in American criminology at the end of the 1970s and the beginning of the 1980s, the immediate repercussions were quite limited. As Vincent Bontems and Yves Gingras have shown for physics,[35] by obliterating existing lines of research—by declaring, for instance, that there are no social variables when it comes to crime—heterodox scientific productions are likely to meet resistance from researchers who have chosen the path of normal science. Jeffery, Ellis, and Fishbein, as well as Wolfgang, were unable to access the institutional resources that would have allowed them to develop their specialty. Even research that did not deal with biology but mobilized individual explanations within a sociological framework were then suspected of contravening the dominant explanations. Thus, when Travis Hirschi and Michael Hindelang argued in an article published in the *American Sociological Review* that delinquents have a lower IQ than nonoffenders and that this explains their lower success in school,[36] "this analysis, even though it was insistently sociological and made no claim whatsoever about biology, raised eyebrows simply by daring to mention the still verboten variable of intelligence."[37] Biological explanations were also severely criticized in leading criminology textbooks. For example, sociologists Edwin H. Sutherland and Donald Cressey wrote in their 1978 edition of *Criminology* that "heredity has no connection whatever with criminal behavior."[38] In the same vein, sociologist Donald Gibbons wrote in 1970 that "biological theories that have been advanced have been scientifically naïve."[39]

VIOLENCE AS A PUBLIC HEALTH ISSUE

Because of the domination of sociologists and the marginalization of biological approaches, Jeffery and his doctoral students, Ellis and Fishbein, were forced to rely on resources they could find outside the field of criminology. As Jeffery explained in an interview for the American Society of Criminology's Oral History Project, he advised his doctoral students to take courses outside the criminology faculty: "You came to me [addressing Fishbein] and asked, 'What can I do with, you know, a master's, doctor's degree,' and I said, 'Get out of criminology and take some experimental psych and psychobiology.'"[40] Unsurprisingly, researchers who participated in the roundtable Jeffery organized at the 1978 ASC meeting on the biological factors of crime were mostly from outside the field of criminology.

The domination of sociologists within the field forced biosocial criminologists into a relationship of dependence vis-à-vis behavior genetics. The genetic knowledge that biosocial criminology currently uses was already available in Jeffery's time. Jeffery, for example, was familiar with the basic equation of quantitative genetics used in the famous twin studies ($Vp = Vg \times Ve$) according to which variation in a given phenotype (e.g., aggressiveness) is due to genotype variation combined with environmental variation and statistical error.[41] Jeffery also identified the importance of twin research,[42] an approach that would go on to become one of the main tools of present-day biosocial criminologists.

Yet the fact that this knowledge was theoretically available did not mean that it also was accessible. Jeffery could of course cite research led by geneticists and psychologists to support his biological argument, but it was considerably more difficult for him to conduct such studies. While biosocial criminologists can now rely on easily available genetic databases (such as Add Health), the 1970s saw the first attempts to build a twin studies database. The beginnings were quite laborious, to the extent that most geneticists continued to collect their own data by sending hundreds of questionnaires to individuals who would then constitute their sample.[43] Moreover, this dependence on behavior geneticists was not only material but also intellectual, as is clear from Jeffery's interview with his former doctoral student Diana Fishbein:

> The bridge [sic] between biology and crime is a vast one, and I'm not sure how you can overcome it. What I would prefer, my own choice, would be to come in as a criminologist, you know, ally myself with a biologist or psychobiological type and use my knowledge as a criminologist and that person's knowledge as a biologist. I would never on my own do it, you know, I just don't have that kind of knowledge.[44]

It was also through data resourced from outside the criminological field that Wolfgang's purely theoretical biosocial proposals began to take shape. In 1959, the Collaborative Perinatal Project was launched. This large-scale biomedical project collected data in a study of neurological disorders among American children: participants comprised approximately forty-two thousand women and fifty-five thousand children. The project covered twelve major U.S. cities, including Philadelphia, the city in which Wolfgang was employed at the University of Pennsylvania. Wolfgang asked for permission to access the data, with the idea that it might be useful to him in the future. With the help of the National Institute of Justice, Wolfgang was able to combine the data from the Collaborative Perinatal Project with Philadelphia Police Department data, linking the neurological disorder data to crime statistics and analyzing possible correlations between these variables.[45]

Rather than process the data himself, Wolfgang, then director of the Center for Studies in Criminology at the University of Pennsylvania, assigned the task to a doctoral student, Deborah Denno. Using data from the combined Collaborative Perinatal Project and Philadelphia police statistics, Denno completed her dissertation on the developmental, biological, and social factors of crime.[46] This "Biosocial Project," as Wolfgang and Denno called it, was not particularly well received by their fellow criminologists. In the book based on her dissertation, Denno exposed at length the difficulties that she had encountered during her doctoral studies and that could have forced her to abandon her research:

Those ten years were immensely enriching, but also frustrating. The Biosocial Project seemed always to be shrouded in politics. From the start, I was continually concerned that the Project might be discontinued because some influential social scientists at the time thought that any studies involving biological data were oppressive or fascist. A number of my colleagues told me that they could not understand why the Criminology Center had agreed to take on the Project because it wasn't "mainstream sociology."[47]

After receiving her doctorate in 1982, Denno was employed by the Center for Studies in Criminology at the University of Pennsylvania for a few years, but only as a lecturer, a status that did not offer her the possibility of becoming a tenured professor. Confronted with her marginality in the criminological field, Denno reoriented herself toward the legal field. She became a partner in a Philadelphia law firm in 1988, and in 1989 earned her JD from the University of Pennsylvania. Following this fork in the road, she obtained a tenured faculty position at Fordham University School of Law, where she now directs the Neuroscience and Law Center, which she founded in 2015.

The importance of resources outside the field of criminology should not, however, be overstated. For example, while Wolfgang and Denno were able to draw on the Collaborative Perinatal Project, their involvement was more a result of Wolfgang's own opportunism than a genuine willingness on the part of the government to involve sociologists and criminologists in their endeavor. This is not to say that politicians were indifferent to crime. The 1960s were a particularly troubled period for the United States: the wave of social protest that had been raging since the birth of the civil rights movement in the 1950s threatened the racial hierarchies of American society.[48] It was in this turbulent context that the medical approach to crime received government support and considerable funding.[49] One of the avenues explored was to fund research on violence to better prevent it. Interestingly, the government did not seek the collaboration of sociologists, even those like Jeffery and Wolfgang who sought to combine sociological and biological variables. Violence and crime were viewed as public health problems, as phenomena to be diagnosed and then treated.[50] The solution was thus entrusted to doctors and psychiatrists, rather than to sociologists and criminologists. For example, the research that Vernon Mark and Frank Ervin, MD, conducted on the alleged links between undiagnosed brain damage and violence[51] was funded by the National Cancer Institute, the National Institute of Mental Health, and the U.S. Public Health Service, that is by the entire "mental health establishment."[52]

A particularly striking illustration of the exclusion of scholars from the criminological field in favor of medical and psychiatric professionals was the project to create a Center for the Study and Reduction of Violence at the prestigious University of California at Los Angeles (UCLA).[53] In 1973, the director of the Institute of Neuropsychiatry at UCLA, Dr. Louis West, proposed the creation of this center, whose goal would be "to study the pathologically violent individual with a view toward earlier diagnosis, treatment and prevention of violent behavior, and its consequences."[54] The Center for the Study and Reduction of Violence was to be funded by the Department of Health and the California Council for Criminal Justice. Robert Litman, a psychiatrist from the University of Southern California, was chosen to head it. Although the center did not see the light of day because of the numerous protests that the project provoked—notably from the Black Panther Party[55]—no sociologists or any other representatives of the criminological field were chosen to direct the operation or even considered as potential interlocutors. By proposing a pathological conception of violence, psychiatrists and physicians imposed themselves as essential partners in the war on crime led by President Richard Nixon.

Jeffery, Wolfgang, and their colleagues thus found themselves locked in a vicious circle: their marginalization in the field of criminology prevented them from advancing their movement, and this lack of visibility reduced their ability to attract funding, which would have enabled them to counteract their marginalization. The trend was, moreover, regressive, as some PhDs in biosocial criminology decided to migrate to fields that seemed more receptive to their work. A former doctoral student in biosocial criminology from this period explained that she preferred to leave criminology, where she had been stuck, to invest in fields more open to biological theory:

> I do not call myself a criminologist. I separated from the field after many years of feeling disinterested in their strictly sociological views and tiring of all the corresponding theories that were rather limited. ASC meetings seemed not to evolve over time, and I had less in common with other criminologists. I also never did study "crime" per se, which is a legal conception and not a behavioral phenotype. So over time I drifted, to use a criminological term! Instead, I pursued experimental laboratory research and then branched out to focusing on neurodevelopmental precursors and consequences of environmental influences, from adversity to intervention.[56]

The lack of symbolic recognition slowed the demographic growth of the movement, forcing the few biosocial criminologists to collaborate with researchers outside their field. When Wolfgang edited a collaborative book devoted to the biological and psychological factors of violence in the early 1980s,[57] he was forced to call on researchers trained in psychology: Sarnoff Mednick and his colleague William Gabrielli, John Monahan, and David Farrington. This dependence was also reflected in the training of younger scholars, since doctoral students in biosocial criminology were forced to turn to psychological literature—and in particular to Mednick's work—to acquire a sense of what had and could be done: "It was a whole new dimension; nobody had ever looked at these variables before, and the person whose work I probably knew best at the time was Sarnoff Mednick. . . . That's actually Adrian Raine's mentor, but he was the one who had looked at twin studies and, you know, sort of biological factors."[58]

The difficulties that Wolfgang and Jeffery encountered in attracting the interest of research funding agencies continued well until the end of the 1990s. Hence, when an international meeting funded by a NATO[59] program on the biosocial factors of violence was held on the island of Rhodes in Greece from May 12 to 21, 1996, the organization was entrusted to four psychologists: Adrian Raine, Patricia Brennan,

David Farrington, and Sarnoff Mednick. Jeffery, Wolfgang, and their former students (Lee Ellis, Diana Fishbein, Deborah Denno) did not even participate in the subsequent collective publication.[60] A similar meeting had already taken place in Italy in 1986. Also funded by a NATO program, it was devoted to the biological basis of antisocial behaviors. Like the event in Greece in the 1990s, this meeting was supervised by two psychologists who were active in the field of behavior genetics, Terrie Moffitt and Sarnoff Mednick.[61] Biosocial criminologists' situation had thus not changed much in a decade. By and large, they remained ignored by public authorities, whether at the local, national, or supranational level.

THEORETICAL ADVANCES IN BIOSOCIAL CRIMINOLOGY WITHIN THE FIELD OF CRIMINOLOGY

It is therefore unsurprising that the 1980s were not particularly favorable to biological theorizations of crime either and that empirical research came mainly from researchers outside the field of criminology. Only three biosocial criminology articles devoted to the genetic factors of crime were published in criminology journals during the 1980s,[62] and their authors were all psychologists. Two of the three articles were written (or coauthored) by researchers already active in behavior genetics, namely Sarnoff Mednick and David Rowe.[63] In other words, there was still no real progress of biosocial criminology within the field of American criminology.

This lack of progress was all the more notable given that the study of biological factors in crime had benefited from the development of the discipline of genetics in the 1980s. As historian Daniel Kevles explained, "Human genetics had grown from being a quiet hobby, involving merely the collection of pedigrees of rare diseases and deformities, to one of the most complicated and demanding disciplines in the whole of science."[64] But genetic knowledge about crime was pursued primarily in genetics and psychology, that is, outside the field of criminology. Researchers trained in criminology, whether in traditional sociology departments or in the more recent doctoral programs in criminology, had very little involvement in the development of this new brand of biocriminology and were content to follow its progress from a distance. There were, of course, a few researchers who were active in the field of criminology and also adopted a biological approach to crime, but they were relegated to marginal universities oriented toward teaching and professional training rather than scientific research, which prevented them from having any real influence on the empirical study of biological factors in crime. In addition to Lee Ellis—a former doctoral student of Jeffery who was hired by the Sociology Department at Minot State University, a small university in North Dakota—Anthony Walsh, likewise going against the grain, practiced biocriminology. Walsh earned his doctorate in criminology at Bowling Green State University in 1983 before joining the Criminal Justice Department at Boise State University in Idaho. It was no coincidence that the first wave of biosocial criminology researchers ended up at less prestigious universities. There seems to have been a tacit agreement between these universities and biosocial criminologists: the universities accepted the scientific heterodoxy—and the controversies that sometimes accompanied it—because Ellis and Walsh committed themselves to publishing their research, thus increasing the scientific visibility of their university:

> My colleagues weren't particularly interested in what I had to say. . . . One thing that kind of helped me was that I was publishing research. And at the university where I was, it wasn't a high-powered publishing institution. . . . It was not a "publish or perish" university. But they liked having somebody that was publishing, and so I was . . . I think they tolerated my odd ideas (*laughs*) about biology being important because I published.[65]

While scholars such as Ellis and Walsh kept the biosocial flame burning within the field of criminology, empirical research remained within the purview of psychologists and behavior geneticists. Yet the latter were careful to reject the label of criminology. In the preface to his *Causes and Cures of Criminality* published in 1989, the psychologist Hans Eysenck made it clear that he did not consider his contribution to be criminological in nature: "This is not a textbook of criminology. It is a book about psychological problems and issues related to crime, and because crimes are committed by people, we believe that psychology is a fundamental discipline which underlies any advances we may make in the prevention of crime, and the treatment of criminals."[66]

Similarly, University of Southern California psychologist Sarnoff Mednick's research on the heredity of crime was first presented to natural scientists, notably in 1982 at the annual meeting of the prestigious American Association for the Advancement of Science. Only afterwards did he share his findings with criminologists in an article published two years later.[67] But publishing in the flagship journal of the criminological field did not prevent him from disseminating his results to the readers of *Science*[68] and in the field of behavior genetics.[69] The same held true for the psychologist David Rowe, who first published his results in *Behavior Genetics*,[70] one of the main journals in the field of behavior genetics, before sharing them with criminologists in an article published three years later in *Criminology*.[71]

To be sure, the situation of these psychologists was not ideal either. Adrian Raine, now one of the leading figures in the neuroscientific study of violence and antisocial behavior,[72] pointed out a few years ago in an interview that this approach had a marginal status in the psychology of the 1980s. Raine revealed the difficulties he had encountered when seeking a professorship after finishing his PhD dissertation on the biological factors of antisocial behavior:

> I wanted an academic job, I mean that's what PhD students want, right? So I applied, I just couldn't get a job, and the only place that would take me was prison. So . . . that's the only job I could get. I couldn't get any academic job, but I could get a job as a prison psychologist, working with, you know, rapists, murderers, psychopaths, pedophiles (*laughs*). . . . Over the four years [of this job in prison], I applied to sixty-seven academic jobs and got sixty-seven straight rejections. I like to brag a little bit, I think I'm the only tenured academic I know who's been rejected by Papua New Guinea (*laughs*). I did apply, they do have a psychology department, I did apply, no, they rejected me. Nobody would take me. . . . I think looking back it just wasn't on anyone's radar screen at all, it didn't ring anyone's bell. You know, biological basis to

antisocial behavior, it's not something that's mainstream anywhere, neither in criminology, nor in psychology either.[73]

In this same interview, Raine also recounted how he was forced by one of the outside members of his dissertation committee to exclude a chapter on the biosocial causes of antisocial behavior, even though it had already been published as an article[74] in the journal *Personality and Individual Differences* founded by psychologist Hans Eysenck.

In the 1990s, the biological study of crime continued to develop outside the criminological field. Several important contributions were published during that period. Deborah Denno, who had at that time migrated to the legal field, published *Biology and Violence*,[75] a book that grew out of her doctoral dissertation completed under the direction of Marvin Wolfgang. Three years later, Raine, who eventually obtained a professorship at the University of Southern California with the support of Sarnoff Mednick, published his *Psychopathology of Crime*,[76] in which he raised the question of whether recidivist criminal behavior was a psychological disorder or psychopathology in the same vein as depression, anxiety, or schizophrenia. That same year, a team of Dutch geneticists published an article in *Science* on the correlation between the now-famous *MAOA* gene and violent behavior.[77] This first attempt at linking the *MAOA* gene to crime was followed by numerous replication attempts. These advances in behavior genetics were accompanied by the growing emergence of neuroscience as we approached the 1990s, "the decade of the brain."[78] It was during this period that the first brain imaging study using a population of murderers was published by Raine and his team.[79]

None of the empirical evidence suggests that the biosocial approach had suddenly garnered consensus among biologists and geneticists. For example, when Raine presented his research on the biological factors of crime at the annual meeting of the American Association for the Advancement of Science in San Francisco in 1994, the participants reacted violently and led a "unified and outspoken assault on biological research in this area," which was accused of being "racist and ideologically motivated."[80] The 1990s, however, marked an epistemological shift in the biological approach to crime, which became less reductive and deterministic. The way researchers conceived of the interaction between the different elements of the biological system was beginning to change. Genes and neurons were placed within the same causal chain leading to crime and antisociality:

> From about 1990, something began to change in the way in which the relations between genetics, neurobiology, and crime were construed. It was no longer a question of the search for a gene for crime, or even of a gene for aggression (even though this was the way that it was sometimes reported in the popular press). Indeed, these studies no longer sought to explain criminality in general, but focused on the impulsive behaviors that were thought to be involved in many criminal or antisocial acts, in particular, acts of aggression. These behaviors seemed to involve something that would once have been understood in terms of the will but that now fell under the rubric of *impaired impulse control*. And those searching for a genetic basis for such impairment now conceptualized the issue in neuromolecular terms.[81]

In other words, the different elements of the biological system formed a coherent whole, and researchers sought to model these coherent yet multifactorial processes. To borrow a metaphor proposed by British biologist Denis Noble, the aim of contemporary biosocial criminology was now to reconstruct the melody of the criminal "music" and to define the role of the different "instruments" that made up its "orchestra":[82] genes, alleles, neurons, neurotransmitters, but also physiological elements such as heart rate or hormone levels, thought to interact with each other. Each element was thus assigned a place and a role in the criminological orchestra.

Paradoxically, these important steps in the development of contemporary biocriminology occurred beyond the control of criminologists. And while we clearly witnessed a rise of biological theories within criminology during the 1990s, it appeared somewhat secondary and largely manifested the difficulties encountered by biosocial criminologists. For example, while there was indeed greater coverage of biological theories in criminology textbooks,[83] criminologists' control over genetic knowledge remained limited, to say the least. Criminologists were still largely dependent on the knowledge produced by researchers in other fields, particularly in psychology and behavior genetics. For example, of the seventeen articles published in the 1990s that used biological knowledge and were published in criminology journals, more than half were the work of behavior geneticists or researchers who were employed and/or trained in disciplines close to this field, including psychology and neuroscience.[84]

Of the remaining eight articles that were written by researchers active in the U.S. criminological field, six were theoretical articles that merely reviewed the literature and programmatically called for the development of biosocial criminology.[85] A paper published by Diana Fishbein in the early 1990s on the psychobiology of aggressive behavior in women provides an excellent example of this type of contribution. The former doctoral student of Clarence Jeffery at Florida State University argued that "pre- or postnatal biological experiences, combined with a socially disadvantageous environment, predispose certain women to antisocial behavior."[86] Fishbein's work, however, was purely theoretical and based on a review of the existing literature. Another example is provided by Lee Ellis and Anthony Walsh, who together published an article in the field's leading journal, *Criminology*. Their aim was to present the evolutionary theories of crime that had "reemerged during the past two decades,"[87] without proposing any empirical test of these theories through case studies. The genetics of crime was presented as a new field of research that would take time to be mastered by criminologists: "Decades of careful empirical testing will be required to assess the merit of many of these hypotheses."[88]

As a result, only two articles qualifying as empirical biosocial articles were written by researchers active in the criminological field: the first on the influence of testosterone on deviant behavior,[89] and the second proposing an empirical test of the theory of deviance developed by psychologist and behavior geneticist Terrie Moffitt.[90] This nearly complete lack of appropriation of genetic knowledge by criminologists was particularly visible in a meta-analysis on the correlation between genotype and criminal behavior published in the ASC journal

Criminology in 1992: virtually none of the studies identified were published in criminology journals.[91]

More generally, the importance of biological knowledge for the understanding of crime continued to be questioned, from both a scientific and a political point of view. At the scientific level, the available evidence remained unconvincing to criminologists. For example, in the aforementioned meta-analysis published in 1992 in *Criminology*, Glenn Walters concluded that there was an inverse relationship between the methodological quality of a study and the strength of the statistical relationship between genes and crime. That is, the best studies were also those that found the least empirical support for the idea that criminal behaviors were somehow linked to one's biology: "Better designed and more recently published studies provided less support for the gene-crime hypothesis than the more poorly designed and earlier published investigations."[92] Similarly, there was no consensus on the interpretation of the quantitative results from an article published in *Criminology* by the sociologists Alan Booth and Wayne Osgood. Using a sample of Vietnam War veterans, they endeavored to evaluate the relationship between testosterone levels and deviance. Their conclusions favored the hormonal factor and the biosocial approach in general: "This pattern of results supports the conclusions that (I) testosterone is one of a larger constellation of factors contributing to a general latent propensity toward deviance and (2) the influence of testosterone on adult deviance is closely tied to social factors. Our findings show that there is considerable promise in a biosocial approach that integrates social and biological explanations, rather than playing them off against one another."[93]

This enthusiasm over the incipient promise of social biological theories was not, however, shared by everyone. In 1994, a year after the publication of Booth and Osgood's article, the first edition of Ronald Akers's *Criminological Theories*, now a reference work in criminology, was published.[94] When it appeared, Akers was a major figure in the field of criminology: he had been president of the American Society of Criminology in 1979, the year in which the *American Sociological Review* published the founding article of his famous theory on the social learning of delinquency.[95] In other words, Akers was the perfect embodiment of the sociological domination of the criminological field. According to Akers, Booth and Osgood's conclusion about the correlation between testosterone and deviance "seriously overstates the relationship found in their research. In fact, the initial relationship between testosterone levels [and deviance] is extremely weak (explaining close to zero percent of the variance in adult deviance), and the relationship disappears when social integration and prior delinquency are taken into account."[96] After reviewing other empirical analyses of the biological factors of crime, including Sarnoff Mednick's work on the heritability of antisocial behavior, Akers was quite skeptical about the contribution of this line of research to the understanding of crime:

> Thus far, newer biological explanations have garnered mixed and generally weak empirical support. Biological theories that posit crime-specific genetic or physiological defects have not been, and are not likely to be, accepted as sound explanations in criminology. The greater the extent to which a biological theory proposes to relate normal physiological and sensory processes to social and environmental variables in explaining criminal behavior, the more likely it will be empirically supported and accepted in criminology.[97]

The rejection of biological theories of crime by sociologists was thus formulated in scientific terms. Biosocial criminologists were evidently insufficiently rigorous in the interpretation of their results since objective analysis should have led to a simple disqualification of existing research. These scientific criticisms, however, were also accompanied by questions targeting the political motivations of researchers interested in the biology of crime. Two significant events seem to have left little doubt as to the real motivations of the researchers participating in the renaissance of biocriminology. The first event was a failed National Institutes of Health conference. In 1992, the NIH convened both critics and proponents of this approach for a conference scheduled to be held at the University of Maryland where biological factors of crime and the potential practical applications of this newly acquired knowledge would be debated. However, a few months before the conference, Frederick Goodwin, then director of the Alcohol, Drug Abuse, and Mental Health Administration, suggested at a National Institutes of Health meeting that the purportedly violent and hypersexualized behavior of African American ghetto youth was similar to that observed among wild monkeys.[98] While these remarks were not directly related to the preparation of the conference, African American organizations used them to attack the event and call for its cancellation. Following this mobilization, the National Institutes of Health decided to withdraw its funding, which amounted to $78,000.[99]

While the funding was eventually reinstated, the 1995 conference was "accompanied by protests and placards reading 'Jobs not Prozac' and 'This Conference Predisposes Me to Disruptive Behavior Disorder.'"[100] In addition to the political frictions that it led to, this event provides yet another example of the marginality of criminologists in the study of criminal biology. Indeed, the collective work published a few years later focused on the ethical, legal, and social implications of the neurogenetics of crime, once again leaving out representatives of the criminological field.[101]

A second important event was the publication of *The Bell Curve* in 1994.[102] The *Bell Curve* is a book of more than eight hundred pages in which the psychologist Richard Herrnstein and the political scientist Charles Murray set out to demonstrate that the social and economic inequalities encountered by African Americans and Latinos in the United States were mainly due to genetic differences in intelligence. These differences in intelligence would also explain why African Americans were overrepresented in crime statistics. The publication of this study gave rise to a major controversy, both in the field of behavior genetics and in the scientific field more generally. While the authors were fiercely attacked and accused of fueling racist ideologies, some behavior geneticists defended them in the name of academic freedom.[103]

Far from being confined to the academic world, the controversy spilled over into some of the most widely read English-language weeklies (*New York Times Magazine, Newsweek*, etc.). The first author, Richard Herrnstein, was no stranger to controversy even before *The Bell*

Curve was published. He had already made a name for himself a decade earlier by publishing a book with another political scientist, James Q. Wilson, that was just as contentious. In *Crime and Human Nature*, Wilson and Herrnstein had proposed a synthetic approach to crime, combining economic, social, psychological, and biological variables. Predictably, it was the biological factors that caused the most stir. Reviewing the work of biology and criminal anthropology, from Lombroso's anthropometric research to quantitative genetic studies on twins, Wilson and Herrnstein provocatively concluded that "the average offender tends to be constitutionally distinctive" from the nonoffender.[104]

Starting in the 1960s, a first generation of biosocial criminologists emerged. Two sociologists, Clarence R. Jeffery and Marvin Wolfgang, each decided to take an interest in the interactions between social and biological factors in the development of deviant behavior. Although they succeeded in training a few doctoral students, the project did not take off. Access to empirical data was scarce; their approach raised indignation and suspicion among their sociological colleagues, who accused them of trying to revive Lombroso; and public authorities turned to psychologists, psychiatrists, and behavior geneticists in their war against violence. These barriers were still in place in the 1990s, and a true biosocial research stream was not yet discernible. The 2000s marked a turning point in several respects.

3 THE TURNING POINT OF THE 2000s

Institutionalizing Biosocial Criminology

THE STRUCTURAL DOMINATION OF SOCIOLOGISTS both stifled and contained Clarence Jeffery's and Marvin Wolfgang's attempt to initiate a biological understanding of crime in the second half of the twentieth century. The beginning of the new millennium, however, marked a turning point. First, genetic data became more accessible, and advances in behavior genetics gradually penetrated the social sciences.[1] The sequencing of the human genome at the beginning of the 2000s marked the end of the Human Genome Project, which had begun a decade earlier, and the transition to the genomic era. Launched in 1990, the Human Genome Project, the "holy grail" of biology, was vaunted as a platform for the next revolution in the discipline.[2] The expectations surrounding DNA research were considerable. Biochemist Daniel Koshland, editor of the prestigious journal *Science* from 1985 to 1995, wrote in October 1990, for example, that "the combination of new tools may not only let us help in reducing crime, but also aid some of our most disadvantaged citizens, the mentally ill."[3] Despite these outsized projections, molecular genetics has yet to revolutionize more traditional approaches in behavior genetics. In fact, as Aaron Panofsky has convincingly shown, the transition to the genomic era has only reinforced preexisting professional and scientific divisions.[4] Nonetheless, the scientific enthusiasm around the Human Genome Project attracted funding for behavior genetics research, accelerating the pace of publication and facilitating the entry of new researchers into the field.[5] Biosocial criminology was not the only scientific movement to benefit from this effervescence. From the 2000s onwards, research combining environmental and genetic variables has flourished throughout the social sciences, from political science[6] to economics.[7]

At the same time, the issue of violence and antisocial behavior became increasingly visible. In 2002, a research team led by psychologists and behavior geneticists Avshalom Caspi and Terrie Moffitt published a now-famous study in *Science* on the interaction between genetic and environmental factors in the development of antisocial behavior. The article, which intended to address the question of "why some children who are maltreated grow up to develop antisocial behavior, whereas others do not,"[8] proposed a biosocial answer: a polymorphism in the *MAOA* (monoamine oxidase A) gene moderated the results of maltreatment. Individuals who were abused but exhibited a high level of *MAOA* expression would be less likely to develop antisocial behavior as they grew up. The discovery of an interaction between genetics (*MAOA*) and environment (child abuse) in the development of antisocial behavior attracted considerable research interest. The *MAOA* gene is now commonly referred to as the "warrior gene,"[9] and the Caspi et al. paper has been cited more than six thousand times.[10] Dozens of studies have attempted to replicate and extend the results of this research. These efforts have had varying degrees of success, however, and the meta-analyses published to date have reached conflicting conclusions. While some have concluded that the Caspi et al. study was largely confirmed,[11] others remain more skeptical of the causal link between genetics and violent behaviors.[12] Beyond these debates on the reliability of its empirical results, this article played a major role in legitimizing the new biological theories of crime. Neurocriminologist Adrian Raine considers it to be "probably the most influential social science paper of the decade."[13] By embodying the serious and truly scientific character of contemporary biocriminology, this publication played an important role in the biosocial dynamic,[14] including for social scientists who were beginning to use genetics to study issues other than crime.[15]

Yet the sheer availability and attractiveness of behavior genetics do not, by themselves, explain the progress of biosocial criminology within the American criminological field. It is equally inadequate to attribute the development of "social genomics" to a crisis in the sciences[16] that would have been leading to the development of "amorphous" scientific fields,[17] as Catherine Bliss has claimed. Notwithstanding the conceptual vagueness of such an assertion, Bliss fails to draw the logical consequences of her own findings. She has clearly shown, for example, that the use of genetics in the social sciences necessarily depends on the ability of agents to maintain permanent, steady institutional positions within their respective disciplinary fields.[18] Disciplinary fields, far from being amorphous, continue to be constitutive of such enterprises.

The importance of institutional resources, both internal and external to the field of criminology, is clearly evident in the development and consolidation of biosocial criminology. The 2000s witnessed the academic and scientific rise of researchers from independent criminology departments. In 2001, Robert Sampson, who graduated in criminal justice at the University of Albany, was distinguished by the ASC Edwin H. Sutherland Award. Two years later, his colleague and coauthor John Laub, also a PhD in criminal justice, became president of the ASC itself. Biosocial criminology took advantage of this favorable situation. Until then, biosocial research had been conducted outside the field of criminology. However, the 2000s saw the birth and crystallization of a more solid research movement led by a few key figures from the criminological field.

THE EROSION OF SOCIOLOGICAL DOMINATION

The growing autonomy of criminology from the 2000s onwards was a central factor in the consolidation of biosocial criminology. In the short and medium term, however, we saw that the institutionalization of criminology resulted in the naturalization of sociologists' scientific domination. This was visible in the main academic associations, journals, and departments of criminology, and it enabled sociologists to contain heterodox scientific productions. But in the long run, the demographic development of autonomous criminological structures led to an erosion of this domination. To say that sociological domination has eroded since the 2000s does not mean that sociologists no longer dominate American criminology. Rather, this domination, while still tangible, is less important than it was in the 1980s and 1990s. In order to document criminology's autonomization vis-à-vis sociology, we will use the same indicators of the distribution of academic and scientific capital that made it possible to account for the domination of sociologists during the period of 1980–2000: the presidency of the two major academic associations (ASC and ACJS), winners of these associations' research awards, researchers most cited in the two associations' flagship journals (*Criminology* and *Justice Quarterly*), and the disciplinary origins of faculty employed in criminology departments.[19]

On the academic level, this erosion translates into a decrease in the number of sociologists heading the ASC and ACJS and in the number of sociologists among the faculty of criminology and criminal justice departments (table 3.1). On the scientific level, this erosion presents itself in the shrinking proportion of sociologists who received ASC and ACJS research awards between 2000 and 2016, as well as in the number of sociologists among the most-cited researchers in the journals *Criminology* and *Justice Quarterly* (table 3.2).

It is thus clear that a non-negligible part of the academic and scientific capital attached to sociology within the criminological field has been transferred to other disciplines. This redistribution has largely benefited PhDs from criminal justice and criminology departments. Beginning in the 2000s, independent criminologists were more frequently elected presidents of both the ASC and ACJS. They were also more likely to be hired by the criminology departments from which they graduated. Furthermore, these advances did not stop at the academic level. In scholarly terms, PhDs in criminology and criminal justice received more research awards than before 2000. Consider the

TABLE 3.1

Changes in the distribution of academic capital between disciplines before and after 2000

Discipline	ASC presidency	ACJS presidency	Criminology departments
Sociology	– 12.5%	– 5.5%	– 5.3%
Criminal justice[a]	+ 22.5%	+ 11.5%	+ 28.2%
Criminology[b]	– 5.0%	+ 24.5%	+ 2.7%
Psychology	– 5.0%	=	– 3.5%
Other	=	– 30.0%	– 20.5%

Note: Two averages per variable were calculated for each discipline: one average for the period 1980–99, and another for the period 2000–2016 (or 2017, based on data available as of January 11, 2017). The percentage increases or decreases shown are the difference between the twenty-first-century average and the twentieth-century average. This means, for example, that there are 12.5 percent fewer sociologists elected as ASC presidents between 2000 and 2016 than there were between 1980 and 1999.

a. This includes doctorates in "criminal justice and criminology."

b. This includes doctorates in "criminology, law and society."

TABLE 3.2

Changes in the distribution of scientific capital between disciplines before and after 2000

Discipline	ASC award	ACJS award	*Criminology* citations	*Justice Quarterly* citations
Sociology	– 44.5%	– 41.0%	– 5.7%	– 0.5%
Criminal justice[a]	+ 15.0%	+ 22.0%	+ 6.2%	+ 3.0%
Criminology[b]	+ 5.0%	+ 12.0%	=	+ 1.3%
Psychology	+ 12.3%	=	– 0.8%	+ 1.0%
Other	+ 12.3%	+ 7.0%	– 0.2%	– 5.7%

Note: Two averages per variable were calculated for each discipline: one average for the period 1980–99, and another for the period 2000–2016 (or 2017, based on data available as of January 11, 2017). The percentage increases or decreases shown are the difference between the twenty-first-century average and the twentieth-century average. This means, for example, that there are 5.7 percent fewer sociologists cited in the journal *Criminology* between 2000 and 2016 than there were between 1980 and 1999.

a. This includes doctorates in "criminal justice and criminology."

b. This includes doctorates in "criminology, law and society."

ASC Edwin H. Sutherland Award: criminal justice PhDs received more awards between 2001 and 2009 (Robert Sampson in 2001, John Laub in 2005, and Nicole Rafter in 2009) than they had in the previous forty years (zero awards from 1960 to 2000). They were also more highly cited for their work in two of the leading journals in American criminology, *Criminology* and *Justice Quarterly*.

The rise of autonomous criminologists was largely structural and demographic. In the 1980s–1990s, there were still few doctoral programs in criminology and criminal justice (table 3.3). Over the years, new programs were established. The number of doctoral degrees in criminology doubled between the mid-1990s and the mid-2000s as a result. Currently, about forty American universities offer a postgraduate degree in criminology. To be clear, when contextualized and compared to the growth of other disciplines, this progress remains relatively modest, given, for example, that the number of doctoral programs exceeds one thousand in a traditional discipline such as psychology.[20] The erosion of sociological domination did not, therefore, amount to a takeover of the criminological field by independent criminologists. Rather, as time progressed and the community of criminologists grew, the criminological field became more and more autonomous vis-à-vis the sociological field. This growing autonomy in turn allowed the development of research programs that most sociologists perceived as heterodox, foremost among which was biosocial criminology.

Not only did the community of independent criminologists grow, but this demographic expansion was accompanied by academic and scientific demands that defied the interests of the sociological field. Thus it was not just an institutional and quantitative growth of the criminological field, but the emergence within that field of new and competing scientific norms. Indeed, a significant segment of criminology led a veritable campaign to have criminology accepted as a full-fledged discipline that would be autonomous from sociology. In other words, while criminology had long been treated as a second nationality, more and more researchers made it their primary field. Numerous articles promoting the discipline's independence have been published

TABLE 3.3

Year of establishment and university of U.S. doctoral programs in criminology and criminal justice

University	Department Name	Year of Creation
Florida State University	Criminology and Criminal Justice	1958
Michigan State University	Criminal Justice	1968
SUNY Albany	Criminal Justice	1968
Sam Houston State University	Criminal Justice and Criminology	1970
Rutgers University, Newark	Criminal Justice	1975
University of Maryland	Criminology and Criminal Justice	1975
John Jay College of Criminal Justice	Criminal Justice	1980
University of California, Irvine	Criminology, Law and Society	1982
Washington State University	Criminal Justice and Criminology	1983
American University	Justice, Law and Criminology	1985
Arizona State University	Criminology and Criminal Justice	1986
Indiana University of Pennsylvania	Criminology and Criminal Justice	1988
University of Delaware	Sociology and Criminal Justice	1989
University of Cincinnati	Criminal Justice	1991
Temple University	Criminal Justice	1993
University of Nebraska, Omaha	Criminology and Criminal Justice	1994
Pennsylvania State University	Sociology and Criminology	1996
University of Missouri, St Louis	Criminology and Criminal Justice	1996
Indiana University, Bloomington	Criminal Justice	1997
University of Illinois, Chicago	Criminology, Law and Justice	1997
University of South Florida	Criminology	1997
University of Central Florida	Criminal Justice	1998
University of Southern Mississippi	Criminal Justice	1998
University of Arkansas, Little Rock	Sociology and Criminal Justice	2000
University of Pennsylvania	Criminology	2001
Prairie View A&M University	Juvenile Justice and Psychology	2001
North Dakota State University	Criminal Justice and Political Science	2002
Minot State University	Criminal Justice	2002
University of Florida	Sociology, Criminology and Law	2004
Northeastern University	Criminology and Criminal Justice	2004
George Mason University	Criminology, Law and Society	2005
University of Texas, Dallas	Criminology	2007
University of South Carolina	Criminology and Criminal Justice	2008
Texas State University, San Marcos	Criminal Justice	2009
Southern Illinois University	Criminology and Criminal Justice	2012
University of Louisville	Criminal Justice	Unknown
Georgia State University	Criminology	Unknown
University of Massachusetts-Lowell	Criminology and Justice Studies	Unknown
Old Dominion University	Sociology and Criminal Justice	Unknown
University of North Dakota	Criminal Justice	Unknown
University of New Haven	Criminal Justice	Unknown

in American criminology journals since the early 2000s by researchers who have no observable connection to biosocial criminology.[21] Biosocial criminologists strategically exploited this movement and aligned themselves with the interests of the proponents of independent criminology, or, to use a Latourian expression, enrolled these allies who, like themselves, sought the field's autonomy. For if criminology was to be an independent discipline, then there would be no reason why the definition of crime should be formulated in strictly sociological terms. To assert that crime is a genetic problem amounts to justifying the academic and scientific independence of criminology from sociology, and to pushing the process of autonomization slightly further.

AUTONOMOUS CRIMINOLOGY, A NICHE FOR BIOSOCIAL CRIMINOLOGY

Unsurprisingly, the empowerment of the criminological field has greatly benefited the development of biosocial criminology. Figure 3.1 shows the parallel evolution of the development of doctoral programs in the discipline and the publication of biosocial criminology articles. Nearly 90 percent of biosocial criminology articles have been published from 2000 onwards, when sociological domination began to wane and the criminological field became increasingly autonomous. While this does not necessarily mean that one causes the other, it is very likely that the two processes are somehow linked. A similar pattern of parallel development of institutions and intellectual movements can be seen, for example, in the case of women's and gender studies in the United States. As sociologist Christine Wood has astutely observed, "The processes of institutional and intellectual expansion were naturally interrelated. Scholars justified the institutional growth of their programs by articulating theoretically ambitious intellectual goals, such as claiming expertise over analysis of gender relations and identities or diversifying the faculty roster so as to represent a wider range of knowledge about women."[22]

This example nicely illustrates a fact well known to historians and sociologists of science, namely that "scientific activity depends on the extrascientific factor that is most closely related to it, namely

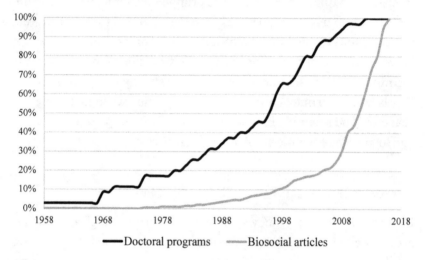

FIGURE 3.1

Parallel evolution of the percentage of doctoral programs in criminology (n= 35) and biosocial criminology articles (n= 188), 1958–2016

the organizational forms within which the research is carried out."[23] Similarly, the development of biosocial criminology has been facilitated by the growth of independent criminological structures, while at the same time providing them with scientific legitimacy. Just as the organization of the Collège de France allowed Parisian doctors to develop the organicist doctrine and to oppose the vitalism of the Montpellier school during the first half of the nineteenth century, criminological institutions—departments, doctoral programs, journals, associations—created the social conditions for the development of novel scientific products, including biosocial criminology.

This is just one indicator of the increasing autonomy of criminology, also reflected in the implementation of specialized journals, which in turn have promoted the development of biosocial criminology. Journals play a fundamental role in the development of scientific movements, as they allow for the "creation of communities" and the "circulation of concepts and references."[24] While biosocial criminologists have not—yet—created their own journal, they have taken control of the editorial line of an existing criminology journal, the *Journal of Criminal Justice*. Matt DeLisi, one of the most productive researchers in biosocial criminology, became its editor in chief in 2010, and several members of the biosocial movement have joined the editorial board over the years (including J. C. Barnes, Kevin Beaver, Brian Boutwell, Terrie Moffitt, and Michael Vaughn). This academic capital is an invaluable resource for the dissemination of biosocial criminology. Since Matt DeLisi became editor, thirty-three biosocial criminology articles from the corpus constituted for this book have been published in the *Journal of Criminal Justice*, representing approximately one-third (28.7 percent) of the total number of articles published during the 2010–16 period.

The parallel drawn between the development of doctoral programs in criminology and biosocial criminology also explains why one of the primary demands of biosocial criminologists is that of autonomy, especially vis-à-vis sociology. As an interdisciplinary discipline, that is, as a field without disciplinary boundaries, criminology serves researchers who have an interest in challenging sociological domination. Put differently, the issue of the fate of criminology as an independent discipline cannot be detached from the scientific considerations of the actors who participate in this struggle over the relationships between criminology and sociology. Science and academic politics are but two sides of the same coin. That can be seen by comparing comments from Robert Sampson, a criminal justice PhD who then served as a sociology professor at the University of Chicago and Harvard University, and who was also president of the ASC in 2012, with those from biosocial criminologist Kevin Beaver, also a criminal justice PhD who then became a professor of criminology at Florida State University and has been a member of the Biosocial Criminology Research Group. Sampson believes that criminology is not a discipline and that it would benefit from being even more open to sociology.[25] He is, moreover, skeptical of the "current fascination with DNA sequencing and brain imaging."[26] Kevin Beaver takes the exact opposite view, praising the fact that criminology departments have helped loosen sociologists' grip on the study of crime.[27] When Sampson encourages proximity with sociology, Beaver and his colleagues argue that "it may be time to cut the intellectual chord [sic] with sociology and to recognize that criminology and criminal justice are highly multidisciplinary."[28] This brings us back to the opposition that marked the birth of criminology at the end of the nineteenth century. Researchers like Robert Sampson do not view criminology as an autonomous field and maintain a primary attachment to another discipline, in this case sociology. Opposed are researchers who are solely involved in the field of criminology and who advocate for its autonomy.

The parallel evolution of the autonomization of the criminological field and the development of biosocial criminology is not only visible at the macrosocial level. One of the key characteristics of the biosocial movement is that it is predominantly composed of early-career PhDs from independent criminology departments. Sociologists, conversely, constitute a marginal portion of this movement (table 3.4). Not only do criminology and criminal justice PhDs provide biosocial research with the bulk of its workforce through doctoral students, but these academic structures also provide a sheltered space within which biosocial criminologists can pursue a stable career. PhDs in criminology are not, however, the only contributors to the field. A significant portion of those who publish in biosocial criminology have been trained in psychology (table 3.4).

Although one might think that the presence of psychologists would dilute the preponderant role of criminological structures in the development of biosocial criminology, a bibliometric analysis contradicts this hypothesis. Indeed, even though there are about as many PhDs in criminology as in psychology, the relative contribution of these two groups to biosocial criminology is far from equal. Of 188 articles, over 60 percent were written by a PhD in criminology, compared to approximately 20 percent by psychologists.[29] In other words, the relative contribution of PhDs in criminology to biosocial criminology is three times greater than that of psychologists. This result can be explained by the fact that psychologists working in the field of criminology have remained attached to their original discipline. Indeed, Aaron Panof-

TABLE 3.4

Doctoral training of biosocial criminologists (n = 182)

Criterion (*n* authors)		Percentage share
PhD discipline (161)	Criminology[a]	39.1%
	Psychology	38.5%
	Sociology	14.9%
	Other	7.5%
Graduation year (155)	Before 2000	36.8%
	After 2000	63.2%
THE rank[b] (149)	0–10	0.7%
	11–50	11.4%
	51–200	33.6%
	> 200	54.4%

a. This includes PhDs in criminal justice.

b. For this criterion, only authors who completed their PhD at a U.S. university were included. For *The Times*'s higher education (THE) rankings, see "World University Rankings 2015–2016," accessed February 7, 2020, https://www.timeshighereduca tion.com/world-university-rankings/2016/world-ranking.

sky has clearly shown that psychologists who deploy genetics consider their participation in other scientific fields, for example in criminology, as a means of producing scientific capital that they then seek to reimport into their field of origin.[30]

Another notable characteristic of biosocial criminology is the overrepresentation of early-career researchers, with 63.2 percent of biosocial criminologists having graduated on or after 2000. The role of doctoral students and young researchers in scientific innovation is well documented.[31] Student recruitment has played a role in the development of research movements as diverse as radio astronomy,[32] medieval history[33] and the study of stem cells.[34] Conversely, the inability to recruit doctoral students usually leads to the end of a scientific specialty. To borrow the terminology of the sociologists Joseph Ben-David and Randall Collins, not only do the "founders" of a scientific discipline or specialty need to be able to recruit "followers,"[35] but the latter must in turn be able to educate doctoral students who then extend the research domain.[36] This is what the first generation of biosocial criminology lacked. Jeffery, the founder, was able to recruit only two followers, Lee Ellis and Diana Fishbein, who were isolated and unable to train biosocial criminologists.

In contrast, the second generation of biosocial criminologists found a pool of potential followers in criminology departments (table 3.5). This explains why most biosocial criminologists earned their doctorates after 2000. This second generation interacts with four subgenerations of researchers. The first generation, the founders, is composed of criminologists who did not complete a dissertation in biosocial criminology. They became interested in genetic factors later in their career

TABLE 3.5

A selection of recent biosocial criminology dissertations

Name	Graduation Year	Dissertation Title
Kevin Beaver	2006	*The intersection of genes, the environment, and crime and delinquency: A longitudinal study of offending*
Jamie Vaske	2009	*The role of genes and abuse in the etiology of offending*
J. C. Barnes	2010	*Analyzing the biosocial selection into life-course transitions*
Brian Boutwell	2010	*School-level moderators of genetic influences on antisocial behaviors*
Jamie Newsome	2013	*Resilience and vulnerability in adolescents at risk for delinquency: A behavioral genetic study of differential response to risk*
Marie Ratchford	2013	*Gene-environment interactions in the prediction of antisocial phenotypes: A test of integrated systems theory*
Eric Connolly	2014	*Examining gene-environment interactions between antisocial behavior, neighborhood disadvantage, and collective efficacy*
Melissa Petkovsek	2014	*Molecular genetic scaffolding of maladaptive behaviors and victimization*
Dylan Jackson	2015	*Do nutritional factors influence externalizing behavior during early childhood? A genetically informed analysis*

once they had obtained a permanent position at a university. One example is John Paul Wright, a professor at the University of Cincinnati who devoted his dissertation to sociological theories of crime before turning to biosocial criminology for the first time in a 2005 paper co-authored with his doctoral student Kevin Beaver.[37]

The second subgeneration, the followers, corresponds to researchers who have completed a dissertation in biosocial criminology under the direction of one of the founders. The first occurrence of this trajectory can be traced back to 2006 and Kevin Beaver's dissertation on genetic and environmental factors in crime. The third subgeneration is made up of researchers who have completed a dissertation in biosocial criminology under the direction of followers, that is, researchers from the second subgeneration. For example, Brian Boutwell completed his dissertation on moderators of genetic influences under the direction of Kevin Beaver. Signaling the dynamism and reproduction of the movement, members of the third subgeneration have themselves begun to train biosocial criminologists. Brian Boutwell, for example, recently directed Melissa Petkovsek's (2014) criminology dissertation at Sam Houston State University.

In the process, some universities in the United States have become hubs for the reproduction of biosocial criminology. Seven universities have trained more than one-third of biosocial criminologists (35.7 percent; table 3.6). This concentration of biosocial criminology in a small number of institutions is reminiscent of the situation described by Aaron Panofsky in relation to behavior genetics. Panofsky interprets this maneuver as a consequence of the controversial nature of the field. Repeatedly exposed to criticism from other researchers, behavior geneticists have turned their field into a protective "bunker." Concentration in a few academic institutions is part of this strategy of "bunkerization."[38] Interestingly, some of the centers of biosocial criminology are also bastions of behavior genetics. For example, the University of Colorado is one of the historical centers of behavior genetics.[39] The University of Southern California also has an institute that has produced many of the psychologists active in behavior genetics, including David Rowe, Terrie Moffitt, and Adrian Raine.

TABLE 3.6

Top doctoral universities for biosocial criminologists

University	Department(s)	Trained Biosocial Criminologists
Florida State University	Criminology, psychology, sociology	15
University of Cincinnati	Criminology	13
University of Southern California	Psychology, sociology	11
University of Colorado	Psychology, sociology	9
Sam Houston State University	Criminology	6
University of Maryland	Criminology, psychology	6
University of Pennsylvania	Criminology, psychology	5

The presence of other institutions is better explained by the activity and importance of their criminology departments, confirming once again the fundamental role that the development of the criminological field has played in the development and consolidation of biosocial approaches to crime. Since biosocial criminology is a recently established research movement led by a handful of highly productive researchers, it seems logical that the institutional centers of this current are the home institutions of the few individuals who give it its impetus. Kevin Beaver, for example, completed his dissertation under the direction of John Paul Wright at the University of Cincinnati before becoming a professor in the Criminology Department at Florida State University, the same department that had employed Jeffery thirty years earlier. Beaver went on to train numerous biosocial criminologists at FSU, while regularly serving on the dissertation committees of his colleagues at Cincinnati.

This concentration also circumvents—and explains—the controversial nature of biosocial criminology among a significant portion of American criminologists. In an interview, a young professor who had completed his dissertation under the direction of one of the most active biosocial criminologists touched upon the difficulties he experienced in finding a permanent academic job. Despite an impeccable

CV and numerous publications in peer-reviewed journals, only a criminology department at a small regional university was willing to offer him a position. This department, where he is still employed, is headed by a longtime friend of his former supervisor:

> Julien Larregue: When you were on the job market, had you encountered any difficulties? Or was the fact that you published a lot an advantage and do you think it played a role?
>
> Interviewee 2: I do think that publishing in biosocial criminology probably turned some schools off to me. When I was coming out of my PhD I had a pretty strong record . . . but I only got an interview on one school, which kind of surprised me, the school that I ended at now . . . when I had other colleagues that maybe were publishing in less . . . I don't know . . . controversial fields and may have had fewer publications and had multiple job offers. So I think it probably impacted my navigation in the job market a little bit.
>
> Julien Larregue: Okay, and do you remember your interview for the job? Did they mention anything about that?
>
> Interviewee 2: No, so at the job that I have right now, the department head is actually one of X's [one of biosocial criminology's leading figures] best friends . . . and so he and X have been friends for thirty-four years, and he [the department head] has always been exposed to biosocial criminology, and he looked at bringing me onto the faculty to move the department forward so . . . and everybody at the department seemed excited about my research.

In addition to the interplay of personal relationships at work, this professor's response hints at the academic considerations that already presided over the recruitment of the first generation of biosocial criminologists in the 1970s and 1980s. This small regional university produces few scientific publications. The department to which this biosocial criminologist belongs is oriented more toward teaching and professional training than scientific research. One sign, among others, of this positioning is that we find police officers among the faculty.

Hiring a biosocial criminologist who published in peer-reviewed journals constituted an opportunity to raise the department's standing and
"move the department forward."

A DISABLING RESOURCE: THE POOR REPUTATION OF AUTONOMOUS CRIMINOLOGY

Although biosocial criminology has found a welcoming niche in the
criminological field, it has also inherited the negative characteristics
associated with it. In particular, the police-based origins of criminological institutions discussed in chapter 1 have affected the position
of criminology departments within U.S. academic hierarchies. Criminology's lack of recognition, which was already apparent from the
outset, has continued to haunt the discipline to the present day. In his
inaugural address as newly elected president of the ASC in 2003, John
Laub lamented the "disdain that prominent academics, policymakers,
and politicians have for our discipline."[40] Laub reminded the crowd of
the contempt that had for instance been expressed by University of
Pennsylvania political scientist John Dilulio, who was quoted as saying
that he "would most definitely rather be governed on crime policy by
the first 100 names in the local phone book than by the first 100 names
on the membership roll of the American Society of Criminology."[41]

Criminology's poor reputation has had repercussions at the institutional level. Following Berkeley's fiasco,[42] no other elite U.S. university
attempted to establish a stand-alone criminology department.[43] When
I spent time at the University of Chicago during my doctorate, one student expressed surprise at the research I was conducting on American criminology by saying, "But there is no criminology at U Chicago,
right?" This anecdote expressed genuine surprise that one might find
"criminology" on the campus of an Ivy League university. To be sure,
prestigious universities do produce knowledge about crime. This process, however, is organized through more established and respected
disciplines, including sociology and psychology.

It might be the case that criminology is yet another instance of an
imitation effect. According to this hypothesis, elite universities would
be reluctant to establish criminology departments because of the re-

sounding failure of one of their peers. The Berkeley effect would thus be the counterpart of the "Harvard effect" that sociologist Fabio Rojas has uncovered regarding the creation of ethnic and African American studies departments.[44] Rojas has shown how, in the United States, "universities do not follow national trends; they belong to peer groups, as defined by the Carnegie classification, and African American studies is diffused through these groups."[45] This hypothesis is supported by the fact that most criminology programs are found in institutions that are oriented toward professional training rather than scientific research (table 3.7), so much so that sociologist Andrew Abbott labeled independent criminology as an "undergraduate discipline."[46]

The social effects of this distribution are significant: a researcher who intends to get a graduate degree in criminology is destined to not attend the most prestigious universities. Compared to other scientific specialties such as neuroeconomics[47] or the history of science,[48] biosocial criminology is associated with less prestigious universities. We

TABLE 3.7

Carnegie classification of the universities offering a master's and/or doctoral degree in criminology (n = 233)

Carnegie Classification	Number of Programs
Master's	128
Doctorate	97
Undergraduate	6
Other	2

Note: The list of criminology programs was obtained from the American Society of Criminology website. Doctoral institutions are those awarding at least twenty doctoral degrees per year. They correspond to the most research-intensive universities. In contrast, master's and bachelor's institutions are those that focus on predoctoral studies (undergraduate and master's degrees). Data source: Indiana University Center for Postsecondary Research, "The Carnegie Classification of Institutions of Higher Education," accessed February 7, 2020, https://carnegieclassifications.acenet.edu.

saw earlier that more than half of biosocial criminologists (54.4 percent) obtained their doctorate in a university outside the top two hundred of the *Times* Higher Education Rankings (table 3.4). Conversely, only one biosocial criminologist was trained in an elite university. It is also striking that the hierarchization of U.S. universities is directly correlated with the disciplinary composition of the faculty in criminology departments. The more prestigious a university, the more it is likely that its criminology department will have a higher number of sociologists among its professors (table 3.8). The fact that this correlation is linear makes it all the more striking. While in low-prestige departments only 21.9 percent of professors are trained in sociology, this rate rises to 27.4 percent for medium-prestige departments and to 49 percent for the most prestigious ones. This demonstrates that the general hierarchy of U.S. universities is deeply intertwined with the disciplinary hierarchies that are specific to the criminological field: the domination of sociology within criminology departments is even more manifest in the most prestigious universities.

This raises the question of whether having been trained in less prestigious universities might explain, to some extent, the decision of some researchers to study the biological factors of crime. Indeed, it is established that "the propensity to address prestigious subjects [is] directly related to the prestige of the places frequented by the researchers" because of the resulting differentiated scientific socialization.[49] Thus it has been observed that Nobel Prize winners were often trained in prestigious universities, often by former Nobel Prize winners.[50] By attending universities that ranked lower in the prestige hierarchies, biosocial criminologists were able to develop deviant research interests that did not conform to the dominant sociological canons. Indeed, by advancing the idea that crime is at least partly genetic in origin, biosocial criminology runs the risk of being perceived as fundamentally antisocial.

In the case of biosocial criminology, it is more than likely that these two variables, the prestige of the institutions attended and the choice of research interests, work in a circle of mutual reinforcement. In fact, the greater presence of sociologists in the most prestigious faculties

TABLE 3.8

Doctoral discipline of faculty employed at thirty-two PhD-awarding departments of criminology according to institutional prestige

Discipline of doctorate	Low prestige[a] 1 to 3	Medium prestige[b] 4 to 6	High prestige[c] 7 to 8
Sociology	21.9%	27.4%	49.0%
Criminal justice	27.7%	24.9%	12.7%
Criminology and criminal justice	18.1%	14.2%	7.4%
Other	12.3%	8.1%	11.3%
Political science[d]	4.5%	9.6%	5.4%
Psychology	5.2%	3.6%	8.8%
Criminology	4.5%	7.1%	2.0%
Criminology, other[e]	4.5%	2.5%	2.4%
Sociology and criminology	1.3%	2.5%	2.4%

a. This category includes eight criminology departments and 155 faculty members.

b. This category includes fourteen criminology departments and 197 faculty members.

c. This category includes ten criminology departments and 204 faculty members.

d. This includes the following disciplines: public policy, public affairs, public administration, political science, government, international relations.

e. This includes the following disciplines: justice studies, administration of justice, criminology law and society, criminology law and justice.

of criminology means that biosocial criminologists are statistically more likely to succeed in institutions where the control of sociologists is weaker, that is, those that are also the least prestigious and therefore the least conducive to the development and further embodiment of a habitus that is in line with the dominant criteria of the criminological field. This hypothesis is supported by the fact that the two institutions that are most highly represented within the biosocial movement are Florida State University and the University of Cincinnati. They have trained fifteen and thirteen biosocial criminologists respectively and lie among the medium-prestige universities in table 3.8, where the presence of social scientists is less important. The overrepresentation of biosocial criminology in the less prestigious criminology departments will likely continue to affect the movement's ability to establish social legitimacy within the field of criminology, as "institutional hierarchy also plays a role in the acceptance or nonacceptance of new findings."[51] Biosocial criminologists will find it even more difficult to gain acceptance for their "Copernican criminology,"[52] as their position within the field of criminology does not work in their favor. But it is not simply in terms of symbolic capital that this dominated position within the field could have harmful effects. We shall see later that there are practical consequences to this marginality, as biosocial criminologists are forced to concentrate their research on some biological factors while neglecting others that are more costly to study (including the brain), yet are considered more advanced and promising on a scientific level.

Although biosocial criminology had been under pressure during the second half of the twentieth century, it experienced a major boom from the 2000s. Several factors explain this takeoff. First, genetic databases were gradually made accessible to social scientists, which made it possible for biosocial criminologists to go beyond theoretical discussions and produce empirical research. However, decisive changes also occurred within the field of criminology itself. The increasing autonomy of criminological institutions (departments, associations, journals, etc.) with respect to sociology opened the space for renewed scientific possibilities. Nonetheless, this resource was not without constraints: criminology's lack of prestige and the fact that the discipline was seldom institutionalized in the most prestigious universities (except for the University of Pennsylvania) continued to weigh on the perception and reception of biosocial criminology. Let us now turn to the internal divisions within this scientific movement.

4 THE SCIENTIFIC HETEROGENEITY OF BIOSOCIAL CRIMINOLOGY

WHAT FRÉDÉRIC LEBARON HAS SAID of economists applies equally to biosocial criminology: this science "is more an indication of an intense—but never accomplished—work of social construction of the group than the proof of a real and well-established unity, based on a clearly delimited and constituted corpus of knowledge, scientific norms, and shared professional procedures."[1] It is telling in this regard that the study by Avshalom Caspi and colleagues published in *Science*,[2] considered to be one of the founding works of the movement,[3] fails to mention the term *biosocial*. This is further evidence that some researchers produce biosocial criminology without identifying themselves with this movement. In fact, when asked, "Would you define yourself as a biosocial criminologist?," seven of the twenty researchers who answered an online questionnaire I circulated answered "no."[4]

Thus one can either view biosocial criminology as a label and include only those researchers and publications that define themselves as "biosocial," or approach this line of research as a composite milieu within which biosocial criminology is sometimes produced without explicitly mobilizing the term. This pattern is not unique to biosocial criminology. For example, many researchers produce work in behavior genetics without claiming to be part of the field,[5] and the debate on criminology in France displays the same phenomenon.[6] Far from being trivial, this management of identities gives rise to flexible categorizations ("them" versus "us") that guide the emergence and resolution of scientific controversies.

FROM SOCIAL TO INTELLECTUAL AFFINITIES: THE NETWORKS OF BIOSOCIAL CRIMINOLOGY

The existence of subgroups can be visualized through an analysis of the collaborative relationships among biosocial criminologists. Underneath the apparent homogeneity of this research movement, a network analysis of article coauthorship reveals that most subgroups have only loose links with each other. The modularity coefficient is 0.724, meaning that the different groups are largely autonomous. This can be seen in figure 4.1: around a central network mainly composed of PhDs in criminology and housing the key representatives of the biosocial movement (Kevin Beaver, Brian Boutwell, J. C. Barnes, Matt DeLisi, and John Paul Wright) gather several small independent networks that do not use the label "biosocial criminology." The authors in these smaller networks are mainly psychologists and sociologists. Notice that prestigious representatives of the biological approach to crime, such as Terrie Moffitt (localized in the center) and Adrian Raine (localized in the upper part), have no collaborative relationship with the core network of biosocial criminologists.

This division of the movement is not purely social and structural but also scientific, as these networks can be categorized according to their proximity to "strong biologism" and "weak biologism,"[7] or, in other words, progenetic biosocial criminology and proenvironmental biosocial criminology. These two positions, progenetic and proenvironmental, are of course ideal types. Some researchers are more difficult to categorize because they adopt an intermediate position that is agnostic with regard to ranking the importance of environmental and genetic factors. According to the agnostics, environmental and genetic factors are a priori equally important. This position can be

FIGURE 4.1

Networks of coauthored articles in biosocial criminology, 2005–2016.

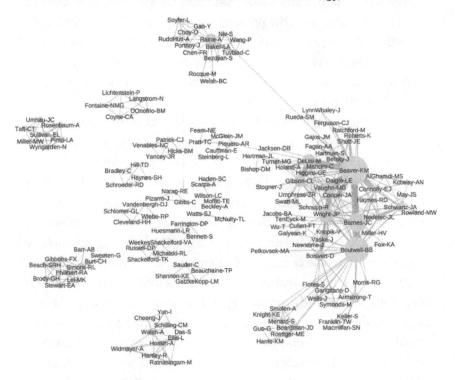

Note: This graph was produced using the software Gephi with the ForceAtlas spatialization algorithm. The size of the nodes, which is a function of the number of collaborations between authors, reflects the centrality of the different authors in the corpus of biosocial criminology articles. The thickness of the links between the different authors depends on the number of coauthored articles. Of the 155 articles in the corpus published between 2005 and 2016, 12 were excluded from this analysis because they were not found in the Web of Science database from which the coauthorship data were harvested.

illustrated with the following passage from an interview: "I mean, I really think they [environment and genetics] are both fifty-fifty. . . . Of course in different circumstances, right? I mean, if I was just to generalize, I would say they are equally important. Of course, for certain traits biology is more important; for other traits, you know, sociology and environment are more important. But I'd say on average they are equally important."[8]

The fact remains that all biosocial criminologists can be positioned on an axis ranging from the progenetic to the proenvironmental, with agnosticism being an intermediate position that reflects, not a refusal of the distribution criterion itself, but the desire of some researchers to distance themselves from what they perceive as more radical postures (biologism and environmentalism).

The scientific heterogeneity of the biosocial movement can also be objectified through an analysis of the references used by these researchers in their scientific productions. Co-citation analysis is used in scientometrics to measure the proximity and theoretical affinities between different authors in a given specialty or discipline. Figure 4.2 presents the results of this type of analysis for biosocial criminology articles published between 2005 and 2016. Whereas the modularity coefficient for article coauthorship networks was 0.724, this time it is 0.297, which, at first glance, seems to indicate that the intellectual homogeneity of biosocial criminology (as measured by citation practices) is greater than its social homogeneity (as measured by coauthorship practices). However, one must consider the relative contribution of different subcommunities to the total number of works cited: given that the core network (Beaver, Boutwell, Barnes, DeLisi, Wright, etc.) publishes far more articles than any other community, the co-citation analysis largely reflects what this group thinks biosocial criminology should be. Unsurprisingly, the five most central authors within this co-citation network (i.e., the authors who are most frequently cited together in biosocial criminology articles), Beaver, Moffitt, Raine, DeLisi, and Alex Piquero, were all trained in criminology or psychology. Most of these authors share a common vision of what biosocial criminology should be, which will become clear below, particularly in the analysis of the controversies opposing progenetic and proenvironmental biosocial criminologists.

Despite this relative homogeneity, we can still identify some dynamics that, although they do not necessarily translate into funda-

FIGURE 4.2

Networks of authors co-cited by biosocial criminology articles, 2005–2016 (threshold of twenty common references).

Note: This graph was produced using the software Gephi with the ForceAtlas spatialization algorithm. To facilitate the readability of the graph, only the names of authors associated with a minimum of ten other authors are displayed. The size of the nodes, which is a function of the number of citations received, reflects the centrality of the different authors in the bibliography of biosocial criminology articles. The thickness of the links between different authors depends on the number of shared citations. As with the previous network analysis, only 143 of the 155 articles published during this period were included.

mental cleavages or disagreements, do reveal interesting theoretical nuances in how different researchers might approach the criminal phenomenon. In particular, a central pole, linked to the criminological field, where we find authors such as Beaver, Piquero, and DeLisi (upper part of the graph), can be contrasted with a pole of evolutionary psychologists where biosocial criminologists such as Lee Ellis are found alongside authors such as David M. Buss or Steven Pinker (bottom of the graph). Occupying a median position, researchers like Moffitt and Raine serve as intellectual intermediaries between these two distant poles.

In contrast, prominent sociologists such as Robert Sampson and Ronald Simons lie at the margins of the network, reflecting their reduced importance in the biosocial criminology literature. Sociologists' marginality is also observed in the type of work cited by biosocial criminologists. For example, restricting ourselves to the period of 2005–16, we see that the journals most cited in biosocial criminology articles (table 4.1), while varied, are mostly concentrated in three disciplines: criminology (1,997 citations), developmental and child psychology (1,169 citations), and psychiatry (1,024 citations). Sociology comes in only eighth with 367 citations, again giving weight to the antisociological posture adopted by prominent members of the biosocial movement.

To a certain extent, the biosocial criminology movement reproduces institutional disciplinary divisions. Disciplinary affiliation alone, however, does not account for the structure of biosocial criminology, as it is also necessary to consider the dynamics of this movement and the way in which competing visions of biosocial criminology clash with each other. As we shall see, there is a clear division of labor between researchers who are trained in psychology and those who are not. Psychologically trained researchers produce knowledge about the neurological factors of crime, while sociologists and criminologists compete for control over the production of genetic knowledge.

TABLE 4.1

Discipline of the journals most cited by biosocial criminology articles published between 2005 and 2016 (n = 143)

Discipline	Citations
Criminology	1,997
Developmental and child psychology	1,169
Psychiatry	1,024
Personality psychology	616
Neurology and neurosurgery	484
Clinical psychology	480
Genetics and heredity	464
Sociology	367
Biomedical research—general	353
Psychology—various	254
Experimental psychology	196
Psychology—general	160
Behavioral science	144
General medicine	124
Pediatrics	120
Illness and dependency	117

Note: Some biosocial criminology articles published in journals not listed in the Web of Science database were not included in the analysis.

CRIMINOLOGY GRADUATES: THE HEART OF THE PROGENETIC BRANCH

Biosocial criminology is most often identified with a small group of controversial researchers who publicly describe themselves as "biosocial criminologists" and who have written articles and books that directly challenge the dominant sociological paradigm found in the U.S. criminological field.[9] Criticisms of biosocial criminology are generally directed at them.[10] One of the main characteristics of this first group is that it is mostly composed of early-career PhDs working in nonprestigious criminology departments (main network in figure 4.1). Not all of them come from these structures, however, as some of their best-known representatives have been trained in other disciplines (box 3). Conversely, not all graduates in criminology who produce biosocial criminology necessarily attack sociological theories of crime, which means it is necessary to go beyond clear disciplinary divisions.

Following relatively informal collaborations such as the Biosocial Criminology Research Group (box 3), an academic association called the Biosocial Criminology Association (BCA) emerged in 2014. Chaired by Eric Connolly, a former doctoral student of Kevin Beaver, the BCA presents itself as "an organization dedicated to understanding the genetic and environmental influences on the development of antisocial behavior."[12] The BCA has held three annual meetings since its foundation: in 2014, 2015, and 2016. Attendance at this event provides a rough idea of the size of the network of criminology graduates. According to one of the Association's executive members, the Association has just over two hundred members, about one-third of whom are crimi-

BOX 3. THE BIOSOCIAL CRIMINOLOGY RESEARCH GROUP

The Biosocial Criminology Research Group is an informal research network founded in 2005[11] with the goal of studying the relationship between social and genetic variables in the development of criminal and antisocial behaviors. It is composed of two criminology graduates (Kevin Beaver and John Paul Wright), a sociologist (Matt DeLisi), and a social work graduate (Michael Vaughn). Wright supervised Beaver's dissertation at the University of Cincinnati, where he earned his doctorate, while DeLisi graduated from the University of Colorado and Vaughn from Washington University St. Louis. Beaver is the only researcher to have completed a dissertation about biosocial criminology (on the intersection of genes and environment and their impact on crime and delinquency). Aside from Wright, all members of the network finished their doctoral studies between 2000 and 2006. Thus we are dealing with a relatively early-career group that entered the academic market at a time when the domination of sociologists within the U.S. criminological field was becoming less flagrant.

nologists, with the remainder of the membership being split between psychology, behavior genetics, social work, sociology, psychiatry, and medicine.[13]

The group seeks to develop biosocial criminological theories to replace the dominant sociological theories[14] that fail to withstand empirical testing once biological variables are considered. John Paul Wright and Kevin Beaver, for example, tested the general theory of crime developed by Michael Gottfredson and Travis Hirschi to show that self-control was not determined, as they claimed, by the education provided by parents.[15] The subversive and antisociological ambitions of these researchers are also reflected in the fact that they claim to follow in the intellectual footsteps of the nineteenth-century Italian criminologist Cesare Lombroso, whom they treat as an unjustly demonized Copernican heretic,[16] reproaching sociologists for having neglected his genuine contributions to criminology.[17] From the perspective of these researchers, biosocial theories are incompatible with traditional sociological perspectives on crime. For example, one of the leaders of this group confided that he began to question the relevance of sociological approaches while he was a doctoral student: "I was beginning to read quite broadly at the time in genetics, neuroscience, and so forth, and I realized that the findings that were coming out of these different fields of study were largely incompatible or at least partially incompatible with what I was learning in my sociology courses."[18]

Rather than an evolution, the shift from sociological pseudoscience to actual biosocial science is thus portrayed as a revolution marked by a Kuhnian paradigm shift.[19] This idea of a before and after is well illustrated by a progenetic biosocial criminologist who earned his PhD in the early 1980s, at a time when the domination of sociologists was still very strong:

> Sociological criminology was like philosophy, philosophizing about the universe, you know? The geocentric model [this model was prior to the scientific revolution sparked by Copernicus and Galileo and presumed the Earth was the center of the universe], you know, the Sun revolved around an Earth that was standing still. Well that made

sense, didn't it? If you think about it, we don't feel that we're spinning. The spins are about a thousand miles an hour, we don't know that, we don't feel that, and we're hurtling through space around the sun 67,000 miles an hour, we don't feel it! We do see the Sun rising in the east and setting in the west, so . . . but once we get a telescope and we can see things, you know? When you get people like Copernicus and Tycho Brahe and people like that, they can actually make observations. Yeah, it makes a difference when you got tools, right? And sociology lacks the tools, you know? It's just philosophy![20]

This group's research borrows heavily from the field of behavior genetics. Conversely, they have little involvement in the neuroscientific side of biosocial criminology, which can be explained in part by their limited access to brain imaging technology: unlike psychologists, these researchers are employed in criminology departments that do not have the equipment and personnel to produce neurological analyses of crime.[21] In contrast, genetic data are readily available, and they are integrated into statistical analysis no differently from the variables traditionally used by criminologists.

PSYCHOLOGISTS AS UNCOMMITTED BYSTANDERS

The second group of biosocial researchers is centered on psychology and is overall more prestigious than the one originating in criminology departments. Its best-known representative is University of Pennsylvania psychologist Adrian Raine, who, although he sometimes uses the term *biosocial,* claims to be from neurocriminology, "a new subdiscipline of Criminology which applies neuroscience techniques to probe the causes and cures of crime and violence."[22] This terminological distinction is not insignificant, for we know that "neuroscience has many more resources, is better integrated, and has avoided the kinds of controversies behavior genetics has suffered (and the publicity it has enjoyed)."[23]

Compared to genes, which seem to be out of reach, Raine and his colleagues emphasize the curative dimension of their research, in short, its social utility. Unlike criminologists, most psychologists and neuroscientists do not take sides in the controversies surrounding biosocial criminology. Focusing on neurological factors rather than genetic factors is therefore a choice between respectability and controversy. This explains why some members of the criminology group, who are less attracted to polemic and do not seek to question the importance of social variables, prefer to invest in neuroscience rather than in the more controversial behavior genetics. A criminology PhD, who is now a professor in a sociology department, explained why he preferred the neurological approach over genetics:

> I'm more interested in brain research because a) I think it makes more sense [than genetic approaches] (everything that happens in terms of behavior, including social causes, must operate at brain level at some point, right?)—after all, H2 research [H2 refers to heritability research based on twin studies] simply suggests that crime is genetic but doesn't really say how or why, and b) it's less controversial. I would say that I am not a person who likes controversy, but I am involved in biosocial research for two reasons: 1) I think biology is important and ignoring it is not beneficial, and 2) I think that even if social scientists want to reject biosocial research, they still need to understand it.[24]

Nevertheless, researchers trained in psychology are not entirely unfamiliar with the controversies surrounding behavior genetics. In fact, several psychologists from the field of behavior genetics, where scientific controversy has become a full-fledged mode of scientific knowledge production,[25] have imported the provocative attitude found among the progenetic fringe of biosocial criminologists. The case of David Rowe is typical. Trained in behavior genetics at the University of Colorado and a professor of psychology at the University of Arizona from 1988 to 2003, Rowe has published several articles in peer-reviewed criminology journals, either as a sole author[26] or with colleagues.[27] He also published a book entitled *Biology and Crime* in 2002.[28] In this book, Rowe takes the same approach—and reaches the same conclusions— that he previously used on the issue of family socialization, namely that environmental factors, such as parental education, "make only a small dent in the sum total of our social problems."[29] Similarly, Rowe believes that "crime is a part of human nature, a legacy of evolution,"[30] and that "many traits related to crime are heritable."[31] The crime issue is thus just another opportunity to produce scientific capital by adopting a heterodox attitude. Nevertheless, Rowe differs from biosocial criminologists who come from criminology departments insofar as these scientific positions are not accompanied by epistemological reflections on the status of criminology, or by a desire to change the distribution of resources within the criminological field.

This is due in part to the fact that, unlike criminologically trained researchers, most psychologists are not invested in the criminological field, which is reflected in their relatively small number of biosocial criminology publications (figure 4.1). As Aaron Panofsky wrote about the interdisciplinary field of behavior genetics, these authors "envision their participation in the field as a means to compete for scientific capital in other fields."[32] This failure to integrate the habitus of the criminological field is particularly apparent in the following interview with a professor of psychology who expressed surprise at the controversial nature of biosocial approaches in American criminology:

> Julien Larregue: You probably know that biosocial criminology is quite controversial in the U.S. Its main proponents regularly attack fellow criminologists and/or are attacked by fellow criminologists. How do you position yourself vis-à-vis this struggle? You said that you would not define yourself as a biosocial criminologist, does it have something to do with its controversial aspect?
>
> Interviewee #9: Regarding controversy, I am not aware of major controversies regarding the biological basis of criminal behavior. Indeed, since there is virtual unanimity that a biopsychosocial approach to understanding all human behavior, including criminality, is the dominant paradigm, I am hard pressed to understand how there could be such a "struggle" between two camps. I

know of no competent, respected recognized authority on criminality who would deny that biological, psychological, sociological influences are all important in understanding antisocial/criminal behavior.

Julien Larregue: Do you attend more criminology-related events, for instance American Society of Criminology's annual meetings, or psychology-related ones? Or both?

Interviewee #9: I do not attend criminology-related events and thus would not be aware of controversies that are discussed in these venues. My opinions are based upon reading the literature that I judge to be representative of the best thinking on the biopsychosocial bases of antisocial behavior. Based upon this literature, I do not detect anything resembling a huge controversy over the perennial nature/nurture issue of human behavior including criminal behavior, but rather a profound convergence, that is, both are very important.

This lack of familiarity with the culture and structure of the criminological field is also common among students who have studied psychology before entering a doctoral program in a criminology department. In an interview, a young professor with a master's degree in psychology explained that she was completely unaware of the controversial nature of biosocial criminology when she entered her graduate program in criminology:

It had to be told to me, though [that biosocial criminology was controversial], because I was not from sociology or criminology before [entering a graduate program in criminology]. Because I got my master's degree in psychology, so I didn't know, and when I started studying with Doctor X [a prominent biosocial criminologist], he said, "I want you to know that in this discipline this is not a . . . This is a controversial topic, you know, not everyone agrees, it's not accepted everywhere." . . . He had to prepare me in case anybody ever said something to me, or I didn't get any scholarship or something like that because of the research.[33]

Despite these different degrees of involvement in the field of criminology, most criminologists and psychologists do share a common vision of what biosocial criminology should be. Psychologists from the field of behavior genetics have long held a genetic determinism that is intended to challenge environmentalist psychology.[34] It is thus easy for them to identify with the criminologists' attempt to challenge the domination of sociologists within the field of criminology as the two undertakings are fundamentally analogous. Above all, research on the individual causes of crime is much more accepted and common in the psychological field than in the criminological field.

Moreover, because of the division of scientific work, with genetics being taken care of by criminologists and neuroscience by psychologists, the two groups do not actually compete. They can therefore collaborate without feeling threatened by each other's activities. Moreover, academically, psychologists occupy a marginal position in the criminological field. Unlike sociologists, therefore, they have nothing to lose by allowing criminologists control of the field.

The affinity between the psychological and criminological fields is evident in the academic profile of the psychologist Adrian Raine. A professor at the University of Pennsylvania, Raine maintains affiliations with the Department of Psychology and the Department of Criminology. This dual identity allows him to recruit doctoral students from both departments and to train biosocial criminologists. For example, he directed Anna Rudo-Hutt's psychology dissertation, "Biological Correlates of Conduct Disorders and Callous-Unemotional Traits" (2014), while concurrently directing Jill Portnoy's criminology dissertation, "Risk Factors for Antisocial Behavior in Juveniles" (2015). These affinities also appear in the account of a criminology doctoral student who began her studies in psychology:

> I became interested in biosocial criminology while I was pursuing my bachelor's degree at Florida State University. I took a class offered by the Criminology Department titled "Human Behavior," which introduced me to the biosocial perspective. At the time, my areas of

study were in psychology and criminology, so I was naturally drawn to the biosocial perspective. Most importantly, I viewed the biosocial perspective as a way to unite the two disciplines [psychology and criminology].[35]

This shows that the interdisciplinarity of biosocial criminologists is "closely linked to logics of access to academic professions."[36] Biosocial criminologists who have accumulated capital in the psychological field—usually in the form of a bachelor's or master's degree—can thus play on both sides of the fence, psychology and criminology, in order to maximize their chances of obtaining a position in a university upon completion of their doctorate.

This shift from biosocial criminology to psychology is made easier by the fact that the affinity between criminologists and psychologists encompasses shared scientific standards. For example, the Biosocial Criminology Association, created and led by criminology graduates, awarded the 2015 Book of the Year Award to the neurocriminologist Adrian Raine for his *Anatomy of Violence: The Biological Roots of Crime*. Similarly, the principal award distributed by the association, the David Rowe Award, named after the psychologist-geneticist, was given in 2016 to the psychologist Terrie Moffitt, who defended the biosocial criminology group in a controversy published in a special issue of *Criminology* (see chapter 5). This rapprochement between criminologists and psychologists was sealed by the publication of a textbook on biosocial criminology in which the best-known representatives of both networks participated (box 4). These awards to renowned psychologists also allow criminologists to benefit from the aura and scientific prestige that researchers such as Raine and Moffitt generate. By associating their names with Raine and Moffitt, criminology graduates appear even more "scientific," even if they have yet to formally collaborate with them.

BOX 4. THE *ROUTLEDGE INTERNATIONAL HANDBOOK OF BIOSOCIAL CRIMINOLOGY*

The *Routledge International Handbook of Biosocial Criminology* was published in 2015 under the editorship of Matt DeLisi and Michael Vaughn. Although it claims international scope, seventy-five of the ninety-one contributors were affiliated with U.S. universities at the time of publication. Some of the most productive biosocial criminologists have contributed: Kevin Beaver, John Paul Wright, Brian Boutwell, J. C. Barnes, and Adrian Raine. The book is divided into five parts. The first, entitled "Criminological Foundations," introduces biosocial theory. It also includes epistemological reflections on the scientific status of criminology. Chapter 2, for example, uses the Kuhnian concept of "paradigm shift."[37] The next three parts present the state of the art in biosocial criminology. Part II focuses on genetic factors, Part III on neurological factors, and Part IV on biosocial mechanisms, that is, the interaction between biological and environmental factors. The last part of the book is devoted to the forensic applications of biosocial criminology.

SOCIOLOGISTS, OR THE HEART OF THE PROENVIRONMENTAL BRANCH

Alongside these two groups who explicitly claim to be biosocial criminologists are several researchers, mainly sociologists, who use biology to study criminal behavior without presenting themselves as biosocial criminologists or questioning the importance of sociology in the understanding of criminal phenomena. In other words, this group does not share the vision of most criminologists and psychologists. Unlike the previous two groups, these researchers are less connected to each other. They do, however, share some common characteristics. More of them completed their doctorate at a prestigious university before the 2000s. Some of them also occupy a more dominant position within the U.S. criminological field. Ronald Simons, for example, is a professor of sociology at the University of Georgia and a fellow of the American Society of Criminology, while Callie Burt began her academic career as an assistant professor in sociology at the University of Washington.

As we shall see, both have publicly opposed the work of criminology graduates.

Unlike most criminologists and psychologists, sociologists mainly use genetics as a means of refining existing sociological theories. Simons and his colleagues, for example, have used genetics to advance the understanding of the culturalist theory of the street code. Developed by sociologist Elijah Anderson from an ethnography of an African American ghetto in Philadelphia, the theory maintains that "when jobs disappear and people are left poor, highly concentrated, and hopeless, the way is paved for the underground economy to become a way of life, an unforgiving way of life organized around a code of violence and predatory activity."[38] The use of genetics by Simons and his colleagues, far from undermining or relativizing the importance of this theory, actually provided an answer to the criticisms that have been leveled at it. Critics wondered, for example, why some ghetto residents adopted the code of the street, while others conformed to the dominant social rules. Simons and his colleagues suggested the following answer: the greater genetic plasticity of some individuals makes them more sensitive to the influences of the surrounding environment.[39]

This proenvironmental approach can be illustrated by another article that combines a neuroscientific approach with the street code theory.[40] Its authors—Michael Rocque, Chad Posick, and Shanna Felix—hold PhDs in criminology and/or are employed in criminology departments, showing that the division of biosocial criminology cannot be reduced to a disciplinary war. As they explained in the introduction to their article, their goal was not to challenge sociological theories of crime. Rather, the authors sought to show "how biosocial work can be integrated within sociological theories of subcultural violence in a way that makes these theories more powerful and scientific."[41] The conclusion of their article was even more explicit in emphasizing the importance of the social origins of crime:

> We wish to emphasize that our argument is not that the social aspects of subcultural theories are invalid and the subculture is entirely a biological process; rather, we believe that environments have a direct and

indirect effect on attitudes and behaviors. After all, the term biosocial implies that both biological and social factors are important in causal process models (see Walsh & Yun, 2014: Wright & Boisvert, 2009). To date, biosocial work has focused on statistical interactions between biological and environmental factors. Our formulation attempts instead to show how the environment "gets under the skin" to affect behavior.[42]

While progenetic criminologists try to reduce the scope of sociological work, the research of Simons and Rocque widens this sphere and strengthens the theoretical basis of criticized notions and hypotheses. In contrast to progenetic biosocial criminologists, then, whose innovation consists in overturning traditional theories of crime, the innovation of proenvironmental biosocial criminologists "takes place through a deepening of the tradition."[43] This explains why Simons and his colleagues oppose the main biosocial network while declaring themselves to be "enthusiastic about truly biosocial research programs."[44] For these researchers, progenetic biosocial criminologists are not really producing biosocial criminology:

> I definitely see that there are some people who . . . I would say claim to be biosocial criminologists [laughs] but forget about the social part. And I think that's a serious issue. . . . I do see that some people in the field are very much more concerned by genetics as opposed to looking at all of the factors, whether they be social in nature, whether they be biological, they be genes, they be brain functioning. . . . And certainly, certain environmental factors can impact your biology.[45]

Hence, these researchers do not question the connection between criminology and sociology. They insist that "environmental influences are more salient in explaining individual differences in complex phenotypes such as criminal behavior, with genetic influences usually being limited to moderating the effect of the environment."[46] To them, biosocial criminology is not a new paradigm that will eventually replace sociological theories and methods but an additional tool that they can borrow to better the latter.

THE REVERSED HIERARCHY: THE DOMINATION OF CRIMINOLOGY GRADUATES

The preceding chapters have shown that within the American criminological field, the sociological view of crime is dominant. Sociologists are the primary representatives of the orthodoxy, in both academic and scientific terms. In contrast, criminology graduates occupy a subaltern academic position due to the absence of criminology departments within the most prestigious universities. This creates a social hierarchy that places sociology at the top of the criminological hierarchy, while autonomous criminology lies in the lower ranks.

In biosocial criminology, this hierarchy is reversed. Researchers from autonomous criminology, who also happen to question the pertinence and scientificity of sociological theories, lead the institutionalization of the movement. The Biosocial Criminology Association (BCA), for example, is chaired by a criminology graduate and rewards researchers from behavior genetics. The name given to the BCA award (David Rowe) is indicative of the organization's orientation. Similarly, unlike criminologists and psychologists, few sociologists have contributed to the *International Handbook of Biosocial Criminology*.[47] Ronald Simons and Callie Burt, for example, were conspicuously absent.

The domination of the criminologist-psychologist alliance within the biosocial movement is particularly visible in terms of productivity. Ronald Simons is the only member of the orthodox sociology group to have published at least five biosocial criminology papers. By comparison, Kevin Beaver has published sixty-one papers. Joseph Schwartz, a former student of Beaver's who completed his PhD in 2014, already has twice as many biosocial criminology papers to his name as Simons (ten). This domination is not only important in the objectified state. In the embodied state, we saw that the most productive biosocial criminologists have been trained mostly by members of the subversive group. Criminology PhDs are thus able to replicate their conception of crime and biosocial criminology by instilling it in their PhD students. Kevin Beaver, for example, completed his dissertation under the direction of John Paul Wright, before he supervised the doctoral research of J. C. Barnes, Brian Boutwell, Joseph Schwartz, Joseph Nedelec, and Eric Connolly.

The marginalization of the sociological view of crime is also reflected in biosocial criminologists' esteem for each other's research. To estimate the theoretical affinities among members of the biosocial movement, the network analyses already presented were complemented by a questionnaire to researchers from the field that included the following question: "Would you say that the following scholars adopt the same vision of crime as yours?" Three responses were possible: "yes," "no," or "I am not familiar with his or her work." The list of referenced researchers included representatives from the different subcommunities of biosocial criminology (criminology, psychology, and sociology). By way of comparison, the list also included the names of two researchers from outside the biosocial stream. Besides Elijah Anderson, who was included for his culturalist street code theory, the questionnaire proposed the name of Robert Sampson, who graduated in criminology and is now a professor of sociology at Harvard University. His theory of social disorganization has made him one of the most cited contemporary criminologists.[48] Sampson's structuralist approach is hardly compatible with the work of progenetic biosocial criminologists, however. In fact, he has been openly skeptical of the entire biocriminological tradition, from "the crude biology of Cesare Lombroso to the current fascination with DNA sequencing and brain imaging as the promise of the future."[49]

Although they must be interpreted with caution because of the small sample size (twenty respondents), the results support the hypothesis that the proenvironmental branch represented by Ronald Simons is dominated within the biosocial movement (table 4.2). It is particularly notable that respondents perceived Simons to be closer to Sampson and Anderson than to the progenetic branch of the biosocial stream represented by Beaver, DeLisi, and Raine. The presence of the sociologist Matt DeLisi among the most popular researchers, alongside criminologist Kevin Beaver and psychologist Adrian Raine, also confirms that this is not simply a disciplinary war. DeLisi, one of the main coauthors

---

TABLE 4.2

Theoretical affinities among biosocial criminologists (n = 20), as shown by answers to "Would you say that the following scholars adopt the same vision of crime as yours?"

Scholar	Yes	No	I don't know
Elijah Anderson	6	9	5
Kevin Beaver	18	2	0
Matt DeLisi	18	1	1
Adrian Raine	17	2	1
Robert Sampson	8	11	1
Ronald Simons	11	6	3

---

of the network of criminologists led by Beaver, takes a progenetic approach that challenges sociological domination. Theoretical affinities between biosocial criminologists thus cross disciplinary boundaries, although researchers' position with respect to the nature-culture debate does depend on their position within the scientific field and thus partly on the discipline to which they belong.

This phenomenon of hierarchical inversion is not unique to biosocial criminology. Aaron Panofsky has observed a similar phenomenon in the field of behavior genetics. Panofsky showed how researchers who worked on animals and who mainly came from biology and genetics were supplanted by social scientists, at the forefront of whom were psychologists such as David Rowe and Terrie Moffitt.[50] The situation in biosocial criminology is somewhat different, however. In behavior genetics, the inversion put the social sciences ahead of the so-called "hard" sciences: that is, it reversed the classical hierarchy of sciences. In biosocial criminology, the opposite has occurred: the classical hierarchy of sciences was reestablished at the expense of the specific hierarchy of the criminological field, with biology and genetics taking the place of sociology at the top of the criminological enterprise.

———

To speak of "biosocial criminology" seems to imply that we are dealing with a homogeneous movement. In reality, however, it is possible
to identify three subnetworks whose views on crime do not always
concur: criminologists (i.e., researchers with a doctorate in criminology), psychologists, and sociologists. Most criminologists participate
in the construction of a progenetic approach: under the guise of biosocial conceptions of crime, it is the role of biological factors that is
often emphasized and considered to be preponderant. In contrast,
sociologists insist on the importance of environmental factors. Psychologists, for their part, while being closer to the progenetic vision of
criminologists, keep their distance from the controversies and prefer
to focus on the role played by the brain. We will see that these internal
divisions in biosocial criminology, far from being merely material,
have repercussions for the conceptual and methodological choices
made by researchers.

5 THE RESILIENCE OF THE NATURE-CULTURE DEBATE

THE CAPACIOUS LABEL "BIOSOCIAL CRIMINOLOGY" might give the impression that we are dealing with a clearly bounded scientific movement characterized by a shared consensus about the origins of crime. This is not so either in terms of the social construction of the group (see chapter 4) or at the scientific level, where heterogeneity reigns. Indeed, the very definition of biosocial criminology has been the subject of an ongoing dispute among researchers. A special issue devoted to the controversy was published in 2015 by what is often regarded as the criminological field's leading journal, *Criminology*. From an outsider perspective, this debate might appear to be a dispute between "pro-" and "anti-" biosocial criminology. Viewed from within, however, the debate was really happening among biosocial criminologists. As Callie Burt and Ronald Simons would clearly point out in their critique of heritability studies (also called twin studies because of their use of twins), "This is not a 'war' between biosocial criminologists and environmental determinists."[1] Rather, the main issue concerned the definition of *legitimate* biosocial criminology. The controversy that has been raging among biosocial criminologists over the relative importance of genetic and environmental factors offers further evidence that "the field of thought that deploys biology today is vaster and more undefined than a theory. It draws polarities, opens debates, and varied, sometimes antagonistic, points of view."[2]

The debate that rocked biosocial criminologists can be summarized as follows: Should genetics be used to complement and enhance sociological theories of crime? Or should genetics become the dominant model, replacing sociology as the theoretical reference? Just as behavior geneticists debated whether their endeavor should be organized around the study of animals or humans,[3] biosocial criminologists remain divided over whether environmental or genetic factors should take precedence. In short, the nature-culture debate has reappeared within a research movement that one might have thought unified. The centrality of the nature-culture debate is one of the most striking characteristics of contemporary biosocial research.[4] The persistence of this polarization is even more intriguing given that the biosocial approach is generally presented as the best way to put an end to an opposition that many consider sterile and simplistic. The case of biosocial criminology thus provides a new illustration of the significant difference that often exists between the discourse and the practices of scientific actors.

The opposition between progenetic and proenvironmental biosocial criminologists can be represented through what sociologist Andrew Abbott has named "fractal distinction." The notion of fractal distinction refers to "the fact that such a distinction repeats a pattern within itself, as geometric fractals do."[5] That is, the dichotomous scientific choices that researchers make (such as nature-culture or quantitative-qualitative) can be subdivided following the same dichotomy. A multilevel tree is created within which institutions, disciplines, researchers, and knowledge can be classified. This is the image of the microcosm: the same divisions that oppose biosocial criminologists to sociologists can be found among biosocial criminologists themselves.

Abbott draws several corollaries with regard to these divisions. First, the median subdivisions of a fractal distinction are often closer to each other than to the subdivisions of their respective branches. To illustrate his point, Abbott offers the example of the history-sociology dichotomy.[6] The sociological approach developed in history and the historical approach developed in sociology share greater affinity with each other than with the main currents of their respective disciplines (history and sociology). This explains why the branches that are on the outside, and which therefore make the same choice at each level (for example, history and then history), are more isolated than the middle branches that share commonalities.

A second corollary concerns the affinities that exist between apparently independent fractal distinctions. For example, scientific positivism is often associated with structural analyses, while interpretivism is more generally used to study culture.[7] In other words, there is a coherence between the various methodological and theoretical choices that a researcher makes, so that apparently independent decisions are in fact interdependent. This idea can be juxtaposed with Noah Friedkin's work on the logical constraints that weigh on the various constituents of a system of thought.[8] When a belief system is composed of several interdependent elements, the modification of one of the components imposes a logical constraint on the system, which must then adapt to the alteration.

As we shall see, the dichotomous choices that form the fractal distinctions are closely associated with the different subcommunities of biosocial criminologists identified in the previous chapter. In other words, the opposition between progenetic and proenvironmental researchers is related to the structure of biosocial criminology and the contradictory approaches that have arisen within it. Far from being purely semantic, this opposition is directly reflected in the conceptual and methodological choices of the various protagonists.

THE G×E MODEL: SOCIOLOGY OF A SCIENTIFIC CONTROVERSY

As Martin Dufresne noted in his analysis of the Caspi et al. study published in *Science*, biosocial criminology combs through genetic, biological, and neurological markers looking for risk variables.[9] The genetic polymorphisms included in the regression analyses are not, strictly speaking, direct causes of delinquency. Rather, they should be seen as "facilitators," as disinhibitory. The idea is therefore not to identify "crime genes" but to identify the genetic variants that are associated with antisocial phenotypes. For example, much research has been conducted on a polymorphism in the *MAOA* gene that presumably predisposes its carriers to violence. The influence of this gene on delinquency is not direct, however. Its effect is expressed only in interaction with the environment of its carrier, as was emphasized by the experts in the Bayout case mentioned in the introduction of this book. Figure 5.1, which is reproduced from a biosocial criminology article, clearly shows how the *MAOA* gene interacts with neuropsychological disorders. This interaction itself influences the individual's self-control and therefore, ultimately, his or her probability of committing delinquent acts.

In this research, the interaction between an individual's genetic makeup and his or her environment is generally measured by the equation G×E ("G" for genetic, "E" for environment). This interaction

FIGURE 5.1

Schematization of the influence of the MAOA gene on delinquency in a biosocial criminology article.

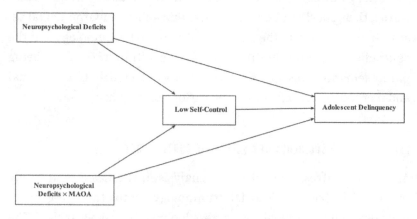

Figure reproduced from Beaver, DeLisi, et al., "Intersection of Genes," 28.

Note: Monoamine oxidase A (MAOA) is not posited to have a direct effect on low self-control or adolescent delinquency.

is more than the sum of the respective influences of the genes and the environment. The added value of the interaction of the two factors is clearly visible in figure 5.2: the adoption of a street code, which itself influences aggressive behavior, is more common in hostile environments or among people with greater genetic plasticity. These effects are thus multiplied among individuals with greater genetic plasticity who also happen to live in a hostile environment ("G×E" box, bottom left). This makes it relatively difficult to "unbox" the two components and estimate their respective contributions to criminal behavior.

As we shall see, proenvironmental and progenetic biosocial criminologists are at odds over the conceptualization of the G×E equation. Yet this opposition is as much about the G×E equation as the debate between Robert Boyle and Thomas Hobbes in the seventeenth century was about the air pump.[10] As Thomas Gieryn has explained,

> The debate between Robert Boyle and Thomas Hobbes in the 1660s was "about" an air pump in the same way that *Moby Dick* is "about" a whale.

FIGURE 5.2

Schematization of the G×E model in a proenvironmental biosocial criminology article.

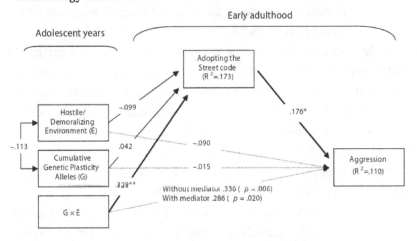

Figure reproduced from Simons, Lei, Stewart, et al., "Social Adversity," 16.

Note: Asterisks indicate statistical significance: **p ≤ .01; *p ≤ .05.

At stake was the delineation of authentic and authoritative knowledge: How was it made? Who could make it? What was it for? The dispute was more than one between Boyle's experimentalism and Hobbes's rationalism, for at issue as well was the constitution of the social order itself in Restoration England.[11]

Just as the Hobbes-Boyle debate was not just about the air pump, the opposition between progenetic and proenvironmental biosocial criminologists is not just about the G×E equation. The G and E factors are in fact symbols of the degree of orthodoxy of the researchers using them. To assert that the G factor is more important than the E factor (and vice versa) is to assert that crime can be understood primarily in genetic (or social) terms, and thus to question (or reinforce) the domination of the criminological field by sociologists.

The same way that the technicality of the Boyle-Hobbes debate concealed some of the more profound issues at stake, the technical debate between progenetic biosocial criminology and proenvironmental biosocial criminology conceals the question of the legitimacy of criminology's domination by sociology. The degree of subversiveness adopted by biosocial criminologists is reflected in very concrete ways, materializing in their modeling of the origins of crime. We will see that the importance that should be given to the environmental factor polarizes researchers, which is visible in their positioning vis-à-vis the field of epigenetics. Indeed, the G in the equation was originally understood as a genetic vulnerability, a deficiency of sorts, whereas the E was conceptualized as a facilitator, a trigger for latent genetic vulnerability. But this apparent consensus conceals a disagreement as to the respective importance of G and E—so much so that this classical understanding of the genetic-environment interactional scheme has split into two branches. Each branch lends different degrees of importance to one of the two terms of the equation.

The first branch, which corresponds to the proenvironmental approach in biosocial criminology, draws mainly on the concept of plasticity. Rather than embracing the classical acceptance of G as genetic vulnerability, the sociologist Ronald Simons and his colleagues have begun to consider the hypothesis of genetic plasticity. The problem is no longer that some genotypes are more vulnerable or deficient than others but rather that they are more receptive to environmental influences.[12] Far from being a purely verbal construct, this reconceptualization of the classical terms of the G×E formula has concrete consequences with regard to the respective importance of G and E. Indeed, if G is nothing more than an increased plasticity, then "individuals most vulnerable to adverse social environments are the same ones who reap the most benefit from environmental support."[13] In other words, a relocation from the least to the most privileged social environments would completely reverse the effect of plasticity. Nothing would therefore distinguish delinquents from socially successful individuals, except "toxic" neighborhoods and milieus. Put differently, the proenvironmental branch of biosocial criminology ultimately reverts to the classical teaching of American criminology: crime is a social problem.

In contrast, the other variant of the G×E model, which is used by the progenetic branch, is more marked in its relativization of sociological factors. In these authors' writings, the mutual interaction that was the G×E relationship has become a one-way correlation: "A person selects into an environment on the basis of his or her genetic propensities," write J. C. Barnes and Kevin Beaver.[14] Whenever they are told that social processes matter, progenetic biosocial criminologists will simply retort that "we all seek environments that are compatible with our genetic dispositions."[15] By always choosing the biological over the sociological, this branch of biosocial criminology adopts an extremist position that is difficult to attack intellectually. Figure 5.3 is revealing in this respect: the genotype, G, simultaneously influences the dependent variable Y (in this case, self-reported delinquency) and the environmental variable E (in this case, association with delinquents), which in turn influences Y. The mere possibility that variable E may influence variable G is not addressed. In short, if we make our way back to the original source of the criminal phenomenon, we will find biological factors. We thus end up with the opposite view to that which resulted from the concept of plasticity used by the proenvironmental

FIGURE 5.3

Schematization of the G×E model in a progenetic biosocial criminology article.

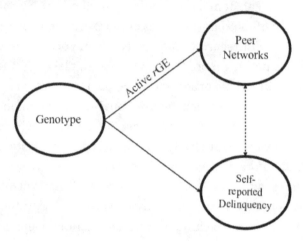

Figure reproduced from TenEyck and Barnes, "Examining the Impact," 7.

branch: genetics takes precedence over the environment, the latter being emptied of its etiological substance. Without an open denial of the importance of the environmental factor, "It is 'nature' that emerges as the decisive victor."[16]

DIFFERENTIATED PERCEPTIONS OF THE MERITS AND LIMITATIONS OF EPIGENETICS

The opposition between proenvironmental and progenetic biosocial criminologists is particularly visible in their perceptions of the merits and weaknesses of epigenetic research. Indeed, one of the primary criticisms that proenvironmental biosocial criminologists level against their opponents is their refusal to consider that environmental factors might, and do, influence genetic processes. It is therefore not surprising that environmentalists are enthusiastic about epigenetics, since this field of research touts the "the possibility that the environment can change the characteristics of living organisms."[17] They are particularly attentive to the possibility that the environment might influence gene expression without actually altering DNA structure. In other words, epigenetics clearly lines up with the proenvironmental approach to biosocial criminology taken by sociologists Burt and Simons:

> Our environment influences us by regulating our genetic activity. As noted, DNA is not self-activating. DNA has to be transcribed to produce RNA and proteins, but before DNA can be transcribed, it must be activated by the epigenome—the complex, biochemical regulatory system that can turn on, silence (leave off), or change the transcriptional activity of genes (Charney, 2012; Martiensen, Riggs, and Russo, 1996). As such, the mere presence of a gene does not ensure that it is going to be used (activated by the cell), and changes in the epigenome can alter the phenotype without any underlying change to the genome (Bernstein, Meissner, and Lander, 2007). In this way, the epigenome regulates gene expression. As the epigenome is responsive to environmental input (both internal and external to the cell), the environment influences gene expression through the epigenome (e.g., Charney, 2012; Jablonka and Lamb, 2006).[18]

The discussion of the merits and weaknesses of epigenetics thus demarcates researchers who propose "truly biosocial" research and those who remain attached to a biological neodeterminism. Thus a biosocial criminologist employed in a sociology department explains that he does not subscribe to the subversive attitude adopted by criminology graduates or to their outright rejection of epigenetics: "My interactions with some biosocial criminologists have convinced me that they are adamantly opposed to any effect of the environment. To be a 'biosocial criminologist' you must by definition think that the environment matters, but apparently they do not. The best example is epigenetics. This is a new and promising line of research that should be taken seriously. Some people dismiss it out of hand, probably because it suggests that the environment matters."[19]

The skepticism expressed by progenetic biosocial criminologists regarding epigenetics is not simply a myth perpetuated by their opponents to promote their own conception of biosocial criminology. While researchers who adopt a proenvironmental stance praise epigenetics on principle, there is no doubt that progenetic biosocial criminologists are more doubtful of the field's maturity. In their view, the emerging research arenas that Maurizio Meloni has gathered under the label of "social biology,"[20] such as epigenetics and social neuroscience, are still in their infancy and do not deserve the enthusiasm displayed by Burt and Simons, among others:

> Instead of partitioning variance, biosocial criminologists, according to Burt and Simons, should explore GxEs, epigenetic processes, and social neuroscience. The problem, however, is that much of the GxE literature is under heavy criticism and epigenetics is in its infancy. Unfortunately, Burt and Simons couched their discussion of epigenetics and GxEs in language that makes it seem as if this body of research is generally accepted and easily replicated by neuroscientists, geneticists, and epigeneticists. In reality, nothing could be further from the truth.[21]

To counter the enthusiasm of proenvironment biosocial criminologists, Barnes and his colleagues called upon the norm of skepticism, which "requires scientists to exercise sustained critical doubt about the findings of their peers."[22] With this overt display of caution, they underscored the unreflective and premature nature of proenvironment biosocial criminologists' interest in this area of research, while positioning themselves as experts in the genetics literature. Barnes and colleagues also appealed to another important argument that related to the reproducibility of experiments conducted in epigenetics. Jeremy Freese and David Peterson have suggested that recent concerns about the reproducibility of scientific results reflect the emergence of a new formulation of the standard of objectivity, namely statistical objectivity, which is unique in that it is assessed on a collective scale, particularly through meta-analyses.[23] In turn, by advancing this argument, progenetic biosocial criminologists placed themselves at the forefront of the latest scientific standards while drawing attention to the lack of epistemological rigor of their opponents. Beyond these references to generic social and epistemological norms, however, it must be emphasized that progenetic biosocial criminologists remain vague about the concrete limits of epigenetics. This is illustrated in an interview with one of their main representatives. When asked about his views on epigenetics in general and the article by Burt and Simons in particular, this person was particularly evasive: "They want to do epigenetics, right? Well, epigenetics is fine, but [laughs] you know . . . The thing is, we're serving it up before its time, you know. I mean it's not as well known as . . . Even the experts in epigenetics realize that . . . it's very, very difficult to study."[24]

This progenetic researcher was unable to precisely explain why studying the influence of environmental factors on genetic processes would not be useful for criminology. The invocation of the standard of skepticism ("It's very difficult") masked his discomfort, allowing him to avoid mentioning the specific reasons for caution. Indeed, it may be noted that biosocial criminologists make selective use of the norms of prudence and replicability. For instance, as we shall see in chapter 7, their position within the scientific field leads them to use molecular genetics methods that have been abandoned by behavior geneticists in favor of genome-wide studies, partially because of problems relating to reproducibility.

An analysis of this controversy thus demonstrates that the issue of epigenetics is much more than a question of how genes might be expressed in different environments. Just as the conceptualization of the terms of the G×E equation ultimately questions the role and importance of social and biological processes in criminal behavior, the debate over the relevance of epigenetics is also a debate over the preservation or subversion of sociological theories of crime. One might think that the development of biosocial criminology would put an end to the nature-culture debate, at least within this research movement. Instead, the nature-culture debate is resurfacing in a new form, with a proenvironment biosocial criminology on the one hand and a progenetic biosocial criminology on the other: while the former merely recognizes the potential influence of biological factors on the correlation between social factors and crime, the latter considers biological factors to be more important than social factors. Thus, just as historical sociology is closer to history as a social science than to mainstream sociology, proenvironmental biosocial criminology has greater affinity with the structuralist criminology of a Robert Sampson than with the work of progenetic biosocial criminologists.[25] This division is all the more interesting in that all the biosocial criminologists, both progenetic[26] and proenvironmental,[27] call for the nature-culture dichotomy to be abandoned. Despite these shared intentions, the opposition between the progenetic and proenvironment branches of biosocial criminology came to the fore in another important controversy displayed in a special issue of *Criminology.*

QUANTIFYING THE HERITABILITY OF ANTISOCIAL BEHAVIOR?

It is considered an established scientific fact among many biologists that it is "almost impossible to separate environmental from genetic effects in an organism that cannot be manipulated experimentally."[28] A given phenotype may be heritable (e.g., aggressiveness, size, eye color), but this does not mean that it is not influenced by the environment. Indeed, geneticists have come to distinguish between the heritability and the plasticity of a phenotype. Plasticity is the influence of the environment on the expression and evolution of a phenotype. In other words, a highly heritable phenotype can also be highly plastic and thus be influenced by the environment of the person who bears it. Some characteristics that are decidedly genetic have, however, very low or even zero heritability coefficients because the trait concerned is found consistently in humans. In the absence of statistical variation in the distribution of the trait across the studied population, the heritability coefficient would indeed be equal to 0. Such is the case for the probability of having two eyes, a trait that is of course genetic but whose heritability coefficient is null.

The complex, entangled nature of these phenomena has not prevented researchers from questioning the respective influence of genetic and environmental factors on human behavior. To do so, researchers in behavior genetics have often relied on twin studies. This branch of behavior genetics is generally called quantitative (or nonmolecular) genetics. In contrast to molecular genetics, which consists of identifying specific genes that are correlated with certain human behaviors (the *MAOA* gene, for example), quantitative genetics seeks to discover to what extent human behaviors are genetically heritable, without necessarily identifying the specific genes involved in this biological process. The results of this research are usually expressed as percentages. The variance of a given phenotype (e.g., aggression) will be attributed to x percent genetic factors and y percent environmental factors. The higher the proportion of genetic factors, the more heritable the phenotype.

It was precisely the complexity of genetic expression and transmissibility that led proenvironmental biosocial criminologists to react to the heritability research carried out by Kevin Beaver and his progenetic colleagues. This controversy was rendered visible to the whole criminological field when it was exposed in a special issue of *Criminology*, the flagship journal of the American Society of Criminology. The methodology of twin studies was initially set out by Francis Galton, a British scientist and cousin of Charles Darwin, infamously renowned for his eugenics ideology, as a way of providing a quantitative response to the nature-culture debate (box 5). More than a century later, the debate lives on among social scientists, whether they are criminologists, economists, political scientists, or sociologists.[29] The controversy over twin studies was important enough to merit the publication of a special issue of *Criminology* because it indirectly raised the question of the legitimacy of sociologists' domination over criminological research since the second half of the twentieth century. This confirms once again that "a controversy, both scientific and public, is more likely to erupt if it challenges dominant interpretations."[30]

The debate confronted the two conceptions of biosocial criminology mentioned above, namely progenetic and proenvironment biosocial criminology. While sociologists Callie Burt and Ronald Simons forcefully invited criminologists to "[pull] back the curtain on heritability studies,"[37] Kevin Beaver and his colleagues, who were also supported by psychologist and behavior geneticist Terrie Moffitt, insisted on the relevance of quantitative genetics to the study of crime.[38] To be

BOX 5. GALTON'S HEIRS

Along with adoption studies, twin studies have been one of the main tools used by geneticists to study the intergenerational transmission of human behavior. Starting from the assumption that monozygotic twins—as opposed to dizygotic twins—have an identical genetic heritage, geneticists have tried to quantify the respective share of genetic and environmental factors in the explanation of diverse phenotypes (violence, intelligence, political behavior, etc.). The invention of twin studies is generally credited to the anthropologist and eugenicist Francis Galton for an article published in 1875 in *Fraser's Magazine*.[31] Although aware of the existence of monozygotic and dizygotic twins, Galton did not exactly use the methodology as we know it today.[32] Going back to the origins of the method is nonetheless interesting because it allows us to grasp the expectations placed on twin studies from their inception. If Galton uses twins, it is indeed to examine "relative powers of nature and nurture." The results, according to him, left little room for doubt: nature is much more important in determining human behavior than culture is.[33]

While the method has been statistically refined over time, the results of research conducted on twins have constantly been used to support naturalist theses. In the early twentieth century, twin studies were invoked to critique Franz Boas's culturalist anthropology.[34] In the latter part of the twentieth century, this method was mobilized to attack environmentalist approaches, particularly in psychology.[35] There are reasons to believe that the success of twin studies is partly due to the fact that this method produces relatively high heritability coefficients, so that researchers in behavior genetics would have strategically preferred twin studies over alternative approaches.[36]

sure, the objections raised by Simons and Burt to the use of twin studies were far from new. Several controversies about the heritability of
human behavior had already erupted in the field of behavior genetics
in the 1970s and 1980s, and it is striking how the structure of the debate
published in *Criminology* largely followed the arguments already invoked in the field of behavior genetics a few decades earlier.[39]

The controversy that opposed the two branches of biosocial criminology can be summarized as follows. The basic idea of the twin studies approach is to infer the variance in a given phenotype from the
genetic variance between monozygotic and dizygotic twins. Monozygotic twins (MZ) have identical genetics (100 percent), while dizygotic
twins (DZ) share only 50 percent of their genetic material. If we also
include half siblings (25 percent) and cousins (12.5 percent), we obtain
the following series running from the highest genetic correlation to
the lowest:[40] MZ > DZ > half-siblings > cousins.

By comparing monozygotic and dizygotic twins and keeping this
proportional distribution in mind, twin studies aim to deduce the
variance of the phenotype that is due to the environment rather than
to genes. Specifically, twin studies start from the assumption that it
is possible to distinguish, through statistical analysis, three sources
of phenotypic variance: genetics (A), shared environment (C), and
nonshared environment (E). The more phenotypic variance (VarP) explained by genetic variance (VarA), the more heritable the trait is. This
is the classical ACE model (figure 5.4), which can be formalized by the
following equation: VarP = VarA + VarC + VarE.

What were the arguments advanced by proenvironmental and
progenetic biosocial criminologists in support of their positions? The
controversy had two phases. Each phase corresponded to a specific
epistemic standard. The first phase dwelt on the plausibility of the
results obtained by progenetic biosocial criminologists using the twin
method. The second phase, related to the first, was primarily concerned with the realism of the results obtained.

The infamous cases of cold fusion[41] and water memory[42] show that
the norm of plausibility is of central importance in the emergence and
resolution of scientific controversies. The norm of verisimilitude re-

FIGURE 5.4

Schematization of the ACE model in a progenetic biosocial criminology article.

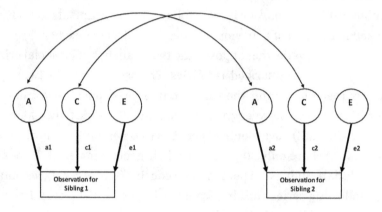

Figure reproduced from Barnes, Beaver, and Boutwell, "Examining the Genetic Underpinnings," 936.

quires researchers to ensure that their work does not "contradict what their peers consider to be established, validated knowledge," since it is up to them to "to provide a valid explanation in accordance with what is already known."[43] Of course, if there were a consensus among researchers about the meaning and context of this standard of reasonableness, its role in controversies would not be so central. In reality, scientific results are constantly interpreted within a particular evidential context, whether it is a specialty, a theory, or a research hypothesis that one wishes to submit to empirical testing.[44] Thus it frequently happens during controversies that researchers interpret identical results in divergent ways according to their position within the scientific field.

The case of cold fusion is exemplary in this respect: while the electrochemists Stanley Pons and Martin Fleischmann found it implausible that the excess heat they observed could be of chemical origin, the physicists who confronted them found it equally implausible that this excess was due to a nuclear reaction. In short, they did not have the same vision of what was (im)probable. The flexible nature of the plausibility standard is also reflected in the twin studies controversy. The evidentiary context invoked by proenvironmental biosocial criminologists is sociology, and more specifically sociological theories of crime that are considered reliable by most of American criminologists. It is perfectly clear that the hypothesis that the origins of criminal behaviors may be primarily biological conflicts with this accumulated knowledge. Unsurprisingly, Burt and Simons expressed their disbelief at empirical results that seemed "implausible"[45] and "astonishing,"[46] insofar as the results called into question decades of knowledge that criminologists had patiently accumulated. This is why to reconcile their own biosocial results with the theories validated by the criminological field, the two sociologists deployed a malleable conception of genetics through the G×E equation.

Conversely, the idea that criminality might be an entirely social behavior seemed highly implausible to progenetic biosocial criminologists. They therefore changed the evidentiary context and shifted the disciplinary reference, from what was commonly accepted in sociology to what was considered plausible in behavior genetics and cognitive psychology, namely that most human behavior is genetic in origin.[47] Their use of twin studies, rather than being part of the continuity of knowledge accumulated to date by their fellow criminologists, had more to do with underlining the implausibility of sociological theories of crime with respect to the knowledge accumulated in behavior genetics. Thus, while Burt and Simons mobilized the standard of plausibility that was generally accepted at the time in the field of criminology to counter the use of twin studies, progenetic biosocial criminologists mobilized the same standard to criticize what seemed plausible to sociologists.

The standard of reasonableness was not the only standard invoked by proenvironmental biosocial criminologists to criticize their opponents. While "plausibility refers less directly to empirical argument than to the summoning of the authority of judged science,"[48] the standard of realism requires critics to judge the relevance and reliability of the evidence provided by their opponents in support of the controversial thesis they support. While distinct, these standards are deeply intertwined: the less plausible scientific propositions seem in a given

evidentiary context, the more likely they are to be scrutinized for realism. It will thus be up to the originators of a controversial proposal
to double down on their efforts to justify the stability and reliability of
the results obtained.

As we have seen, the classic mathematical equation of twin studies
has two unknowns: the shared environment (C) and the nonshared environment (E). Indeed, the initial postulate with regard to the genetic
heritage of the MZ and DZ twins only neutralizes the genetic factor (A).
A second assumption must therefore be adopted to solve the equation
and obtain a heritability coefficient. This second postulate is generally
referred to as the Equal Environment Assumption (EEA). According to
this assumption, the environments of MZ twins are no more similar
than those of DZ twins. In other words, we neutralize the shared environment factor (C), and we are left with a single unknown, the nonshared environment (E). Figure 5.4 provides an example of a schematic
of the ACE model: A and C neutralize each other.

Callie Burt and Ronald Simons criticized progenetic biosocial
criminologists for basing their research on the Equal Environment Assumption, which, they argued, was flawed. Indeed, they wrote, "This
central assumption is flatly contradicted by both empirical evidence
and common sense. Research clearly demonstrates that MZ co-twins
experience more similar social environments than DZ co-twins."[49] Burt
and Simons then cited research that showed that MZ twins are more
likely to be treated similarly by their parents, have the same friends,
spend time together, and so on.[50] To understand the seriousness of this
criticism, we should stress that by locating the issue at a lower level
of the twin studies demonstration chain, the two sociologists put the
quantitative genetics approach used by their opponents at considerable risk. Indeed, Trevor Pinch has clearly shown how the production
of scientific facts can be broken down into various successive stages,
from the collection of raw results to the theorization of these results
through increasingly general statements.[51] Criticisms addressed to
the lower levels of the scientific demonstration have one distinct advantage: in case of success, they lead to the collapse, like a house of
cards, of all the subsequent stages. For example, if a researcher were

to demonstrate that the Geiger counter used by a physicist to detect solar neutrinos was defective, then everything else in the physicist's demonstration would immediately collapse.[52] Similarly, if the Equal Environment Assumption were indeed shown to be flawed, then all the results obtained by the progenetic biosocial criminologists would be defective too, as it would undermine the mathematical equation that underlies the very method of twin studies.

Understandably, the progenetic researchers were particularly careful to justify the realism of this assumption to the readers of *Criminology*. First, they pointed out that any statistical model contains implicit assumptions.[53] More importantly, they added, the numerous empirical tests of the Equal Environment Assumption conducted to date all pointed in the same direction: possible violations of this assumption did not produce significant statistical effects. The share attributed to genetic factors to the detriment of environmental factors would thus be overestimated by at most about 5 percentage points, which seems negligible.[54]

It is important to understand the symbolic violence that the publication of this article represented for progenetic researchers. Their work was accused, in the flagship journal of American criminology, of having "fatal flaws."[55] Simons and Burt did not merely criticize the methodological and conceptual choices of Beaver and his colleagues. By addressing their criticisms to the lower methodological levels, they were ultimately calling for an end to heritability studies. It is not surprising, therefore, that this article was very poorly received by progenetic biosocial criminologists, who felt that they were being personally attacked and censured by the rest of the criminological field:

> It's an interesting piece because I could write a critique of twin-based research, and I could tell of issues within, limitations to it, and I could do so it in a very objective, empirical, quantitative way. They [Simons and Burt] didn't do that. They did it in a very editorialized fashion, where they actually called for an end to research. And so I would ask, you know, we're talking about the top criminology journal! Why would reviewers, authors, and editors allow for someone to make a call for an end to research? They're basically saying, "We need to censor an entire body of research."[56]

The *Criminology* controversy also provided an opportunity for psychologists coming from the field of behavior genetics to support progenetic criminologists. In addition to articles from the two main parties in the conflict (Simons and Burt on one side, Beaver and his colleagues on the other), the issue included the opinions of two apparent bystanders. Terrie Moffitt supported the progenetic criminologists, while Princeton University sociologist Douglas Massey supported Simons and Burt. As we have seen, Moffitt was no stranger to the controversy, as she is also a producer of biosocial criminological knowledge. Indeed, she began her article by admitting that she had used twin studies in the past.[57] Her intervention provides a concrete illustration of the theoretical affinities between the criminologists and the psychologists discussed in the previous chapter.

BEHIND THE SCENES OF THE CONTROVERSY

The controversy surrounding the use of twin studies in criminology replicates the situation we encountered regarding the G×E interaction. The real issue at stake in the various controversies studied lies in the redefinition of the space of possibilities within the American criminological field: that is, in the words of biosocial criminologists, in a possible "paradigm shift."[58] This issue, however, seemed to be relegated to the background. The only issue that remained was the ACE and G×E models, which, as we have seen, questioned the role of social and biological factors in the science of crime. Simons and Burt adopted a biosocial approach that did not question the knowledge accumulated up to that point, in particular the importance of social factors in explaining antisocial behavior. This explains the surprise they felt when reading the work of progenetic biosocial criminologists. Indeed, unlike the former, the latter produced heterodox and subversive knowledge: there was good reason to review the role of sociology in the American criminological field. This situation is reminiscent of what the historian Naomi Oreskes has shown with regard to the issue of global warming, where a few researchers challenged the consensus of the scientific community.[59] Similarly, the progenetic branch questioned the consensus of most American criminologists, who adhered to a sociological and environmental approach to the criminal phenomenon.

The stakes in each case were not, however, the same. In the case of global warming, the interests of the contrarian scientists were mainly financial, industrial, and political. This was not the case for progenetic biosocial criminologists. Although Kevin Beaver, John Paul Wright, and their colleagues sometimes betrayed extrascientific interests when, for example, they intervened as experts in the criminal justice system, or when they presented themselves as politically conserva-tive,[60] there is no evidence to suggest that this was the sole motivation for their subversive orientation. Indeed, some of these extrascientific interests arose because of their scientific heterodoxy: if they inter-vened as experts in criminal proceedings, it was in fact because they had previously made themselves known as "criminologists who study genetic factors." It would thus be tempting to see in the *Criminology* debate a simple opposition between two disinterested scientific theses: Is the methodology of twin studies reliable? What is the best way to conceptualize the interaction between genes and environment?

Yet one of the contributions of Bourdieu's theorization of scien-tific activity was to underline that science "is a social field like any other, with its distribution of power and its monopolies, its struggles and strategies, interests and profits."[61] Neither John Paul Wright and his colleagues nor Ronald Simons and Callie Burt were disinterested, even if the interests that guided their interventions were internal to the scientific field and expressed in a socially acceptable form. Scientific issues did indeed guide the subversive action of the progenetic branch. It was also scientific issues that led Simons and Burt to oppose Kevin Beaver and his colleagues. But this does not mean that the controver-sies between the progenetic and proenvironment branches were mere debates of ideas. Far from it, for the struggle that they engaged in over the definition of legitimate biosocial criminology had consequences for the scientific production system. After Burt and Simons published their article calling for a halt to twin studies,[62] the progenetic branch found itself weakened and in great difficulty. Wright and colleagues explained that Burt and Simons's article was "already being cited as evidence by referees in the peer-review process that twin-based designs are inherently flawed and therefore such studies should not be considered for publication."[63] In addition to illustrating the eminently social and practical dimension of intellectual controversies, this confirms the devastating nature of criticism directed at the lower levels of a scientific demonstration.

To be sure, the standards of realism and plausibility were also mobilized by progenetic biosocial criminologists to refuse the publication of work that did not make sufficient room for genetic factors. Indeed, their takeover of one of the leading journals in the field of criminology, the *Journal of Criminal Justice*, allowed them to impose their definition of crime and the expectations that flowed from it. The following interview with a progenetic biosocial criminologist highlights how the plausibility standard was mobilized by this group to reject work that did not make room for biological variables:

> Although the effect size varies, the impact of biological factors (genes, evolution, etc.) is unlikely to be zero. . . . Since variable z [biology] was not present in the study we were asked to review, we concluded that the paper wasn't acceptable. It was a basic methodological problem. Was the study rigorous, did it take into account all possible sources of bias? In this example the answer was no, it had not reached a certain standard of rigor. We therefore rejected the paper (or recommended revisions).[64]

It is thus utterly difficult to separate the scientific interests of biosocial criminologists, both progenetic and proenvironmental, from their personal and institutional interests. On the one hand, they are convinced of the relevance of their approach, and there is no reason to doubt their sincerity in this respect. On the other hand, it is hard not to see that this approach is attached to academic interests and to the interrogation, or conversely the reproduction, of sociological domination. This Janus-faced issue, scientific and academic, intellectual and temporal, explains why the progenetic branch of biosocial criminology is mainly driven by the work of early-career criminology graduates who also campaign for the independence of criminology from sociology. This again shows that "new entrants tend to prefer 'radical' and 'new' positions without worrying too much about the probative value of the arguments that support them, whereas established agents who feel 'attacked' will have every interest (if they keep their composure) in closely analyzing the arguments of their 'opponents' and insisting on their weaknesses."[65]

These dual interests are even more difficult to disconnect because they form a logical whole. The conflicts between proenvironmental and progenetic biosocial criminologists can be better understood by reconstructing the system of logical choices they have formed.[66] The progenetic branch of biosocial criminology presents a heterodox approach to crime that attacks dominant sociological theories. This approach entails a modeling of the G×E relationship that emphasizes the genetic factor at the expense of the environmental factor, and the use of methodologies such as twin studies that are known to emphasize genetics at the expense of the environment. Conversely, the sociologists Ronald Simons and Callie Burt do not question the attachment of the criminological enterprise to sociology. Not surprisingly, they take a proenvironmental view of biosocial criminology in which the E factor is paramount.

One of the claims made by biosocial criminologists is that they can move beyond the nature-culture debate to nurture an interdisciplinary theorization of criminal behavior. An analysis of the scientific controversies that have pitted progenetic researchers against proenvironmental researchers quickly shows that this is wishful thinking. Whether a controversy concerns the modeling of the interactions between genetic and environmental factors (G×E), the merits of epigenetics, or the conceptual relevance of twin studies, both sides clearly favor either nature or culture. And as we shall now see, the rejection of the "social" is quite clear in the antisociological rhetoric developed by criminology graduates.

6 "COPERNICAN CRIMINOLOGY"

Producing Scientific Capital through Controversy

TRADITIONAL SOCIOLOGY OF SCIENCE OFTEN reminds us that the establishment of a scientific fact requires a "social negotiation of truth."[1] This is particularly evident during a crisis when, for example, an experiment on memory transfer in worms defies replication[2] or when a physical entity such as gravitational waves evades detection.[3] Each party in the dispute must find convincing arguments to support its position. The persuasive character of these arguments is measured against the scientific canons of the field—that is to say, against the evidentiary context of evidence already mentioned—and the methodological and conceptual tools then available.

Social negotiation is not always carried out with the decorum and restraint one might expect in the hushed world of academia. As sociologist Cyril Lemieux has pointed out, "Violence, verbal and even physical, is the constant horizon of any controversy," and it is the role of "any culture of controversy to ward off the risk of violence by wrapping it in a corset of civility."[4] This corset, however, can occasionally come undone. Maude Lajeunesse has shown, for example, how the controversy surrounding the publication of Martin Bernal's *Black Athena* exceeded the limits of academic propriety.[5] Aaron Panofsky has provided another example of violent controversy in his detailed analysis of the way behavior geneticists publicly attacked environmental psychologists from the early 1980s to the late 1990s, unhesitatingly resorting to provocation and presenting themselves "as crusaders who would rout the antigenetics heresy gripping behavioral science."[6]

Faced with criticism from their peers, one might have expected progenetic biosocial criminologists to try to tone things down. One might have thought, for example, that the controversy would be played out in euphemistic terms, and that Kevin Beaver and his colleagues would try to convince the rest of the criminological field in a measured and cordial manner, adopting the negotiating attitude that sociologists of science habitually describe. Such expectations would be even more realistic given that most of their direct opponents were researchers who, like Ronald Simons and Callie Burt, shared the desire to develop a biosocial criminology. Yet, as will quickly become apparent, the multiple controversies surrounding the work carried out by progenetic biosocial criminologists lay far from the ideal of nonviolent scientific disagreement. This is even more startling insofar as the polemical and sometimes frankly aggressive tone of the protagonists, in what undeniably was a gendered performance, was not restricted to the backstage of the controversy, as is often the case. People sometimes wonder how it is possible to have biological theories of crime revived despite their dark history of successive scientific failures and egregious political instrumentalizations. As Oliver Rollins made clear in his study of neuroscientific research on violence, this biocriminological program "has endured and even thrived because of, and not despite, its notorious legacy."[7]

To understand this polemical attitude, recall the findings established in the previous chapters. The biosocial current is dominated by the progenetic biosocial criminologists, while those who favor the influence of environmental factors are marginalized and excluded from the institutionalization process of biosocial criminology. This reversal of the hierarchy of the criminological sciences remains, however, limited to the circumscribed space that is the biosocial movement. The rest of the criminological field remains dominated by the social sciences in general, and by sociology in particular. Progenetic biosocial criminologists attacked this domination by insisting on the greater scientificity of behavior genetics and by presenting sociology as an ideological pseudoscience. This dual discourse promoting biosocial (progenetic) criminology and denouncing sociology can be analyzed with the help of the concept of boundary-work.[8] Boundary-work is the historical process through which scientists erect boundaries separating science from pseudoscience. Scientists may thus seek to demarcate themselves from other professions that produce intellectual knowledge, such as religion or engineering, but they may also seek to erect a boundary to exclude other groups that claim to be scientific. What criteria guide this work of demarcation between science and pseudoscience? How do researchers define the cultural boundaries of science? Integrating the concept of boundary-work into the framework of field theory allows us to better understand the demarcation work undertaken by researchers,[9] notably because the definition of "good science" depends on the nature and the amount of scientific capital held by the different protagonists.[10] This is, at least, what the case of biosocial criminology demonstrates.

BIOSOCIAL SCIENCE VERSUS SOCIOLOGICAL PSEUDOSCIENCE

Boundary-work is a necessary step in the development of any novel scientific program. To legitimize their existence, progenetic biosocial criminologists sought to differentiate themselves from sociology, which they presented as unscientific. Ironically, some of the arguments deployed by progenetic biosocial criminologists against sociology had already been used by nineteenth-century anatomists to exclude phrenologists from the scientific field. Generally considered one of the main historical ancestors of biocriminology, phrenology was governed by the idea that "the action of particular faculties or 'powers' of the mind correspond to specific regions or 'seats' of the brain."[11] One could thus identify the aggressive or combative tendencies of individuals by examining their cranial protuberances. Thomas Gieryn used the controversy between phrenologists and anatomists as an illustration of the demarcation process between science and pseudoscience, observing that "traditional divisions of labor within the university (anatomists studied the structure of the body, moral philosophers studied its mental and behavioral functioning) were threatened by phrenologists' claim that 'theirs was the only complete science of man.'"[12]

While the anatomists of the time worked to preserve the state of the scientific field, progenetic biosocial criminologists have attacked dominant criminology in an attempt to overthrow the field's hierarchies. The argumentative strategies used by both groups are nevertheless very similar. The first strategy deployed by anatomists to discredit phrenology was indeed to "expose its political and especially religious ambitions,"[13] which they claimed prevented phrenologists from being completely objective, unbiased observers of human behavior. In the same vein, progenetic biosocial criminologists portray sociologists as biased ideologues who are vehemently opposed to any use of biology in the understanding of criminal behavior. Two representatives of the progenetic branch thus write that "political concerns can influence, if not entirely shape, important academic debates."[14] In this case, the ideological root of the problem is said to be the "leftist political orientation"[15] of American academics, especially in sociology, which would be responsible for the rejection of biology in the explanation of any criminal phenomenon. In short, according to progenetic biosocial criminologists, ideology remains "criminology's Achilles' heel."[16]

Interestingly, some of these criticisms have been directed at researchers who have themselves called for the use of genetics in criminology. For example, in their response to the criticisms leveled by proenvironmental biosocial criminologists Callie Burt and Ronald Simons, progenetic biosocial criminologists asserted that "there is no room for subjective opinion or agreements to disagree: There is only algebra."[17] J. C. Barnes and colleagues even accused Burt and Simons of mobilizing the work of "political ideologues" by passing them off as "experts."[18] Progenetic biosocial criminologists thus attempted to draw a line between scientific and political enterprises through a supposedly neutral call for "a criminology that is disinterested."[19]

According to progenetic biosocial criminologists, one of the main manifestations of the ideological bias of mainstream criminology lies in its treatment of race. As Oliver Rollins and I have demonstrated, these researchers adhere to a "partial social constructionism of race, that is a logic of difference that attempts to accommodate both a social and biological interpretation of race," which translates into a "renewed commitment to the bio-criminalization of race."[20] Indeed, if we are to follow progenetic biosocial criminologists, "The scientific evidence indicates that race is both a biological construct and a social construct."[21] Yet because of their progressive ideology, criminologists—especially those trained in sociology—would not want to accept this simple empirical fact. John Paul Wright, for example, believes that "race and crime is the holy grail [*sic*] of criminology. Touch it and you expose yourself to wrath and fury."[22] Analogously, in a *Quillette* article, Brian Boutwell used the metaphor of the Bermuda Triangle to describe the criminological field as "a place where careers disappear more often than ships."[23]

A second angle of attack used by the anatomists against the phrenologists concerned the religious dimension of the opponent's scientific output. Similarly, progenetic biosocial criminologists frequently compare sociologists' reactions to their research to the dogmatism of the Catholic Church. Biosocial criminology is framed as a heretical science, or, in Matt DeLisi and Wright's terms, as a "Copernican criminology": "While not as extreme, criminology is now faced with a decision similar to that of Galileo. Do we, as criminologists, admit that hundreds of studies now implicate biological and genetic factors in the etiology of criminal behavior, or do we continue to ignore the evidence, sanction its advocates, and remain attached to 'approved' theories?"[24]

Galileo is not the only historical case deployed by biosocial criminologists. They have also recalled how Darwin's writings were considered dangerous by the theologians of the Anglican Church.[25] The use of Galileo and Darwin allows them to emphasize the ideological dimension of the rejection of biosocial criminology. But progenetic biosocial criminologists can sometimes be even more provocative. For example, in a collective work published in 2008, they compared sociology to the creationist theory of intelligent design: "Many contemporary socio-logical perspectives remain just a step or two away from invoking the supernatural. Indeed, sociological criminology sometimes parallels the 'intelligent design' perspective. This perspective views an invisible force as responsible for the organization of life on earth. Preachers refer to this force as God, to sociologists it is referred to as 'environ-ment,' 'stratification,' 'culture,' or 'socialization.' Like God, these fac-tors are omnipotent and beyond reproach."[26]

The strategy of passing off the opponents' position as a moral stance is obviously well known to historians and sociologists of science. In his analysis of the development of science in ancient Greece, Geoffrey Lloyd showed how empirical science was constituted in direct opposi-tion to beliefs and anything that could be considered magical.[27] Closer to the era of biosocial criminology and to its references, the examples of Copernicus and Galileo had already been mobilized by Italian bio-criminologist Cesare Lombroso at the end of the nineteenth century: "To claim that human liberty is ruined by denying certain principles of morality is to repeat the example of those who reproached Galileo and Copernicus for disturbing and destroying the solar system when they taught that the Earth rotates and the Sun remains motionless. The solar system endures forever; so will the moral world, no matter what criterion is used to examine it. Doctrines remain in the books, facts continue their course."[28]

Similarly, Italian criminologist Enrico Ferri, a student of Lom-broso, compared his master to Galileo, writing in 1921 that "the Gali-leo method of observing the criminal is a Lombrosian innovation not destined to perish."[29] Like the accusation of ideological bias, compar-ing sociology to religious dogma allows biosocial criminologists to emphasize the irrationality of the so-called rejection of biology. To biocriminologists, this was not scientific debate but the barely veiled attempt by an "authoritarian science"[30] to impose censorship on an approach that ran contrary to its doctrine, be it political or religious. Just as Galileo was unjustly condemned by the church for the inade-quacy of his scientific conclusions with respect to the official doctrine, biosocial criminologists accuse sociologists of being more interested in defending moral principles than in pursuing scientific truth.

To complete their boundary-work, biosocial criminologists have also sought to drape themselves in the characteristics valued in science. In his study of the biological field, the sociologist Jean-Louis Fabiani has shown that one of the recognition strategies used by researchers in ecology "consisted in reinforcing the technical dimension of their activity by increasing the use of formalization and the borrowing of instruments from sectors considered to be more advanced."[31] Similarly, the attitude of progenetic biosocial criminologists was not simply to receive genetic resources. They used genetics as a strategy to reinforce the legitimacy of their research, while at the same time questioning, head-on, the scientificity of sociological work and sociologists' "stubborn refusal to accept the help offered by the more fundamental sciences."[32]

By portraying sociology as dogmatic and nonrigorous, progenetic biosocial criminologists made biosocial criminology appear even more objective and scientific. They presented their research as a modern approach that would replace an aging sociological paradigm. The contrast is particularly clear when it comes to the issue of causal explanations in science. According to biosocial criminologists, the elevation of criminology to a true science would require systematic data collection and processing, Aristotelian empiricism over Platonic rationalism, quantitative approaches over qualitative methods, and critical realism over constructivist nominalism:

> It is obvious that human beings must exist before we can realistically talk about humanness; only a Platonic metaphysician would argue otherwise. It is equally obvious that while no one has ever seen other abstractions such as "intelligence," "empathy," or "low-self-control" (as well as a multitude of "social facts"), we see them demonstrated by humans every day. They can even be measured, albeit imperfectly, to assess how they affect human behavior. To say that because they do not have shape or occupy space they do not exist as human commonalities, differentially experienced and expressed, is absurd.[33]

All of this would, according to biosocial criminologists, allow them to propose explanations for the criminal phenomenon, and not just a multitude of Durkheim-like descriptions, which "beg a multitude of questions rather than explanations."[34] Instead of this "poor science,"[35] progenetic biosocial criminologists promise their readers they can offer explanations. This rhetoric is greatly facilitated by the apparent simplicity of genetics. A basic problem in social science research is to establish causal relationships. Behavior genetics allows one to "cut through much of the complexity"[36] by assuming that genetic factors are at the base of the causal chain and are not influenced by other variables. This advantage, lacking in sociology, allows biosocial criminologists to attack the scientific rigor of mainstream criminological theories.

This contrast is evident in an article written by Anthony Walsh and John Paul Wright in response to Canadian-based criminologists who criticized progenetic biosocial criminologists for "Ptolemizing Lombroso."[37] Walsh and Wright countered that the methods used by social scientists were similar to those used by Ptolemy, as they merely *"describe* what they see with the 'naked eye' and they complain that to go further below the surface to uncover *explanations* for what they see is gratuitous reductionism."[38] Thus, while "social scientists observe that crime is most prevalent in poor, socially disorganized neighborhoods and conclude that poverty and slums cause crime," biosocial criminology "takes the path of science and seeks to go beyond the readily observable to the underlying 'causes of the causes' by utilizing the techniques provided for us by geneticists and neuroscientists."[39]

CRIMINOLOGICAL HERESY: A CONSERVATIVE SCIENCE

The demarcation between sociological pseudoscience and biosocial science has also led progenetic criminologists to cultivate their orthodoxy. Rather than ironing out their singularities, they have come to value characteristics that they think are heretical in the eyes of the dominant, in a phenomenon not unlike "the posture of the pamphleteer journalist . . . who presents himself as a 'rebel' because he does not respect the codes of the *'bien-pensants.'*"[40] Thus, while sociology has been portrayed as progressive and allergic to Lombroso's heritage, some progenetic biosocial criminologists have campaigned for a conservative criminology and revisited the work of the Italian criminologist.

The progressive political orientation of American academics, which should not be conflated with a so-called liberal bias,[41] is a well-documented phenomenon.[42] While liberalism is prevalent in the humanities and social sciences, it is also pervasive in natural science disciplines such as biology. Conservatives, in turn, are overrepresented in professional faculties, such as nursing, accounting, and criminal justice programs. It would thus be quite easy to interpret the development of biosocial criminology as yet another expression of the conservative movement that has developed in the American academic field over the past fifty years. Several politically conservative universities were created in the 1970s, such as Liberty University in 1971, Regent University in 1978, and Thomas More College in 1978,[43] and the last few decades have seen the development of political activism among conservative students.[44] It was in this context that the Marxist criminologists Paul Takagi and Tony Platt argued that Clarence R. Jeffery's biosocial criminology was part of the new conservative trend of the 1970s.[45] This interpretation is all the more credible given that the majority of biosocial criminologists come from departments of criminology and criminal justice, that is, institutions that are, on average, more conservative than other departments in the humanities and social sciences.

While biosocial criminology may have benefited from the advance of the conservative movement among academics, the political explanation might not be entirely satisfactory if we are to grant some credit to the results of a questionnaire submitted to biosocial criminologists. One of the questions asked which party, Democrat or Republican, they supported during the 2012 presidential election opposing Barack Obama and Mitt Romney. Of the twenty respondents, nine declared having voted for Obama, compared to five for Romney (the rest either did not vote or supported another party). The gap was even wider for the 2016 presidential election: eight declared having supported Hillary Clinton, compared to only two for Donald Trump. While caution should be exercised in interpreting these data, the results do show that biosocial criminology is not inherently a right-wing science. These results confirm those of a larger survey of members of the American Society of Criminology conducted in the late 2000s. Of the small pool of twenty-one criminologists (out of a total of 770 respondents) who reported adopting a biosocial approach in their research, five identified themselves as conservative, five as centrist, and eleven as liberal.[46]

To be sure, these questionnaires must be handled with care, especially since it is possible that some of the respondents simply conformed to the social expectations of the pollsters.[47] The results do confirm, however, a well-established fact about biological thinking, namely that it is politically flexible and can fit into political agendas ranging from the extreme left to the extreme right.[48] This is also true of research on the biological factors of crime. Historian of criminology Mary Gibson has shown that Lombroso's criminal anthropology, which gave a semblance of scientific solidity to the Nazi regime's extermination plans,[49] was nevertheless compatible with many ideologies, from socialism to liberalism to fascism.[50]

Why, then, would biosocial criminologists insist on their conservative orientation? Why publish a collection of essays entitled *Conservative Criminology*[51] or maintain a similarly titled blog?[52] As think tanks and conservative movement expert Thomas Medvetz has explained, political marginality can be an advantage in the academic world, as it allows one to gain visibility that would be more difficult to obtain when blending in with the liberal masses.[53] Precisely because they stand apart from the majority values of their field, biosocial criminologists are visible. As Wright and DeLisi write in the introduction to *Conservative Criminology*, "There is something almost odd, out of place, even counterintuitive about a book with the title of 'Conservative Criminology.' . . . This is part of the reason our book is so unique. As politically conservative social scientists we are a true minority on campus."[54]

Biosocial criminologists are singularly identifiable because their discourse is provocative and stands out even within the minority of conservative scholars. Indeed, not all conservative intellectuals adopt such a polemical attitude toward liberal domination. In their study of political mobilization among American students, sociologists Amy Binder and Kate Wood have shown that conservatives can be divided into two styles: a "civil" style that emphasizes intellectual exchange and discussion with liberals, typically found on elite university campuses, and a "provocative" style, which is more combative and includes participation in controversial events, a style typically found at less prestigious public universities.[55] There is no doubt that the mobilization of progenetic biosocial criminologists corresponds to the provocative style, which is consistent with the link made by Binder and Wood between institutional positioning and the type of political mobilization. Indeed, we saw in the previous chapters that because progenetic biosocial criminologists are predominantly criminology graduates, they have been structurally excluded from the most prestigious American universities.

Like behavior geneticists before them, progenetic biosocial criminologists cultivate a "bad boy"[56] image rooted in a masculine ethos of physical confrontation. Using pugilistic metaphors ("punching bag")[57] and overtly rebelling against the field's norms, the most vocal biosocial criminologists are trying hard to appear as tough, fearless men. This combative, masculine style of scientific discussion can, for instance, be observed in the introduction to *Conservative Criminology*, notably when biosocial criminologists ironically present themselves as "racists, sexists, and homophobic Neanderthals who wish only to impose [their] morality over others."[58] In addition to insisting on the heterodoxy of their political opinions, they present sociologists as "mortal enemies," to use Panofsky's expression.[59] Thus they explain how "being branded 'conservative' frequently results in loss of jobs, reduced professional status, and having your scholarly work impugned."[60] Brian Boutwell's language is equally unequivocal when he warns his colleagues of the risks of studying race from a biosocial perspective: "Someone may slip quietly up behind you and slide a cold piece of steel in between the ribs of your budding research career."[61]

Raewyn Connell has shown how "violence can become a way of

claiming or asserting masculinity in group struggles."[62] Much as industrial labor and its associated skills (endurance, strength, toughness,
etc.) helped to define working-class masculinity,[63] controversies constitute a privileged avenue to define and forge certain forms of masculinities within the scientific field.[64] Moreover, it would appear that the
gender structure is key not only to the management and resolution of
scientific controversies relating to the biological origins of crime but
also to the internal dynamics of the movement itself. Hence, during
an interview, a biosocial criminologist who identifies as a woman confided to me that she had decided to keep her distance from the most
prominent progenetic biosocial criminologists because of the asym-
metrical gender relations that had developed between her and them
over time. While it remains difficult to assess the relative importance
of the gender structure in the historical development of biosocial criminology, we can at least conclude from this material that it has affected
scientific collaborations among researchers.

Coincidentally, the subversive and sometimes provocative attitude
adopted by these researchers also helps to explain the lack of internal
coherence in their discourse. On the one hand, biosocial criminologists attack sociology and present it as a pseudoscience that is more
ideological than empirical. On the other hand, they claim to be conservative and, as such, proponents of a "political ideology."[65] It would
thus be easy to turn their criticism of sociology against them and argue
that biosocial criminology itself "has become increasingly politically
motivated, hiding its true intent behind the façade of objective empirical inquiry."[66]

SATAN WORSHIPPERS: REHABILITATING CESARE LOMBROSO

In addition to promoting a conservative criminology, progenetic biosocial criminologists associate their name with that of nineteenth-
century Italian physician-anthropologist Cesare Lombroso, whose
theories on crime are now typically viewed as grotesque dead ends in
the history of criminology. Lombroso does occupy a rather paradoxical position in the field. On the one hand, he is frequently presented as

the "father of criminology" and therefore as one of the classic figures of the discipline, not only in the United States[67] but also in France,[68] among other countries. At the same time, his theory of atavism, which claimed to explain "the behavior of a significant number of criminals by a return to a 'savage' type in which crime would be the norm," is generally used as an example "of what not to do."[69] As historians Mary Gibson and Nicole Rafter observe in their introduction to the English-language reprint of Lombroso's major work, *The Criminal Man*, "Lombroso's methodology appears unscientific and even laughable."[70] Highly respected biologists have made devastating criticisms of his work, pointing out the numerous errors and contradictions that one can identify in his writings.[71]

Despite the somewhat risible aspects of Lombroso's work today, it is undeniable that the gradual return of the biological understanding of crime has been accompanied by increasing references to the work of the Italian criminologist, to the extent that some researchers have wondered whether we were witnessing the "return of Lombroso."[72] In an article on positivist criminology, legal scholar Jonathan Simon even argued that Lombroso "continues to haunt American crime control at the beginning of the twenty-first."[73]

Biosocial criminology is not foreign to this renewed interest. Far from it: the nineteenth-century Italian criminologist is regularly cited by progenetic biosocial criminologists.[74] Not that they intend to revive Italian positivist criminology, for even biosocial criminologists agree that Lombroso produced "bad science." Matt DeLisi thus underlines that the Italian criminologist "had a disquieting habit of making sweeping generalizations about criminal offenders with little to no data in the way of empirical justification and support."[75] Biosocial criminologists also frequently complain that their research is spontaneously identified with that of Lombroso. In their view, "Comparing biosocial approaches to Lombroso is like comparing medieval medicine to modern medicine."[76]

Why, then, should sociologists be blamed for unfairly ignoring "Lombroso's legacy"?[77] What interest could biosocial criminologists possibly have in regularly invoking Lombroso, or even revisiting his work, while conceding that his criminology was "crude, racist, and insensitive"?[78] The answer can be found in the semiotic dimension of these references, and more particularly in the meaning they have acquired over time in the specific context of the American criminological field. First, the Italian criminologist embodies a crime science apparently free of moral considerations, a knowledge based on the methodical collection of empirical facts. In short, Lombroso is the symbol of a criminological tradition that progenetic biosocial criminologists are trying to revive. This explains why they can skewer the publications of the Italian criminologist, all the while claiming that "there was value in Lombroso's work."[79]

Perhaps more importantly, Lombroso is often used by biological criminologists as a symbol of sociologists' ideological bias. The Italian criminologist had been excluded from the common heritage of American criminology following the abandonment of the biological paradigm in the first half of the twentieth century. Sociologists of the time even came to dispute that he indeed was the "father of criminology."[80] Because progenetic biosocial criminologists felt that they, like Lombroso, were the object of sociologists' "derision and sometimes hostility,"[81] they could not help but feel sympathy for the treatment meted out to the Italian anthropologist. Quoting Lombroso thus serves to restore an icon long despised by mainstream criminology. Criticized for "Ptolemizing Lombroso,"[82] biosocial criminologists continue to revisit the work of the Italian criminologist, retracing his career and research, knowing full well that "some criminologists, especially those with a more critical or leftist orientation, detest Lombroso's work and legacy."[83] Far from being simply an opportunity to recall the broad outlines of the history of criminology, the use of Lombroso by biosocial criminologists can thus be interpreted as an attempt to socially rehabilitate him as an important figure in the discipline, and thus to indirectly discredit those who have excluded him.

Last, mentioning the Italian criminologist and readdressing his work is also a way to provoke mainstream criminology by raising polemical issues. To some extent, it is not so much Lombroso himself that intrigues progenetic biosocial criminologists as the reactions that any mention of the Italian criminologist generally elicits. In this sense, Lombroso is just another tool to fuel the controversy surrounding bio-social criminology, in the same way that the provocative conservative activism of *Conservative Criminology* or the prominent display of Her-rnstein and Murray's much-maligned *The Bell Curve* on one's university desk would be.[84]

CONTROVERSY AS A VEHICLE FOR VISIBILITY: A RISKY STRATEGY THAT SOMETIMES PAYS OFF

The symbolic violence that characterizes the criticisms directed against sociologists by progenetic biosocial criminologists should therefore not to be attributed to an aggressive temperament (even of genetic origin). Indeed, we saw in the introduction to this chapter that this is a recurrent phenomenon in scientific controversies. We thus observed in the cases of Martin Bernal and of behavior geneticists that provocation and polemical attitudes are not the result of uncontrolled slippage. Aggression does not simply surface during a momentary fit of anger. Far from being temporary, these controversies have been spread over several years and through dozens of writings: articles, re-views, books, collective works. How then can we explain these public outpourings?

To understand the actions of biosocial criminologists, it is useful to draw a parallel with similar controversies. When Bernal published the first volume of his work, he was largely unknown to classicists. A sinologist, he had until then concentrated his research on "modern China, Vietnam, the Indochina War and socialism in the Far East."[85] His position as a dominated outsider played an important role during the controversy, as his opponents did not hesitate to question his quali-fications and to call him an amateur. At the same time, as Maude Lajeu-nesse has made clear, Bernal exaggerated his outsider status. Rather than seeking recognition from his opponents, Bernal deliberately em-phasized his "status as a self-proclaimed heretic,"[86] a pattern also seen in pamphleteers such as Édouard Drumont and Éric Zemmour in the French context.[87] The same process can be observed in behavior genetics. Although behavior geneticists were less isolated than Bernal was from the classicists, they were still exposed to biting criticism from their peers and were forced to retreat into their "bunker."[88] Academically, their "community was small and research funds were scarce."[89] Scientifically, psychology (the discipline from which many of them came) was dominated by environmentalist approaches. Like Bernal confronting the classicists, these researchers did not seek recognition from their peers by keeping a low profile and trying to find common ground. On the contrary, "Behavior geneticists raised scientific capital by igniting and fueling controversy and conflict, not by ending controversies and convincing their detractors."[90]

Like Bernal and the behavioral geneticists before them, the strategy of progenetic biosocial criminologists was not to be conciliatory or responsive to the criticisms directed at them. In Panofsky's words, their strategy towards their opponents consisted in "hitting them over the head," "constructing one's intellectual interlocutors as mortal enemies and attacking them in spectacular, polemical fashion."[91] The fact that combativeness is a frequent feature of scientific controversies makes it necessary to look for sociological explanations that go beyond the personalities of the researchers involved. As Lajeunesse has explained, "Investing in a controversy against a dominant agent in an academic field can be a profitable strategy that yields symbolic profits in terms of visibility for researchers occupying dominant positions in this same field."[92] Panofsky concurs, pointing out how "behavior geneticists found ways to make dissensus, controversy, and provocation scientifically 'profitable.'"[93] As Gérard Noiriel sums up, "Loading your pen with venom can make you a lot of money."[94]

Although the profitable nature of scientific controversies rarely translates into economic gains, symbolic benefits can be objectified with the help of scientometric data, specifically through an analysis of the evolution of citations received by researchers involved in such events. In a recent book devoted to the "memory of water" controversy, Pascal Ragouet thus showed how Benveniste's failure to convince his peers of the plausibility and realism of his demonstration led to a clear "reputational and positional downgrading,"[95] one of the results of which was a significant drop in the number of citations Benveniste received for his work, including research articles published before the controversy. But participation in controversial research movements can sometimes be beneficial for the researchers concerned. In genopolitics, for example, a research movement that seeks to identify the genetic factors influencing political behavior, it turns out that the controversies have enabled some researchers to amass scientific capital and increase citations to their work.[96] Importantly, this beneficial effect has also been noticeable among senior academics who spent the first part of their trajectory free of any major controversy.

The positive effect of controversies on the scientific capital held by researchers is verifiably the case of biosocial criminology. Depicting sociology as pseudoscientific, valuing characteristics perceived as heretical by the rest of the criminological field, or adopting a provocative and combative attitude has allowed them to respond to critics with more and more genetics and empirical results, to receive citations, to publish new results, and so on. As a result, during the period 2009–13, progenetic biosocial criminologists were among the most productive American criminologists: Kevin Beaver was in second place, Matt DeLisi in fourth, Michael Vaughn in fifth, followed by Adrian Raine (thirteenth) and J. C. Barnes (twenty-third).[97]

Similarly, if we examine the individual careers of a few progenetic biosocial criminologists, then the consolidation of the field from 2007–8 onwards and the controversies that ensued correspond to peaks in visibility—in terms of citations received—of researchers belonging to different generations (figure 6.1). One would normally expect researchers of different generations—Anthony Walsh received his PhD in 1983, John Paul Wright in 1996, Matt DeLisi in 2000, and Kevin Beaver in 2006—to reach the peak of their visibility in a staggered manner. The fact that this was not the case suggests that it is not a matter of scientific maturity, which can be defined as the number of years since receiving a PhD, but rather the result of the positive effects of controversy and scientific jousting.

In other words, the subversive attitude of biosocial criminologists has effectively allowed them to accumulate scientific capital within the

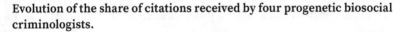

FIGURE 6.1

Evolution of the share of citations received by four progenetic biosocial criminologists.

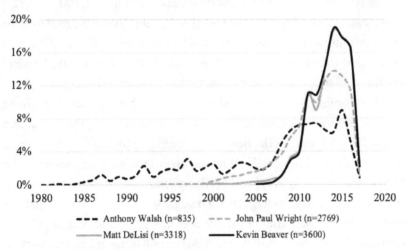

- - - Anthony Walsh (n=835)   - - - John Paul Wright (n=2769)
——— Matt DeLisi (n=3318)   ——— Kevin Beaver (n=3600)

Date source: Scopus, accessed July 16, 2018.

criminological field. In their classic work *Social Stratification in Science*, sociologists Jonathan Cole and Stephen Cole showed that the age of researchers did not necessarily influence their visibility, although a peak was generally observed around the age of sixty.[98] The present results confirm this observation, showing that the provocative attitude of progenetic biosocial criminologists has led to greater visibility within the criminological field, regardless of the age and career stage of the individuals concerned.

"THERE'S A SPACE FOR THAT IN CRIMINOLOGY": SOCIOLOGISTS' ATTITUDE OF DETACHMENT VIS-À-VIS THE PROVOCATIONS OF BIOSOCIAL CRIMINOLOGISTS

Although biosocial criminologists may tout the merits of their genetics of crime, they continue to expend significant efforts attacking the dominant sociological paradigm. Indeed, the negative boundary-work takes up far more space than the positive work of promoting biosocial criminology. In fact, progenetic biosocial criminologists began

attacking sociology long before their research was criticized. Progenetic biosocial criminology is controversial because it does everything
it can to be controversial, with a polemical style and an acerbic tone.
But apart from the two articles by Ronald Simons and Callie Burt,[99]
American criminologists have remained generally indifferent to their
provocations. Burt and Simons noted in the introduction to their first
article that they were "perplexed by the lack of response" and "critical
attention"[100] to the work of progenetic biosocial criminologists.

This is reminiscent of the situation described by Mathieu Albert
and his colleagues regarding the relationship between the social and
biomedical sciences in the field of health.[101] The "defensive and critical
posture" adopted by social scientists toward their colleagues from the
biomedical sciences is typical of disciplines that, endowed with "low
scientific authority," engage in a "struggle to increase their legitimacy
by trying to reorder the hierarchy between scientific practices."[102] In
contrast, those who dominate the field remain quite indifferent to their
self-proclaimed opponents because they have confidence in the scientificity of their work and do not feel threatened by the emancipatory
claims of social scientists.

The situation of biosocial criminology within the criminological
field is similar. Sociologists have so far been content to pursue their
research on crime without concern for the rise of biosocial criminology. Predominantly from less-than-prestigious universities and with
doctorates in criminology that are sometimes mocked, biosocial criminologists are not in tune with the dominant canons of the criminological field, which is why sociologists do not really feel threatened by the
development of this movement. Simons and Burt, the only American
researchers who have taken a stand against the research conducted by
the most visible biosocial criminologists, have done so because they
wish to impose their own conception of biosocial criminology.

This also explains why psychologists and neuroscience-oriented researchers, who have some scientific affinity with progenetic biosocial
criminologists, do not find it useful to participate in the controversies
provoked by the latter. This is true of the most well-known representative of neurocriminology, Adrian Raine, a professor at the prestigious

University of Pennsylvania, who has ample material and scientific resources to carry out his research program. In contrast, criminologists
are dependent on the data and genetic models to which they are granted
access (see chapter 7), so they are forced to defend themselves fiercely
against any form of criticism. Beaver and his colleagues were so combative when Burt and Simons criticized twin studies precisely because
they had few options other than heritability research and their scientific success entirely depended on it. As one of them confessed:

> When they come along and they try to take away your livelihood by
> taking away your ability to publish in criminology journals, by taking
> away the methods and in some cases the data that you use, I think that
> you're almost pushed into a corner. What else are you gonna do? Are
> you gonna continue to sit there and take it, are you gonna continue to
> sit there and let yourself be a punching bag? Or are you gonna fight
> back and at some point say, "Enough is enough?" And I think that's
> really . . . It came to that point for me, and I think it came to that point
> for other people as well.[103]

In contrast, the detached attitude of sociologists can be illustrated
by an interview with one of the leading sociologists in the American
criminological field. After completing her dissertation in sociology
under the supervision of a former president of the Criminology Section
of the American Sociological Association, this person became a professor of criminology and sociology at a renowned Californian university,
as well as a member of the executive committee of the American Society of Criminology. Her research has been published in prestigious
mainstream social science journals, including the *American Journal of
Sociology*. How does this scholar perceive the development of biosocial
criminology?

> I think it's important [biosocial criminology], but it's not where my
> emphasis is. And so, I mean, I don't agree with people who say that it
> has no place, that that research has no place and shouldn't be there,
> and there's a lot of people who think that way. And I think that's a ridic-
> ulous standpoint or viewpoint because to say that, you know, genetics

and bio, you know . . . What's important to me is the social part of the biosocial [laughs]. So, I mean, do I include measures of this in my model, do I acknowledge it, no I don't, right? That doesn't mean that I don't think that that's important, but the sort of questions that I'm interested in are not directly relevant or connecting with that literature. So, my thing is that there's a space for that in criminology. I just question, in light of the recent debate that went on with Callie Burt and others [the debate published in the special issue of *Criminology*], about the quality and the precision of that work. I haven't read enough about that debate or that literature to weigh in, but I suspect that the concerns that Callie Burt and others have raised, Ron Simons . . . I think that's a healthy debate to be having, that the field needs to be having. But I guess I'm not . . . I don't agree with colleagues of mine who say, you know, "We shouldn't hire in that area" [biosocial criminology], or "That area is not sociological and therefore it shouldn't be included." I mean criminology is inherently interdisciplinary.[104]

In the same way that biomedical researchers "conceived social science as a different kind of activity than their own,"[105] this sociologist does not feel threatened by the development of biosocial criminology. Not only does this field not encroach on her research interests, but the marginal position of this movement means that her scientific activity is unaffected. For example, she is not forced to include biosocial variables in her statistical analyses, or to seriously consider the biological origins of crime. Her positioning also betrays her confidence in the quality and relevance of her structuralist sociological research, which remains important even though crime would be partly affected by biological factors.

This interview is not the only illustration of the confidence displayed by the dominant scholars of the criminological field. Another sociologist with a great deal of scientific and academic capital—a former president of a major association in the field of criminology and winner of a prestigious award—explains why he feels unthreatened by the development of biosocial criminology:

No I don't feel threatened by that at all. . . . The fact that there is some biological variation doesn't mean that therefore biology explains it all, or that biology is destiny. . . . My prediction is, and my belief is, that we'll never reach a point where we find that most of the variance in criminal behavior is explained by biological variation. It's still going to be primarily sociological or sociopsychological variation that accounts for differences in individual behavior and across groups.[106]

That social scientists do not feel threatened by biosocial criminology does not mean that it is not controversial. The study of biological factors in crime has garnered little support in the U.S. criminological field, and many researchers still question the scientific value of this research. One of the leaders of the progenetic group, for example, mentioned the warnings he had received from friends and colleagues when he first began to study the biological factors of crime: "You should know that when I started along this line of research [biosocial criminology], everybody, and do I mean everybody (*laughs*), my close friends, my colleagues, told me to not do it because it will . . . As one of my best friends said, 'It will end your career and kill your reputation'" (*laughs*).[107]

When interrogated about the so-called price that biosocial criminologists have to pay for their heterodox views on crime, the same scholar highlighted the informal, almost impalpable nature of the stigmatizing processes at play:

A lot of it has been sort of a private backroom stuff, a lot of it has been the commentary behind the scenes, the anonymous posts on electronic media that call you out and mischaracterize who you are, your students, or your motives. . . . But let's not forget that the field, the discipline itself, has a long, long history of being quite antagonistic to anything biological, and that antagonism has played through in a number of ways. . . . One journal, I think it was *Crime and Delinquency* or one of the others, essentially banned the use of the Add Health data [Add Health is a database that includes genetic variables and as such is one of the primary sources used by biosocial criminologists] for anything associated with biology, that's unprecedented! You can use it for anything else, but you couldn't use it for that apparently. We've had students, simply outstanding students with excellent records, scholarship, unable to find a job. Oftentimes, you know, people on the committee reporting back to us why, because of what they study, or what people on the committee thought their motives were.[108]

The confidence displayed by social scientists can be seen as a means to channel the activity of biosocial criminologists without giving their work too much publicity. As Aaron Panofsky pointed out in relation to behavioral genetics, "ignoring and passively isolating provocative individuals and ideas" can be a way to manage scientific controversy.[109] Criticizing biosocial criminology publicly would only fuel the combative rhetoric of biosocial criminologists and their strategy of demarcating biosocial science from sociological pseudoscience. When criticized, progenetic biosocial criminologists respond with their usual accusations of ideological bias and quasi-religious fanaticism. They do so to the extent that even criticisms that are seemingly purely methodological or conceptual, such as those of Callie Burt and Ronald Simons, are instrumentalized by progenetic biosocial criminologists as yet another example of criminologists' stubborn allegiance to sociological theories of crime.

This defensive attitude tends to exasperate a number of criminologists who feel that progenetic biosocial criminologists are posing as victims and grossly exaggerating the scope of the criticisms that are directed at their work. A researcher occupying a dominant position in the field—professor of sociology, fellow of the American Society of Criminology, and member of the editorial board of *Criminology*—thus explains that he is more disturbed by the attitude of progenetic biosocial criminologists than by the actual content of their research:

> Interviewee #10: These bio people [biosocial criminologists] are pretty combative in criminology. That group is pretty combative, feeling persecuted by the other side, and they're sometimes too combative.
>
> Julien Larregue: Do you have an example of this too-combative attitude?
>
> Interviewee #10: Oh yes, look in *Criminology*, the top journal in criminology, which is called *Criminology*, there is an exchange between Beaver and those people, and then Ron Simons.

Julien Larregue: Yeah, I read it.

Interviewee #10: Yeah. So that was . . . There was anger in the exchange, and then Matt DeLisi is on the bio side, and he's gotten some difficulties, you know about that, editing a journal [*Journal of Criminal Justice*] and publishing his own stuff. (*laughs*) Yeah . . . You know, he's part of that school, so . . . Anyway, there is some tension there.

Matt DeLisi, one of the leaders of biosocial criminology, was indeed accused in an article published in *The Criminologist*, the official newsletter of the American Society of Criminology, of artificially inflating the impact factor of the journal he edited (*Journal of Criminal Justice*) through a disproportionate resort to self-citation.[110] As a result, the journal's impact factor increased by 155 percent between 2012 and 2014, dethroning the leading journal in the field, *Criminology*. These accusations clearly lie in the more global context of opposition to research conducted by biosocial criminologists, with the *Journal of Criminal Justice* being one of the primary outlets for biosocial theses. But this latest controversy also shows that the exasperated reaction of the dominant scholars is not simply due to the idea that crime may have a biological component. Even though his research shows that he can be receptive to biological theorizations of crime, this interviewee is quite weary of the combative and provocative attitude of Kevin Beaver and his colleagues.

This opposition is also reflected institutionally. Rather than create a specific division or section within the American Society of Criminology, the more subversive progenetic biosocial criminologists have preferred to isolate themselves from the rest of the field by creating the Biosocial Criminology Association. One of them makes it clear that this autarkic attitude was adopted as a result of the criticisms from the rest of the field:

Some people on the outside say, "Oh you guys are a bunch of crybabies, you whine about everything." We got that criticism too. And I think the only thing that we've ever wanted was the recognition that our work was sufficiently scholarly that it had its place in the discipline. And that . . . you know, if we're gonna advance the area we ought to have room in that area. But the reaction from the discipline has been to shut things down, the reaction from the discipline has been to (*bitter laugh*) either ignore [biosocial criminology] or to confront, or to put up hurdles. So I think what you see with the BCA [Biosocial Criminology Association] was our group's recognition that we don't need ASC [American Society of Criminology]! We do not need (*laughs*), we don't need the discipline. We can conduct our research, publish it elsewhere, write about it elsewhere, and . . . from my point of view, and maybe this is a bit little arrogant, you know, the rest of the discipline can go to hell.[111]

Again, the point is not to examine biosocial criminologists' psychology. Rather, it is to show that the uncompromising attitude adopted by some of them stems from their strategy of subverting sociology. None of the biosocial criminologists that I interviewed declared liking controversy. Their intransigence stems from the state of domination in which they find themselves. When cornered, they have no choice but to staunchly defend their research and career, which paradoxically leads them to become even more isolated because they make themselves unpalatable to researchers who are fundamentally open to biosocial approaches.

Underneath its hushed and polite appearance, the scientific field sometimes conceals oppositions whose symbolic violence is palpable. A minority of progenetic biosocial criminologists have thus developed a confrontational rhetoric that places them in open conflict with the rest of the criminological field. Politically conservative, they are convinced that race is an important factor in crime, they revisit the work of Lombroso, and they accuse sociology of being an ideological pseudoscience. This position is surprising, to say the least. It is nonetheless profitable, as demonstrated by the visibility acquired by these researchers. Increasingly cited, they have used the controversies to acquire scientific capital. For their part, dominant sociologists do not feel truly threatened by these attacks. Convinced that their conception of crime is the most scientifically sound, they are content to ignore the provocations of this vocal minority.

7 THE PROGRAMMED OBSOLESCENCE OF BIOSOCIAL CRIMINOLOGY

TO SAY THAT NONSCIENTIFIC FACTORS, such as material resources and funding, influence scientific production is today commonly accepted. As sociologist Karin Knorr-Cetina pointed out, scientists "are aware of the material opportunities they encounter at a given place, and they exploit them to achieve their projects. At the same time, they recognise what is feasible, and adjust or develop their projects accordingly."[1] The issue of feasibility is particularly acute in interdisciplinary research movements that, like biosocial criminology, are resource intensive. In this case, "Implementing research or building a career requires practitioners to temporarily cross disciplinary boundaries to seek out techniques, data, concepts, and cooperation from colleagues in related disciplines."[2]

The question arises, however, to what extent the material resources available to researchers influence their ability to cross the boundaries of their discipline and to mobilize concepts and data from neighboring fields. Surprisingly, this problem is largely ignored in the literature on interdisciplinarity. The comprehensive *Oxford Handbook of Interdisciplinarity*, for example, contains no discussion of the question of the physical feasibility of interdisciplinary research programs.[3] Yet, given the unequal repartition of resources within the scientific field, one would expect that the interdisciplinary potential of a researcher depends on their social, symbolic, and economic capital. In other words, there is every reason to believe that interdisciplinarity is not equally available to everyone and that it takes specific forms from one researcher to another.

Of course, this raises the question of what is and is not feasible. The notion of feasibility draws our attention to the fact that "ideas are triggered by the resources and facilities available at a given place and time."[4] So far, the notion of feasibility has been used mainly by ethnomethodologists at the micro-local level, which makes it less obvious why the doability of a project "varies by local and temporal conditions, by institutional and organizational location, and by discipline or profession."[5] These are all questions that a field approach might likely answer. Indeed, an interdisciplinary research program can be considered feasible when the intellectual, material, and technological resources needed to pursue it are available in a given social space or in a neighboring space to which the agents have access.

As shown in the previous chapters, the affinity between biosocial criminology and departments of criminology diminishes the symbolic prestige of this scientific movement. Another consequence of this proximity is the reduced material and financial resources available to biosocial criminologists to carry out their research program. Given that criminology departments lack status and are located primarily in universities oriented toward teaching and professionalization rather than fundamental scientific activities, biosocial criminologists have relatively limited means to carry out their research program. As we will see, feasibility constraints affect the empirical content of biosocial criminology at several levels.

First, the problem of feasibility explains why biosocial criminologists, among the wide range of biological factors they could potentially study, choose to focus overwhelmingly on genetics, even to the detriment of other research fields such as neuroscience that are perceived as more respectable. Only researchers possessing significant symbolic and economic capital, such as Adrian Raine at the University of Penn-

sylvania, can afford to link biosocial criminology to neuroscience because they have access to costly brain imaging technologies.

Second, biosocial criminologists cannot conduct just any type of
genetic research. The most complex genome-wide association studies
are just as inaccessible as neuroscience. They must therefore choose
methodologies that are doomed to obsolescence and are often criticized for their lack of reliability, namely candidate gene studies. This
would have been a problem if biosocial criminologists had intended to
establish themselves in behavior genetics. In the criminological field,
however, where researchers are trained in the social sciences and are
unfamiliar with genetic methods and notions, it remains possible to
use methods that have been gradually abandoned by geneticists without incurring the censure of the field. This confirms the Bachelardian
hypothesis according to which scientific objectivity and quality reside
in the gaze of the other,[6] that is, in the social control operated by the
field. Just as it is possible to resort to impoverished and vague conceptions of social processes in neuroscience,[7] it is equally permissible to
mobilize unsophisticated genetic methodologies in criminology.

"FAST SCIENCE": THE MOBILIZATION OF GENETIC
KNOWLEDGE IN BIOSOCIAL CRIMINOLOGY

When presenting their research, biosocial criminologists often divide
their program into five main categories: quantitative genetics, molecular genetics, neurocriminology, biological criminology, and evolutionary psychology. Although they insist on the importance of each of these
branches and on their interdependence,[8] these specialties clearly do
not occupy an equal place in their research (table 7.1). Indeed, nearly
70 percent of empirical articles in biosocial criminology focus on genetics, either quantitative or molecular. In contrast, only 19 of 117 articles address neurological factors of criminal behavior.

That biosocial criminologists prefer genetics to neuroscience may
seem surprising. Indeed, unlike genetics, neurocriminology deploys
the latest technological advances and seems to break with the determinism of the older biological theories of crime. The more noble and

TABLE 7.1

Primary scientific focus of 117 empirical biosocial criminology articles

Specialty	Articles
Quantitative genetics	52
Molecular genetics	29
Neurocriminology	19
Biological criminology	12
Evolutionary psychology	5

Note: Since these different domains are not completely autonomous, some articles may contain elements from two or more categories. In this case, we have placed the article in the category that seemed to be the most predominant. This distribution should therefore be considered only as indicative of trends.

scientific nature of neuroscience is evident in the words of a prominent American law professor who, although generally critical of biological understandings of crime, tends to see brain research as distinctly more respectable:

> When you say biology, it invokes everything from Lombroso's phrenology or whatever. But I mean probably the most promising, if you will, would be brain physiology. My wife is a death penalty appeal lawyer, and her conferences are dominated by neurologists who lay these findings on frontal lobe, you know, conditioning that may make people more aggressive and violent and . . . It seems to me very different than focusing on the endocrine system, as some criminologists of the 1950s thought it was all about hormones, and masculinity, and things like that.[9]

While the search for genetic predispositions to crime is often seen by critics as a return to scientific racism and eugenics,[10] neuroscientists have somewhat successfully defused such accusations by avoiding politically controversial issues.[11] How, then, can we explain biosocial criminologists' greater attraction to genetics? In *Misbehaving Science*, sociologist Aaron Panofsky showed that one of the main strategies used by behavior geneticists to develop their field has been to be "generous" to outsiders.[12] Rather than raising the cost of entry into their field, behavior geneticists have endeavored to share their methods, theories, and data to make them as widely available as possible. Far from being purely symbolic, this generous—albeit self-serving—attitude has had very concrete effects on the use of genetics, especially in the social sciences. Following the creation of easily accessible databases and registers of twins from the 1970s onwards, several biosocial research programs have developed, ranging from political science[13] to criminology, sociology, and economics.[14] Unlike those in other scientific fields such as biomedical research,[15] social scientists do not need to be members of a select club to produce research in behavior genetics. Biosocial criminologists have rightly pointed out that the research they conduct "does not require the use of expensive laboratory equipment or restricted datasets."[16] In short, they "can gain the association with genetics without having to retreat into the lab to stir test tubes or study fruit flies or mice."[17]

The decisive nature of behavior geneticists' generosity becomes perfectly clear when we analyze the type of data that biosocial criminologists mobilize in their work. Most publications rely on secondhand databases developed by geneticists over the years (table 7.2). In particular, dozens of articles use Add Health, a registry that was set up under the direction of psychologist David Rowe at the Institute of Behavior Genetics in Colorado.[18] In contrast, only 15 of 117 articles report using primary data collected by the authors.

This largely explains why biosocial criminologists are primarily interested in the genetic origins of crime, sometimes neglecting more expensive and less accessible areas of study. This is so, not because they are necessarily more interested in genetics, but because they need to produce research for career advancement. One early-career professor who studied psychology before obtaining her PhD in criminology explained that, despite her attraction to neuroscience, it was difficult for her to invest in this discipline because it required specialized equipment and she could not afford, at this stage of her career, to wait for funding before having her work published:

TABLE 7.2

Source of the data used in 117 empirical biosocial criminology articles

Data Source	Articles
National Longitudinal Study of Adolescent to Adult Health (Add Health)	64
Other secondary sources	24
Primary data collected by authors	15
Early Childhood Longitudinal Study	7
National Longitudinal Survey of Youth	7

Julien Larregue: What's your main interest [in biosocial criminology]?

Interviewee #11: Hum . . . Currently I do more molecular genetics, hum . . . But my main interest, if I could have enough money (*laughs*), would be neuroscience. But unfortunately it is . . . I'm working on sort of making these connections so that I can work with medical doctors to research the brain. But I would say for me I'm more molecular genetics and neuroscience, if I could choose.

Julien Larregue: Can you develop just a little bit about these financial problems regarding neuroscience?

Interviewee #11: Well, in the state that I live in, recently there were government budget cuts for university, for higher education, and otherwise I would have to try to apply for government-funded grants to get funded to work with an MRI [magnetic resonance imaging] machine, or even another kind of lower-level brain scan. . . . But at this point I'm a young professor, and so it is not time-efficient for me to work on that kind of research primarily, I have to work on that secondarily because we have to make tenure, and so I have to do so much work before tenure, and waiting on money from grants and waiting on the time that it would take to collect that data, it's something that I can worry about after tenure (*laughs*) and I have more time and I don't have to worry about tenure.

It is quite clear in this interview that this biosocial criminologist decided to focus on genetics even though her primary research interest lies in neuroscience. Her position in a criminology department at a small public university, however, prevents her from accessing the financial and technological resources that brain research requires. In the United States, the cost of a monthly rental for an MRI machine can range from $25,000 to $50,000.[19] The more advanced and state-of-the-art the machine, the higher the price. The purchase of an MRI machine is even more expensive than a simple rental. Before he was recruited by the University of Pennsylvania in 2007, psychologist Adrian Raine and his colleagues at the University of Southern California obtained funding from the National Science Foundation to purchase a state-of-the-art MRI machine. The award, which covered the purchase of a single machine, was for $1,240,504.[20]

In contrast, the costs associated with the use of genetic data seem negligible. For example, access to the National Longitudinal Study of Adolescent to Adult Health, the primary data source used by biosocial criminologists (table 7.2), requires an $850 fee and the signing of a confidentiality agreement. As a result, biosocial criminologists who still seek to pursue neuroscience must resort to some rather original expedients. For instance, a professor of sociology explained to me that he recycled the data and results obtained by the leading proponent of neurocriminology, Adrian Raine: "Partly I rely on . . . kind of reviewing the literature, so working on papers of Adrian Raine, I do a kind of overview of the research using his research."[21]

Although these secondary adaptations allow biosocial criminologists to further their interest in the brain and neuroscience, the scientific credit they can legitimately claim is quite limited. As a result, they are forced to turn to other fields of research to diversify their explanations of the criminal phenomenon. Genetic data are not the only biological data that are accessible and inexpensive. Another early-career criminology professor explained that she had acquired a heart rate sensor to collect data on the link between heart rate and crime:

Interviewee #2: It's a very small university, so you don't have access to a lot of gene studies, and it's not like I got money to do that research, so that was, you know, not feasible. And then I wondered, "Okay, is there fMRI [functional magnetic resonance imaging] around here?," and there is an fMRI that's about an hour away from school, and I thought, "Okay, well that's not gonna work." So then I started looking at things like physiological functions, like heart rate. You know that can easily be measured so that kind of . . . But you can tie that to psychological functioning, so that's kind of where I am now.

Julien Larregue: How do you have access to these [data]?

Interviewee #2: Hum . . . So for that I basically just purchased a thing for your finger where it measures your pulse and, you know, it's very cost-effective, it's about, you know, thirty to seventy dollars.

The various explanations provided by biosocial criminologists clearly illustrate researchers' "ability to grasp the material and intellectual opportunities of the situation and to redefine [their] research strategy accordingly."[22] The notion of feasibility sheds light on the technical and material dimensions of scientific activity. In other words, researchers' choices are not only guided by intellectual considerations. In addition to being scientifically interesting, the chosen lines of research must be materially doable. For example, the interviewee mentioned earlier chose to focus on molecular genetics because her position within the scientific field did not allow her the funding or time for the research interests she would have liked to pursue. Hence, the intellectual interest of a given project is constantly weighed against its feasibility. However, biosocial criminologists try hard to not reduce their research program to its material and financial dimensions alone. Thus the professor who declared being more interested in neuroscience than genetics also emphasized that molecular approaches were relevant to brain research as well:

Julien Larregue: Okay, and so you chose molecular genetics because it's easier and maybe more accessible?

Interviewee #11: It's actually not more accessible (*laughs*). But I
think any research in biosocial is more difficult than research
in sociology because we need more than just a survey, or more
than just an observation. We need twins, or we need genetics, or
we need, you know . . . something else. So, hum . . . It can be
more difficult to collect data because it's more expensive and more
time-consuming, and needs special populations like twins. So the
reason I focus on molecular genetics is because I have some access
to some data, and molecular genetics to me is, hum . . . involved
in brain processes, so it's very related to neuroscience, the chemical processes that occur. So to me they're sort of similar, they're
related to each other, we have to understand both. And I'm just
lucky that I have some access to some data where I can explore molecular genetics, while I'm waiting for money for an MRI (*laughs*).

While they could be interpreted as an attempt to rationalize a purely
contextual decision, the explanations provided by this scholar clearly
show that even when faced with a restricted range of scientific options,
biosocial criminologists think about how best to approximate what
their research program would look like in a constraints-free world.

THE CAUSAL SIMPLICITY OF GENETICS

The less accessible nature of neuroscience lies not only in the cost of
brain imaging technologies but also in the purported causal directness
of behavior genetics. While the methodologies used in behavior genetics borrow heavily from the regression analyses classically used in
criminology, understanding the functioning of the brain and master-
ing the interpretation of imaging data are more time consuming. It is
no coincidence that the main proponent of neurocriminology, Adrian
Raine, was trained in psychology and psychiatry. In comparison, one
of the major strengths of behavior genetics is its conceptual simplicity. Because behavior geneticists assume that genes are at the base of

the causal chain and are not influenced by other factors, it is much easier to identify cause-and-effect relationships. While social variables such as poverty or divorce rate may themselves be influenced by the variable being explained (crime rate), one of the leading textbooks in behavior genetics points out that "DNA differences can cause the behavioral differences but not the other way around." For this reason, "DNA variation has a unique causal status in explaining behavior."[23]

Biosocial criminologists subscribe to this approach, insisting that "greater progress in understanding and conceptualizing causal processes is essential"[24] to explaining criminal phenomena. Where sociological variables fail, biosocial criminology picks up the trail and documents the "chain of causal mechanisms linking underlying genetic influences with neural substrates."[25] Thus we have a causal sequence that begins with an individual's genetic makeup and ends with deviant behaviors. By being able to argue that "x probably causes y,"[26] biosocial criminologists can claim greater scientific effectiveness than sociological theories of crime.

In contrast, neuroscience does not appear to be as straightforward. In the behavior circuit presented by biosocial criminologists, the brain lies between the genes and the behavior under study: the genes are the risk factors that will influence the functioning of the brain. The brain itself is "responsible" for the antisocial behavior. In other words, unlike genes, the brain does not lie at the beginning of the causal chain, so it is more difficult to claim to have discovered the primary causes of an individual's criminality by studying his or her brain rather than genetic makeup. Adrian Raine, the leader in neurocriminology, concedes this irreducible difficulty:

> Yes, the causal direction of the relationship between prefrontal dysfunction and violence is certainly open to question. Imaging does not demonstrate causality. There is only an association, and many possible counter-explanations. We'll never know what Bustamante's brain scan looked like the day before the homicide. We'll never know if Bustamante's poor orbitofrontal functioning caused him—in one way or another—to morph from an altar boy into a killer who beat an old man to death.[27]

The epistemological advantage that genetics has over neuroscience is reinforced by the attitude of behavior geneticists. As Aaron Panofsky has explained, the generosity of geneticists translates into an increased tolerance toward researchers who use these tools without having proper training in biology.[28] David Rowe offers a particularly lucid example of this generosity. On the back cover of his *Biology and Crime*, he advises readers that "a background in the biological sciences is not required."[29] He concludes by inviting his colleagues "to participate in these disciplines examining the biological basis of criminal dispositions." Whether they are "a consumer, a user, or a beginning researcher" matters little.[30]

Biosocial criminologists can simply plunder data from genetic databases without having to worry about the methodology used to collect them. The genetic factor becomes one more variable in a statistical analysis, just as one would add a control for gender, race, or age. This also implies that biosocial criminologists do not need to collaborate with geneticists to conduct their research. With the data and methodological tools readily available and easy to use, Beaver and his colleagues can base their work on behavior genetics without being active in the field, and thus be content with a consumer role. As progenetic biosocial criminologist Anthony Walsh explains: "Criminologists do not have to become (nor can they expect to become) experts in the deep arcana of these disciplines. All they have to do is learn the rudiments of genetics, neurobiology, and evolutionary biology to the extent that they can read, appreciate, and apply the relevant literature to criminological issues. This is no different from having to learn the rudiments of statistics well enough to conduct credible research."[31]

In contrast, results from a neuroscientific analysis are more difficult to interpret than the coefficients obtained from a regression analysis that includes genetic variables. Interpreting brain imaging requires a specific knowledge that is less accessible and is generally acquired through extensive training in graduate, specialized programs.[32]

THE LIMITS TO GENETICISTS' GENEROSITY: DOING CANDIDATE
GENE STUDIES IN THE GENOME-WIDE ERA

The data available to biosocial criminologists through Add Health and
other databases allow them to conduct candidate gene studies, that is,
to measure the statistical correlation between a set of genes and deviant behaviors. For example, several of their publications[33] focus on
the gene that is responsible for making monoamine oxidase A (MAOA),
better known as the warrior gene[34] because of its suspected link to
violent and aggressive behavior. Candidate genes are usually included
as independent variables in regression analyses, which allows for their
correlation with other independent variables (e.g., environmental
variables) and of course with the selected dependent variable(s) (delinquency, violence, drug use, etc.) to be measured. The effect of these
genes on deviant behavior is not necessarily direct, as it can be medi-
ated by factors such as attention disorders,[35] depression or anxiety,[36]
stress,[37] or psychopathic personality traits.[38] In other words, genes influence the expression of mediators, which themselves increase the
probability of developing antisocial behavior.

Since the sequencing of the human genome in the early 2000s, candidate gene studies have been progressively replaced by genome-wide
association studies (GWAS).[39] Rather than measuring the statistical
correlation between a few genes and a given phenotype, as biosocial
criminologists do with *MAOA*, the genome-wide approach "scans" the
entire human genome to detect which genes (from a handful to several thousand) are associated with the phenotype. Because of their
inductive nature, GWAS do not require any prior knowledge of the
correlations that might exist between a gene and a given behavior.[40]
Although this nuance may seem trivial at first, GWAS have allowed
geneticists to significantly reduce the risk of false positives, that is,
finding correlations between one or more genes and a dependent variable that could be explained by the action of genes not included in the
analyses.[41] However, this progress has a significant cost, as genome-
wide studies require vast databases. Moreover, unlike the few dozen
genes that are coded in databases such as Add Health, the implemen-

tation of genome-wide databases is still in its infancy. This explains why genome-wide studies are the work of consortia that often draw together dozens of researchers from all over the world. One example is the Social Science Genetic Association Consortium (SSGAC), which was created in 2011 by three "genoeconomists": Daniel Benjamin (University of Southern California), David Cesarini (New York University), and Philipp Koellinger (Vrije Universiteit Amsterdam).

This development directly concerns biosocial criminology insofar as most results that had been obtained under candidate gene studies were not reproduced by GWAS,[42] which means that they were probably false positives. The realization of the irreproducible nature of some of the results obtained from candidate gene studies motivated the creation of the SSGAC. Some of the mediators and phenotypes that interest biosocial criminologists were directly affected by this failure. For example, a genome-wide meta-analysis that included more than one million genetic polymorphisms was unable to find any statistically significant correlation between the selected polymorphisms and depression.[43] Similarly, the authors of a genome-wide meta-analysis of attention deficit hyperactivity disorder concluded that "the effects of common ADHD risk variants must, individually, be very small."[44] At the time this book was being written, there was no genome-wide meta-analysis focusing directly on violent and aggressive phenotypes. Thus it was not yet possible to determine the extent to which the molecular results obtained by biosocial criminologists are false positives. Nonetheless, some behavior geneticists are very cautious and, indeed, somewhat skeptical about the possibility of identifying a molecular basis for personality traits in general. Another genome-wide meta-analysis published in the journal *Molecular Psychiatry* in 2012 stated, "The findings of this study show that large-scale collaborative studies with combined sample sizes in the order of thousands or ten thousands still have difficulties in identifying common genetic variants that influence complex phenotypes such as personality traits. It could be that the effects of many SNPs are even smaller than the 0.2% that we were able to detect in this study at a genome-wide significance level."[45]

Thus, even if biosocial criminologists' results were not false positives, the statistical correlations they obtained would likely be only a microscopic portion of the genetic processes at play. Although this problem is largely ignored by biosocial criminologists, one can legitimately ask how their research can continue to be published if the data and methods they mobilize are considered obsolete in some parts of the scientific field. The answer lies once again in the structure of the scientific field, and more precisely in the division of labor between disciplines. Biosocial criminologists' results are primarily published in criminology journals, presented at criminology conferences, and taught in criminology courses. Biosocial criminologists do not seek to migrate into behavior genetics, and their research is mostly read by researchers unfamiliar with genetics and biology. As we have seen in previous chapters, the domination of sociologists within the U.S. criminological field remains robust. The habitus of the American criminologist is formed through immersion in sociological literature, not through reading *Nature, Science,* or biology textbooks. This specialization is not surprising and should not be viewed as pathological. As Andrew Abbott has pointed out, one of the organizational and cultural roles of disciplines is to "define what it is permissible not to know and thereby limit the body of books one must have read."[46] The interstitial position of biosocial criminologists, between criminology and behavior genetics, allows them to reap the symbolic benefits of behavior genetics—scientificity, originality, epistemological simplicity—without being subject to the constraints and social control that normally accompany disciplinary involvement. They can publish genetic results in criminology journals and be evaluated by criminologists who are mostly trained in sociology, or else by another biosocial criminologist. In either case, the control of the institutions of legitimacy that make up the field of behavior genetics is carefully circumvented.[47] This case illustrates the issues raised by interdisciplinary practices in the context of peer review.[48]

Another equally fundamental issue concerns the lack of integration of biosocial criminologists into the collective dynamics of biosocial research that have been at work in the social sciences in recent years.[49] It is striking, for example, that the management team and researchers associated with the SSGAC do not include any biosocial criminologists. One plausible explanation lies in the desire of social scientists who mobilize genetics to avoid research questions that are too controversial, such as crime or intelligence. In keeping with this strategy, the SSGAC focuses its research on education, individual well-being, fertility, trust, risk aversion, and optimism.[50] It is clear from this list that the aim of these researchers is to foreground the politically progressive character of their work and to distinguish themselves from past sociobiological approaches, which have often been accused of providing scientific justification for social inequalities, and sometimes even of verging on scientific racism.[51] Research into the biological causes of crime is precisely often criticized for its conservative political orientation, which culminated in its instrumental use by the Nazi regime.[52] Even if we limit ourselves to a more recent period, one of the best-known pieces of research in the field is Richard Herrnstein and Charles Murray's highly controversial work *The Bell Curve*,[53] in which one of the central propositions sourced the problems affecting African Americans (unemployment, imprisonment, etc.) to an overall lower intelligence than that of other racial groups. It is therefore easy to understand why the founders of the SSGAC could have been trying to distance themselves from biosocial criminologists, who, while openly rejecting charges of scientific racism, have intellectual affinities with controversial figures such as Herrnstein and Murray, particularly on the issue of race,[54] while also claiming to be part of a new "conservative criminology."[55]

WHICH WAY OUT? A REPETITIVE AND APPLIED CRIMINOLOGY

Biosocial criminologists are well aware of the issues relating to data availability. Some regret that the databases to which they have access are limited and do not allow them to go further in identifying risk factors.[56] In fact, most empirical studies in biosocial criminology focus on the following five genes: *MAOA, DRD2, DRD4, DAT1,* and *5HTT*.

The obvious risk is that they will run into a scientific dead end and be forced to completely reshape their research program. To circumvent this problem, biosocial criminologists have adopted a mode of scientific production based on repetitiveness and cumulativeness reminiscent of the practices of behavior geneticists.[57] To maintain diversity in their results, biosocial criminologists keep the same independent variables—*MAOA, DRD2, DRD4, DAT1,* and *5HTT*—while integrating more or less novel dependent variables. Thanks to existing databases—in particular Add Health and its 306 monozygotic and 451 dizygotic twin pairs—biosocial criminologists have been able to produce a large number of studies on a wide range of behaviors in just a few years. They have thus set out to show that everything that could be of interest to criminologists is in fact genetic: gang membership,[58] anger,[59] smoking and drinking,[60] self-control,[61] marriage decisions,[62] parental perceptions,[63] carrying a weapon,[64] violence,[65] and psychopathy.[66]

This repetition also allows them to maintain their line of defense against social scientists. Rather than confronting the criticisms of their peers, biosocial criminologists seek to make biosocial criminology an "accumulative science." Mimicking the attitude of behavior geneticists, Kevin Beaver and his colleagues "did not convince their opponents, settle controversies, and resolve the critiques of their paradigm; instead, they buried their opponents under a pile of repetitive results."[67] The repetitive nature of scientific production is not, however, endorsed by all proponents of the biosocial approach. Weary of an insistence that seems unproductive to them, some former coauthors of Beaver and his colleagues have thus reoriented themselves over the last five years toward what they feel are new and more interesting aspects:

> We know that genes are important, we know that certain genes are important, let's move forward with that. I feel like we've done all this theory testing, we have done a crap ton of theory testing, I think that we know that right now. Let's talk about what this looks like in the policy world, let's talk about how we can integrate these ideas into

programming and correctional counseling, and into, like, real-world policies.[68]

When asked about the repetitive character of some research conducted in biosocial criminology, this same scholar concurs: "Yeah, yeah, exactly, I think that's the right word, repetitive, that captures it perfectly."[69] This interview illustrates the lack of consensus among biosocial criminologists when it comes to the purposes and definition of a useful and relevant research program. Rather than adopting a repetitive mode of scientific production, this criminologist would prefer to settle for the results already obtained with the available data and to invest in the legal and correctional environment to implement them. In other words, while the most productive biosocial criminologists promote the scientific dimension of their project, others seek the development of an applied criminology that finds a way out in the criminal justice system.

To be sure, this practical focus is not fundamentally incompatible with the repetitive approach espoused by other biosocial criminologists. Indeed, biocriminology has always had a close relationship with the legal system and criminal policy more globally. Lombroso's theory of the born criminal was frequently used in criminal trials[70] and was a cornerstone of the Nazi criminal justice system.[71] In the 1960s, as the supernumerary (XYY) chromosome theory spread through the media, lawyers around the world began to invoke their client's biological condition as a mitigating factor, sometimes even as a cause of criminal irresponsibility. In the United States, Dr. Arnold Hutschnecker, one of President Nixon's medical advisers, proposed in 1971 a national corrective therapy program for six-year-olds who would present the XYY chromosomal anomaly.[72]

This affinity can be observed in the field of biosocial criminology itself. Since the 1990s, a growing number of criminal courts use neurological and genetic expertise.[73] As part of this movement, biosocial criminologists regularly accompany their articles with policy recommendations.[74] And their intervention in the legal field is sometimes even more direct, particularly when they intervene personally in specific cases. Matt DeLisi, for example, has been appointed as an expert in various homicide cases, while also serving as a consultant to the Iowa Probation and Pretrial Services.[75]

Interestingly, such practical activities can sometimes open up new scientific avenues. The neurocriminological movement led by Adrian Raine and his team provides an excellent illustration of the role of forensic resources in the development of biosocial criminology. Indeed, as the psychologist explains in his latest book:

> But one reason I emigrated from England to California in 1987 was that in addition to the good weather, there were plenty of murderers who could be recruited into my research studies. Credit for recruiting the unusual sample I studied goes to my colleague Monte Buchsbaum, who was just down the road from me at the University of California in Irvine. We identified the subjects through referrals from defense attorneys. Because California has the death penalty, their clients would die unless mitigating circumstances like brain abnormalities could be documented. We were able to build up a unique and sizable research sample.[76]

This firsthand data allowed Raine and his team to publish the first neuroscientific study of murderers' brains.[77] This study and those that followed were instrumental in building Raine's reputation and establishing his position as a global expert in neurocriminology, demonstrating how resources from outside the scientific field are useful in the development of emerging research programs, particularly when they are heterodox and unlikely to receive support from their discipline.

———

As we have seen in the previous chapters, the 2000s marked a turning point in the access to genetic data. This undeniable evolution should not, however, obscure another equally crucial fact: social scientists do not have access to just any kind of biological data. This greatly limits their room to maneuver. In the era of genome-wide and brain imaging studies, a significant number of biosocial criminologists continue to use methods that have been progressively abandoned, including candidate gene and traditional twin studies. Because they belong to the criminological field, these researchers are also able to bypass the peer review process, as their evaluators might not always be informed of the latest developments in biological research. Nevertheless, biosocial thinking has had a significant influence on legal practices and public policies.

CONCLUSION
CRIMINOLOGICAL IMAGINATION
IN THE BIOSOCIAL ERA

ASKED WHETHER "criminological discourse [was] useful only to give a semblance of good conscience to judges," Michel Foucault unhesitatingly answered: "Yes. Or rather, indispensable in order to make it possible to judge."[1] This rather bold assertion can perhaps be explained by Foucault's observation of French penal practices during the 1960s and 1970s, particularly the more-than-favorable reception the criminal justice system gave to psychiatric discourses on the abnormal individual. Foucault's response is, however, much less appropriate with regard to the current state of the criminological field, at least in the United States. We have indeed demonstrated that there is no single criminological discourse. Rather, there are competing discourses from various disciplines (sociology, psychology, criminology, behavior genetics, etc.) that continually clash, both intellectually and institutionally, in an attempt to impose their vision of the origins of crime. Foucault's remark nevertheless raises a fundamental question about biosocial criminology: What should be the practical use of research that claims to reveal the biological origins of antisocial behaviors? In other words, what is the social utility of biosocial criminology, or better yet, what arguments are proponents of this movement deploying to shape our perception of the practical utility of biological theories of crime?

THE LEGAL USE OF BIOSOCIAL CRIMINOLOGY

The development of biosocial criminology has not only redefined the space of possibilities within the U.S. criminological field. It would be a mistake to limit our understanding of this movement to the strictly scientific publications that researchers read, comment on, and attempt to confirm or refute. Since the 1990s, a growing number of U.S. criminal courts have adopted the ideas expressed by proponents of a biosocial approach to crime. The number of judicial opinions mentioning neuroscience in U.S. criminal law quadrupled between 2005 and 2015, from one hundred to more than four hundred per year.[2] Similarly, between 2007 and 2011, there were a total of thirty-three criminal cases (thirty-two of which involved the death penalty) in which U.S. judges used genetic evidence.[3]

This use of biosocial criminology may at first sight seem surprising. After all, we saw earlier that the social credibility of this research is not well established, as the methods and data mobilized by most of these researchers lag behind the latest standards of genetic research. However, in addition to the fact that the biological study of crime cannot be reduced to its manifestations within the criminological field, there is a clear gap between the state of knowledge within the scientific field and the knowledge implemented by criminal courts that passes as "scientific." This gap, which has been emphasized on many occasions,[4] has been particularly salient in the history of biocriminology, from Cesare Lombroso's theory of the born criminal to that of the XYY syndrome developed in the 1960s. The fact that this work was never consensual among scientists did not prevent legal practitioners from using it. The situation with biosocial criminology is similar today.

How is biocriminology used by the legal system? Abdelmalek Bayout's case presented in the introduction of this book provides the beginning of an answer. Recall the main points. In the first judgment, the accused was subjected to a psychiatric examination at the request of his lawyer. On appeal, the accused was subjected to another expert exam, which focused on his brain and genes. The two experts concluded that Bayout not only had cerebral abnormalities but also bore the version of the *MAOA* gene that predisposed its carriers to violence when this genetic deficiency was associated with an unfavorable environment. This likely affected the appellate judge's decision to reduce Bayout's prison sentence by one year.

This brief overview leads to several observations. First, contrary to the hypothesis of an elective affinity between biological theories of crime and repressive practices, biocriminology is better characterized as politically flexible.[5] It can provide scientific support for conservative and even totalitarian policies, as illustrated by the use of Lombroso's theories by the Nazi regime,[6] as well as it can serve progressive ideologies. Thus, in the Bayout case, the defense lawyer initiated the expert examination procedure in order to plead for the diminished criminal responsibility of her client. Far from being an isolated case, analyses of American jurisprudence show that defense lawyers are the first to invoke neurogenetic expertise to ensure that their clients benefit from mitigating circumstances, thus avoiding the death penalty.

Second, neurogenetic expertise is related to the examination procedure rather than to the investigation procedure.[7] In the Bayout case, for example, the aim was not to provide evidence regarding the circumstances of the murder, which was already well established, but to shed light on what criminal law practitioners call the "personality" of the accused. Neurogenetic expertise serves to draw a line between the normal and the pathological: Bayout was not biologically normal, so neither was his behavior. In addition to his brain abnormalities, he carried a deviant variant of the *MAOA* gene. The importance of this case thus also lies in its support for the idea that crime, and violence in particular, has a biological basis: Bayout is the embodiment of the difficult transition from the statistical study of criminal brains to the concrete application of this knowledge to individual cases.[8]

Third, neurogenetic expertise reveals the fundamentally unbalanced nature of the collaboration between legal practitioners and their scientific partners. Theoretically, the expertise could have led to the conclusion that Bayout lacked criminal responsibility, as he might have been considered not to be fully in control of himself because of the biological anomalies detected by the two appointed experts. But only the judge can make the final decision and decide whether to take into account the expertise, and if so, how. In other words, the therapeutic diagnosis is dissociated from the sentencing: the experts confer legitimacy on the final decision without, however, taking any part in its final formulation. They are simply a "go-between."[9] In fact, the partnership established between criminal justice and scientific and medical expertise can be seen as a power struggle between competing professional fields.[10]

Finally, the interventions of experts in neuroscience and genetics do not combine, but rather, in some respects, seem to compete, with the psychiatric knowledge classically mobilized in the criminal justice system. This is once again evident in the Bayout case. The psychiatric expertise produced during the first stage of the trial was then replaced by the neurogenetic expertise that ultimately led the judge to reduce the prison sentence by one year. Thus not only are the experts involved not the same, but their reports were not equally effective, from the point of view of the defense, with respect to the court's decision.

The lessons that can be drawn from the singular Bayout case are much more general than one might think, as they shed new light on trends that are currently at work in various countries. This conclusion will address two of them. First, biosocial criminology is closely linked to the process of redefining crime, and particularly violence, as a public health problem.[11] Second, the Bayout case, as well as the development of biosocial criminology, betrays the growing role that neuroscience and behavior genetics play in the design and implementation of various public policies.

FROM THE CRIMINAL CODE TO THE *DSM* AND BACK

In his popular book *The Anatomy of Violence*, neurocriminologist Adrian Raine took a stab at science fiction and imagined the implementation, in the United States of 2034, of a criminal screening program called LOMBROSO. LOMBROSO, which provocatively stands for Legal Offensive on Murder: Brain Research Operation for the Screening of Offenders, is designed to identify dangerous individuals before they actually commit any crime.[12] To do so, the program would oblige all men—Raine does not justify the need for this gendered dimension—aged eighteen and over to go to the nearest hospital to be registered in a generalized biosocial file. In addition to questions about their personal circumstances and demographic profile, they would undergo a brain scan and DNA sampling to search for the type of abnormalities identified in the scientific literature as predictive of antisocial behavior. These data would then be used to put individuals into several categories, based on their latent dangerousness and the statistical likelihood of their committing a certain type of offense (violent, sexual, etc.). Those in the most dangerous categories would be held indefinitely in detention centers until they were "cured," even though they had not committed any crime yet.[13]

It was not the first time that Raine offered seemingly simple medical solutions to crime. In a BBC documentary entitled *If . . . We Could Stop the Violence* (2004), the neurocriminologist had already laid out some of the elements he would later expand on in his LOMBROSO program. As sociologist Nikolas Rose pertinently observed in commenting on this earlier intervention, "Raine's speculations join those of popular journalism and science fiction: he imagines a future in which new drugs might correct the neurotransmitter brain abnormalities that cause violence, and where reparative brain surgery might be carried out on prisoners to correct the faulty neural circuits that give rise to violence."[14]

It would be easy enough to laugh at Raine's fiction if this old dream—already evoked by Lombroso in the early days of biocriminology—had not already been partially realized. In France, for instance, the "rétention de sûreté" introduced into criminal law in 2008 allows indefinite detention for individuals who have been sentenced to prison for a list of crimes considered particularly serious. The rapporteur of the law commission at the time, Member of Parliament Georges Fenech, who also happened to be a former judge, pointed out that this measure of detention was inspired by a German law dating from 1933. Ironically, the law adopted under the Weimar Republic and initialed by the chancellor at the time, Adolf Hitler, was itself largely inspired by Lombroso's theory of the born criminal.

In the same vein, the controversial INSERM report mentioned in the Introduction[15] was followed by a bill in which Nicolas Sarkozy, then minister of the Interior, proposed the implementation of a systematic screening of children presenting the symptoms described by the group of experts. This proposal, although finally withdrawn from the text of the law, clearly translated the political expectations invested in the biosocial study of deviance. A similar experiment was initiated in the United States in the early 1990s when a National Violence Initiative was launched by the National Institute of Mental Health.[16] It would therefore be quite unwise to wait for the realization of these fantasies before taking Raine's futuristic visions seriously, especially since they provide insight on the ideology of biosocial criminologists, at least those who tend to advocate a biological vision of crime.

Among his various propositions, Raine projected that the care of individuals declared dangerous would no longer devolve to the prison administration but to medicalized detention centers that would resemble a hospital, "a bit like being in a summer camp but without having to pay."[17] Medical staff would thus take over all or part of the prison population, and diagnosis would once again be backed up by therapeutic management. This suggestion contains a problem raised repeatedly since at least the nineteenth century: Are certain forms of criminality medical rather than legal problems? In other words, should we not entrust the problem of crime to medicine rather than to justice?

While the medicalization of crime is far from new, the transformation of violence into a public health problem is a more recent phenomenon. It seems to have been under way as early as the 1980s and to have become only more important since that time.[18] In 1995, the National Institute of Mental Health solemnly declared that "the effects of violence and trauma [constituted] a major public health problem for all Americans."[19] Importantly, two events that occurred during 1996 allowed biocriminologists to establish themselves as active players in this process. First, when an international meeting funded by a NATO program on the biosocial factors of violence was held on the island of Rhodes in Greece from May 12 to 21, the organization and direction of the debates were entrusted to four psychologists renowned for their studies on violence, including Raine himself (with Patricia Brennan, David Farrington, and Sarnoff Mednick). Second, the forty-ninth international summit of the World Health Organization was held in Geneva from May 20 to 25. In its Resolution 49.25, the Assembly declared violence to be a "public health priority," along with tobacco consumption and iodine deficiency.[20]

A few years later, the World Health Organization published a widely distributed report on "violence and health"[21] with a foreword by Nelson Mandela. This report, which calls for more interventions of the health sector in violence prevention, promotes the work of biosocial criminologists. Chapter 2, devoted to youth violence, thus contains a whole section on individual risk factors, including biological, psychological, and behavioral variables. References are made to research conducted by Terrie Moffitt, Adrian Raine, Patricia Brennan, Sarnoff Mednick, David Farrington, and Deborah Denno.

How can this be justified from a theoretical point of view? How can behaviors whose definition and diagnosis have so far depended on criminal law, which we know varies in time and space, become treatable diseases? To be completely legitimate, such propositions must first redefine criminal behavior as a pathology, which explains the cautious, yet highly strategic distinction, made by some biosocial criminologists and neuroscientists working on violence,[22] between crime and antisocial behaviors, the latter notion being directly borrowed from the *Diagnostic and Statistical Manual of Mental Disorders*, which is published by the American Psychiatric Association. This explains why Raine tried to construe crime as a psychopathology,[23] as well as the psycho-medical references found in biosocial criminologists' writings: "behavioral disorders,"[24] "disease,"[25] "treatment,"[26] and so on.

I would suggest that the development of biosocial criminology constitutes one of the main stages in this process of theoretical re-definition, which may, in the long run, also lead to an institutional reconfiguration of how deviant populations are handled by public and private organizations alike. Thus, concomitant to the internal strug-gles taking place within the scientific field, which have been analyzed at length in this book, the diffusion and concrete application of bioso-cial criminology might amount to a passing of the baton between law and medicine. But this step, however necessary, is alone insufficient to bring about the transformation that Raine and others call for. First, some penal categories, such as psychopathy, might be misdiagnosed as a sign of medicalization when they in fact lead to more punishment rather than to any form of treatment.[27] Second, the theoretical redefini-tion undertaken by biosocial criminologists would have to be followed by a reorientation of public policies and a remapping of the various professional jurisdictions that would be concerned by this shift. This would necessarily imply overcoming the resistance (legal, political, institutional, cultural, etc.) that would undoubtedly arise if the past struggles between doctors and lawyers are any indication.[28]

If this general reconfiguration is not self-evident, we can never-theless note that this passing of the baton has already occurred sev-eral times, in both directions, during the short history of these two totalitarian institutions, the prison and the asylum. Combining the statistical sources available in the United States for the period from 1934 to 2001, Bernard Harcourt has indeed found that the occupancy rates of prisons and mental hospitals have evolved in tandem: when one decreases, the other increases, and vice versa (figure 8.1). This intriguing pattern is not unique to the United States: it can be found in France, Italy, and Belgium.[29]

It would be tempting to conclude that these inversions reflect popu-lation transfers between prisons and mental hospitals. American and also French demographic data, however, contradict this hypothesis: while the typical prison clientele is composed of young men, the typi-

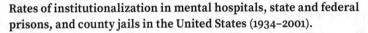

FIGURE 8.1

Rates of institutionalization in mental hospitals, state and federal prisons, and county jails in the United States (1934–2001).

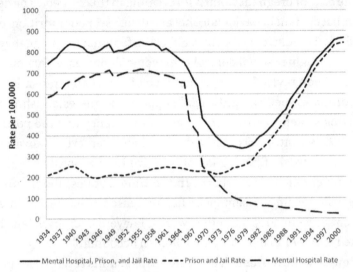

Figure reproduced from Harcourt, The Illusion of Free Markets, *224.*

cal psychiatric hospital clientele is much more feminine and elderly.[30] This seems to indicate that the redefinition of crime as a pathology promoted by some biosocial criminologists does not exactly correspond to the institutional trends described above. In Raine's case, for example, it is indeed men, young and old, that is, the core of the prison clientele, who are destined to be the subjects of medicalization, and not women, who are not even mentioned as potential targets of his program.

Future research will determine to what extent these various factors can explain the failed or successful implementation of the types of programs envisioned by the likes of Raine. It is important to note, however, in connection with the preceding observations, that some failures might sometimes conceal small yet decisive successes, particularly when it comes to groups qualified by public authorities as vulnerable, including children, adolescents, and women. Rather than the revolution that Raine calls for, it is thus possible that reconfigurations in the realm of social control will take the form of compromises and hybrid models allowing for relatively peaceful collaborations between lawyers, scientists, and doctors.

The case of pregnant women is revealing in this respect. The desire to combat deviant behavior (alcohol and drug use, poor nutrition, emotional detachment, etc.) that may affect the fetus during pregnancy has led to ever-tighter social control over women's bodies, a phenomenon that has been revived through the issue of epigenetic transmission.[31] In addition to medical and social support and the establishment of reporting systems at different stages of pregnancy and the postnatal period, this control has resulted in an increased criminalization of mothers accused of having had a negative impact on the health and development of their newborn. In the United States, the number of states using criminal sentences has increased from twelve in 2000 to twenty-five in 2015.[32] In other words, lawyers and physicians have worked together to hold pregnant women accountable.

Similarly, the movement to create hospital units reserved for prison populations—such as the Medical Center for Federal Prisoners—seems to indicate a shift toward hybrid forms of detention that lie between the prison and the hospital, between law and medicine. Not only have prisons become more hospital-like, but health professionals have also taken an active part in punishment. Prison doctors do not just care for prisoners, they also participate to their execution.[33] In short, physicians often work hand in hand with the criminal justice system, which is quite visible when it comes to mental health issues, where the institutional trend bends toward a "penalization of psychiatric care."[34] But the larger scientific, cultural, and political context also demands a more thorough sociological analysis, as biosocial criminologists share common interests with a major ally. The presence of one ally whose role in the development of biosocial criminology is so obvious that it almost becomes elusive: I am here referring to the biosocial lingua franca.

THE BIOSOCIAL LINGUA FRANCA

One striking phenomenon in the recent history of the social sciences is the development of an entire suite of research specialties relying on biological data. In addition to biosocial criminology, we can mention neuroeconomics,[35] sociogenomics,[36] neuromarketing,[37] genopolitics,[38] and, of course, neurolaw.[39] All this clearly indicates that a first iteration of a biosocial lingua franca, likely to evolve further, is already commonplace. This is not to say that scientific disciplines are simply disappearing to make room for this generic model but that they are integrating the model and using it as a megaphone. One of the ways in which this lingua franca disseminates is through the generic instruments associated with genetics and neuroscience, such as twin studies[40] and brain imaging, both of which are increasingly used as "[technologies] of human abnormality."[41]

The influence of this lingua franca is being felt well beyond the borders of the scientific field in which it originated. In recent years, a number of diagnoses and reform proposals affecting different areas of public policy (education, justice, health, etc.) have been expressed not so much from within the conceptual or theoretical frame of reference of a particular discipline as on the basis of "[technical] modes of action, [of] ways of speaking, [of] seeing, [of] representing oneself and [of] thinking"[42] whose primary vocation is to cut across professional jurisdictions. It is clear, however, that the prestige and prominence of neuroscience have been fundamental in this process. "Brain culture"[43] is a prime mediator of the biosocial lingua franca, as it serves to build bridges across social fields. Thus the advisory board of Harvard University's Center for Law, Brain and Behavior, which intends to "[put] the most accurate and actionable neuroscience in the hands of judges, lawyers, policymakers and journalists,"[44] is composed of professionals representing healthcare, legal, government, entertainment, and business circles.

Importantly, the successful diffusion and practical implementation of biosocial theses does not necessarily depend on the social credibility that they possess within the scientific field. To this day,

MacLean's long-discredited theory of the triune (or "lizard") brain continues to inspire journal articles, personal coaches, and marketing programs around the world.[45] "Why can't we stop scrolling or eating Haribo? Blame the lizard brain," wrote British writer Eli Goldstone in *The Guardian*.[46] Another type of brain that has been rendered socially meaningful is that of teenagers. The neuroscientific discourse on the cerebral and cognitive immaturity of adolescents has been taken up by the Supreme Court in the *Roper* decision in 2005, the *Graham* decision in 2010, and the *Miller* decision in 2012. This led to a dramatic reversal of criminal policies aimed at young offenders. Once seen as "super-predators," these offenders suddenly became "vulnerable" persons[47] who could not be sentenced to capital punishment. As demonstrated by sociologist William Wannyn, the active mobilization of professional associations, including the American Psychological Association, the American Psychiatric Association, and the American Medical Association, which intervened in these legal proceedings through amicus curiae briefs, has been decisive in this sociopolitical shift.[48] Yet the scientific contours of this so-called adolescent immaturity remain debated.

Over the years, the biosocial lingua franca has developed intimate connections with other trends that have affected the shaping of public policies in the last decades. It is no coincidence that biosocial criminologists frequently refer to risk management, which translates to probabilistic models of the development of antisocial behavior, as well as to a preventive ideal that requires intervention before the onset of any unwanted behavior. In so doing, biosocial criminology has prolonged movements whose manifestations were already identifiable in the mental medicine of the 1960s–1970s,[49] as well as in the criminal justice system of the 1970s–1980s.[50] In our present actuarial age,[51] the advocates of objective risk management invite us to break with the individualistic subjectivism represented by the clinical approach and the therapeutic practices traditionally associated with it (psychotherapy, psychoanalysis, etc.).

This desire for neutrality and effectiveness is also expressed by many criminologists in their use of the biosocial model. Not only does their approach have the merit of meeting the expectations of medical objectivism, since the linkage of antisocial behavior to biochemical processes—notably genetic and cerebral—allows for the application of drug treatments,[52] but it also benefits from the social prestige of neuroscience, whose growing presence in the general culture is now evident. The biosocial lingua franca thus serves to euphemize political issues, which come to be expressed in an apparently neutral and objective language, that of science and technology. It is, however, imperative to question this posture and to further examine "how existing racial, socioeconomic, and gendered life chances are encoded, and read through, these seemingly benign measures."[53]

To conclude this excursus, let us recall once again that neurolaw, like biosocial criminology, is only one of the avatars of the biosocial lingua franca. One of the latter's main strengths lies in its ability to link together seemingly independent issues, from smoking to delinquency, to consumer behavior and obesity: all of these become risky behaviors that require anticipation, control, and treatment. Put differently, the biosocial approach is not only important for the *imaginaire*[54] that it supports but also for the possibility of international and interinstitutional exchanges that it suggests, incites, and facilitates. For each topic, each problem, there are one or more scientific and professional communities waiting to unite or confront each other, to join forces or to tear each other apart. Yet, despite all disagreements, communities that were once intellectually independent now share a homogenizing language made of genes, brains, environments, interactions, propensities, and risks. They speak *biosocial.*

NOTES

Introduction

1. Feresin, "Lighter Sentence for Murderer"; Musumeci, "New Natural Born Killers?"

2. Court of Appeal of Trieste, cited in Musumeci, "New Natural Born Killers?"

3. It is appropriate at this point to distinguish between DNA samples, which are commonly used by police and criminal justice agencies as evidence to tie an individual to a crime scene or a criminal object (weapons, drugs, etc.), and the behavior genetic tests we are concerned with here. The latter are designed to analyze a person's genetic makeup to identify factors that might explain his or her actions and allow one to assess future dangerousness.

4. Caspi et al., "Role of Genotype."

5. Feresin, "Lighter Sentence for Murderer."

6. Eichelberger and Barnes, "Biosocial Criminology," 1.

7. Rafter, *Criminal Brain*, 250.

8. Caspi et al., "Role of Genotype."

9. Dartigues, "Irrésistible ascension?"; Pickersgill, "Connecting Neuroscience and Law."

10. Appelbaum, "Law and Psychiatry"; Bernet et al., "Bad Nature, Bad Nurture"; Farahany, "Neuroscience and Behavioral Genetics."

11. Catley and Claydon, "Use of Neuroscientific Evidence."

12. Forzano et al., "Italian Appeal Court."

13. Chandler, "Use of Neuroscientific Evidence."

14. de Kogel and Westgeest, "Neuroscientific and Behavioral Genetic Information."

15. Desmoulin-Canselier, "France à 'l'ère du neurodroit'?"

16. According to the Bioethics Act of July 7, 2011, Article 16-14 of the Civil Code: "Brain imaging techniques may only be used for medical or scientific research purposes, or in the context of judicial expertise. The express consent of the person must be obtained in writing before the examination is carried out, after the person has been duly informed of its nature and purpose. The consent shall mention the purpose of the examination. It may be revoked without form and at any time."

17. Denno, "Courts' Increasing Consideration."

18. Greely and Farahany, "Neuroscience," 453.

19. Rose, "Normality and Pathology."

20. Inizan, "Juge italien."

21. Ahuja, "Get Out of Jail Free Gene."

22. Tsouderos, "Exploring Links."

23. Inserm, "Trouble des conduites."

24. Collectif Pas de zéro de conduite, *Pas de zéro de conduite*.

25. Collectif Pas de zéro de conduite, "Le texte de l'appel 'Pas de zéro de conduite pour les enfants de trois ans,'" March 10, 2006, no longer accessible online, accessed February 4, 2020.

26. Cartuyvels, "Troubles de conduite," 62.

27. Inserm, "Trouble des conduites," 377.

28. Conrad, *Medicalization of Society*; Morel, *Médicalisation de l'échec scolaire*; Richardson, *Maternal Imprint*; Rose and Abi-Rached, *Neuro*; Rollins, *Conviction*.

29. Abbott, *System of Professions*, 280–314.

30. Foucault, *Surveiller et punir*; Kaluszynski, "Identités professionnelles, identités politiques."

31. Larregue, "Nouvelle orange mécanique."

32. Lombroso, *Uomo bianco*; Lombroso, *Homme criminel*.

33. Darwin, *On the Origin of Species*.

34. Atavism can be defined as "the unexpected appearance, in an individual, of one or more characteristics that had been present in one of his ancestors and had disappeared for one or more generations." Translation of definition in *Dictionnaire Larousse français*, https://www.larousse.fr/dictionnaires/.

35. Gibson, *Nati per il crimine*, 139.

36. Lombroso, *Criminal Man*, 45.

37. Villa, *Deviante e i suoi segni*, 148–49.

38. Rafter, *Criminal Brain*, 70.

39. Gibson and Rafter, "Editors' Introduction," 376.

40. Milicia, "Protesta 'No Lombroso.'" The Neo-Bourbons seek the reconstitution of the Kingdom of the Two Sicilies that, until 1861, contained the current Sicily and the Kingdom of Naples.

41. Goring, *English Convict*.

42. Rafter, "Criminology's Darkest Hour." Cesare Lombroso was already dead by this time.

43. Knepper and Ystehede, introduction to *Cesare Lombroso Handbook*, 1–2.

44. Knepper and Ystehede, introduction to *Cesare Lombroso Handbook*, 1.

45. Gibson, "Cesare Lombroso and Italian Criminology"; Rafter, "Criminology's Darkest Hour," 300.

46. Rafter, "Criminology's Darkest Hour," 290.

47. Gellately and Stoltzfus, *Social Outsiders*, 5.

48. Rafter, "Criminology's Darkest Hour," 298.

49. Rafter, "Criminology's Darkest Hour," 303.

50. Chapoutot, *Révolution culturelle nazie*.

51. Petit, "Lombroso et l'Amérique."

52. Aldon Morris, *Scholar Denied*, 19.

53. Aldon Morris, *Scholar Denied*, 19.

54. See chapter 5.

55. Aldon Morris, *Scholar Denied*, 48.

56. Work, "Crime among the Negroes," 222–23.

57. Work, "Crime among the Negroes," 222.

58. Short and Hughes, "Criminology, Criminologists," 609.

59. Sutherland, *Principles of Criminology*.

60. Laub and Sampson, "Sutherland-Glueck Debate."

61. Becker and Wetzell, *Criminals and Their Scientists*; Beirne, *Inventing Criminology*; Gibson, *Born to Crime*; Mucchielli, *Histoire de la criminologie française*; Nye, "Heredity or Milieu"; Renneville, *Langage des crânes*.

62. Becker, "Coming of a Neurocentric Age?"; Rafter, *Criminal Brain*.

63. Rollins, *Conviction*, 12.

64. Rollins, *Conviction*, 12–13.

65. Rafter, *Criminal Brain*.

66. Rafter, *Criminal Brain*, 199.

67. Dufresne, "How Does a Gene"; see also Dufresne and Robert, "Biographie d'un gène."

68. Dufresne, "How Does a Gene," 37.

69. Caspi et al., "Role of Genotype."

70. Bliss, *Social by Nature*; Lemerle, *Singe, le gène*; Panofsky, *Misbehaving Science*.

71. Abi-Rached and Rose, "Historiciser les neurosciences," 51.

72. Duster, "Behavioral Genetics"; Duster, "Selective Arrests."

73. Nelkin and Lindee, *DNA Mystique*, 2.

74. Dufresne, "How Does a Gene."

75. Caspi et al., "Role of Genotype."

76. DeLisi and Vaughn, *Routledge International Handbook*.

77. Heilbron and Gingras, "Résilience des disciplines," 8.

78. Rafter, *Criminal Brain*.

79. Shinn and Ragouet, *Controverses sur la science*, 189.

80. Bourdieu, *Science of Science*; Gingras, "Champ scientifique."

81. Bourdieu and Wacquant, *Invitation to Reflexive Sociology*, 97.

82. Heilbron and Gingras, "Résilience des disciplines," 8.

83. Frickel, Albert, and Prainsack, *Investigating Interdisciplinary Collaboration*; Louvel, *Policies and Politics*.

84. Merton, "Matthew Effect in Science"; Rossiter, "Matthew Matilda Effect."

85. Fligstein and McAdam, *Theory of Fields*, 13.

86. Lemieux, "À quoi sert l'analyse," 192.

87. Bourdieu, *Homo Academicus*, 11.

88. Hess, "Bourdieu and Science Studies."

89. Panofsky, *Misbehaving Science*.

90. Fligstein and McAdam, *Theory of Fields*, 13–14.

91. Bourdieu, "Specificity," 24.

92. According to the definition given by Scott Frickel and Neil Gross, a scientific movement is a relatively coherent research program that contradicts the dominant orthodoxy and therefore has the potential to lead to a reconfiguration of positional spaces and social hierarchies within the concerned fields: Frickel and Gross, "General Theory."

93. Fallin, Whooley, and Barker, "Criminalizing the Brain."

94. The corpus of articles was constituted with Web of Science and Google Scholar. The bibliography of the identified articles was screened to identify possible omissions. The practical utility of the Web of Science lies in the disciplinary classification of scientific journals, which makes it possible to avoid an arbitrary delimitation of the research field. Thus, to define what a criminology journal was, I selected the category "Criminology & Penology" used by the Web of Science.

95. Bourdieu and Wacquant, *Invitation to Reflexive Sociology*, 71.

96. Bloor, *Knowledge and Social Imagery*.

97. Dubois, Gingras, and Rosental, "Pratiques et rhétoriques."

98. Gingras, "Formes spécifiques," 34.

99. Sapiro, "Champ est-il national?," 71.

100. Fourcade, *Economists and Societies.*

Chapter 1

1. Frickel and Gross, "General Theory," 213.

2. Frickel, *Chemical Consequences,* 65–66.

3. Frickel and Gross, "General Theory," 214–17.

4. Laub and Sampson, "Sutherland-Glueck Debate."

5. The field of criminology is referred to by a range of terms that are "simultaneously synonymous and different, distinct yet overlapping" (Frickel, *Chemical Consequences,* 19). Although a distinction is classically made between criminology and criminal justice, the former referring to the scientific study of the criminal phenomenon and the latter to the study of the functioning of the criminal justice system, the two are often used synonymously or together, not only in the scientific literature but also in the names of departments and degrees (Frost and Clear, "Doctoral Education in Criminology"). In addition to this classic division, there is the influence of other intellectual movements, such as Law and Society, which is sometimes added to the study of crime and the criminal justice system. Thus the Department of Criminology, Law, and Society at the University of California Irvine, which is considered to be one of the best in the world, is home to researchers who do not work solely on crime. Last, not only are different terms used to refer to the U.S. criminological field, but their meaning depends on who is using them and in what context. For example, the term *criminology* can simultaneously refer to an autonomous scientific discipline and to a subfield of sociology. In sum, the actual meaning of *criminology* remains disputed.

6. Cambrosio and Keating, "Disciplinary Stake," 323–24.

7. Morn, *Academic Politics.*

8. Lebaron, *Croyance économique,* 246.

9. Criminologists, who have every interest in maintaining this ambiguity to promote the scientific nature of their work, have unsurprisingly been quick to speak of "the Nobel Prize in Criminology"; see, for example, Normandeau, "Prix Nobel de Criminologie."

10. Morn, *Academic Politics;* Albert Morris, "American Society of Criminology."

11. Koehler, "Development and Fracture."

12. Under the impetus of the disciples of August Vollmer, a major figure in the movement of police professionalization, several other criminology programs were developed at public universities such as San Jose State University and Washington State University during the first half of the twentieth cen-

tury. While the programs developed at local universities were designed to train street police officers, the Berkeley program was aimed at training future executive officers. This division of labor reflects the social position of these institutions in the U.S. academic hierarchy: while San Jose State University and Washington State University are local institutions oriented toward professionalization, the University of California Berkeley is a prestigious research institution.

13. Morn, *Academic Politics*, 57.

14. President's Commission on Law Enforcement and Administration of Justice, *Challenge of Crime*, 615–16.

15. That tuition usually amounted to several thousand dollars.

16. Morn, *Academic Politics*, 88.

17. Fabianic, "PhD Program Prestige," 563.

18. Kobetz, *Law Enforcement*.

19. Nemeth, *Anderson's Directory*.

20. Akers, "Linking Sociology," 8.

21. Abbott, "Linked Ecologies," 267.

22. Morn, *Academic Politics*, 77.

23. Laub, *Criminology in the Making*, 186.

24. *Scientific capital* refers to the symbolic recognition that a given researcher obtains for his or her work, for example through prizes or citations. *Academic capital* refers to the temporal dimension of the scientific field (direction of a laboratory, editorship of a journal, etc.). These two types of capital are obviously not entirely separate and influence each other.

25. The American Society of Criminology is not the only academic association that brings together specialists in crime and the criminal justice system. It is, however, the oldest and most important, in terms of both membership and scientific and academic visibility. Its official journal, *Criminology*, is one the leading scientific journals of criminology in the world. Such is the importance of this association that its members have been surveyed on several of occasions to determine the state of criminological knowledge: Cooper, Walsh, and Ellis, "Is Criminology Moving"; Ellis, Cooper, and Walsh, "Criminologists' Opinions"; Walsh and Ellis, "Political Ideology."

26. Sorensen, Widmayer, and Scarpitti, "Examining the Criminal Justice and Criminological Paradigms," 156–58.

27. Kennedy and Kennedy, "Sociology in American Colleges."

28. Kennedy and Kennedy, "Sociology in American Colleges," 672.

29. Ward and Webb, *Quest for Quality*, 129.

30. Ward and Webb, *Quest for Quality*, 129.

31. No Bruce Smith Sr. Award was given in 1988.

32. Wolfgang, Figlio, and Thornberry, *Evaluating Criminology*, 96.

33. Bourdieu, "Specificity," 30.

34. Myren, *Education in Criminal Justice*, 29.

35. Rafter, *Criminal Brain*, 199.

36. The gradual development of an autonomous field of criminology did not sit well with crime researchers. In 1953, the American Society of Criminology had only thirty-two members, compared to approximately four thousand today. See Akers, "Linking Sociology," 7; Cooper, Walsh, and Ellis, "Is Criminology Moving"; Morn, *Academic Politics*, 75.

37. Bourdieu, "Opinion publique n'existe pas," 224.

38. Fligstein and McAdam, *Theory of Fields*, 14.

39. Cohen, "Review"; Vold, "Edwin Hardin Sutherland."

40. Akers, "Linking Sociology," 1.

41. Akers, "Linking Sociology," 8.

42. Cambrosio and Keating, "Disciplinary Stake."

43. Panofsky, *Misbehaving Science*, 33.

44. Abbott, "Linked Ecologies," 267.

Chapter 2

1. Mucchielli, "Penser le crime," 468.

2. Lemerle, *Singe, le gène*, 21.

3. Rafter, *Criminal Brain*, 200.

4. Lemerle, "Trois formes contemporaines," 86.

5. Wolfgang and Ferracuti, *Subculture of Violence*.

6. Sellin, *Culture Conflict and Crime*.

7. See, for example, Ball-Rokeach, "Values and Violence"; Dixon and Lizotte, "Gun Ownership"; Messner, "Regional and Racial Effects."

8. Wolfgang and Ferracuti, *Subculture of Violence*, 19–94.

9. Wolfgang, "Criminology and the Criminologist," 156.

10. Laub and Sampson, "Sutherland-Glueck Debate."

11. Jeffery, "Structure of American Criminological Thinking."

12. Jeffery, "Criminal Behavior," 300.

13. Jeffery and Zahm, "Crime Prevention," 330.

14. Jeffery, *Crime Prevention*, 243–44.

15. Jeffery and Zahm, "Crime Prevention."

16. Jeffery, "Criminology," 160.

17. Jeffery, "Criminology," 157.

18. Jeffery, *Biology and Crime*.

19. Jeffery, *Biology and Crime*, 7.

20. Kuhn, *Structure of Scientific Revolutions*.

21. Jeffery, *Biology and Crime*, 8.

22. Akers, "Linking Sociology," 6.

23. Jeffery, "Criminology," 160.

24. Arnold Binder, "Criminology," 59.

25. Jeffery, *Biology and Crime*, 9.

26. Jeffery, *Clarence R. Jeffery Interviewed*.

27. Platt and Takagi, "Biosocial Criminology," 7.

28. Platt and Takagi, "Biosocial Criminology," 10.

29. Jeffery, *Biology and Crime*, 10–12.

30. Meloni, *Political Biology*.

31. Ellis, "Genetics."

32. Ellis, "Criminal Behavior."

33. Fishbein, "Contribution."

34. Interviewee No. 1.

35. The late scientific conversions of Jeffery and Wolfgang are reminiscent of Laurent Nottale's career in physics. As Vincent Bontems and Yves Gingras have explained, "By working in a separate theoretical framework, instead of being part of an established research tradition, Nottale had difficulty finding support among his colleagues," despite the scientific and academic capital he had accumulated up to the time of his conversion; Bontems and Gingras, "De la science normale," 644.

36. Hirschi and Hindelang, "Intelligence and Delinquency."

37. Rafter, *Criminal Brain*, 207.

38. Sutherland and Cressey, *Criminology*, 123.

39. D. Gibbons, *Delinquent Behavior*, 75.

40. Jeffery, *Clarence R. Jeffery Interviewed*.

41. Jeffery, *Crime Prevention*, 243.

42. Jeffery, *Crime Prevention*, 258.

43. Panofsky, *Misbehaving Science*, 147–48.

44. Jeffery, *Clarence R. Jeffery Interviewed*.

45. Wolfgang, foreword to *Biology and Violence*, ix.

46. Denno, "Sex Differences."

47. Denno, *Biology and Violence*, xi.

48. Aldon Morris, *Origins of the Civil Rights Movement*.

49. Nelson, *Body and Soul*, 153–80.

50. Moran, "Biomedical Research."

51. Mark and Ervin, *Violence and the Brain*.

52. Moran, "Biomedical Research," 343.

53. Nelkin and Swazey, "Science and Social Control."

54. Gaylin and Macklin, "Pitfalls," 14.

55. Nelson, *Body and Soul*.

56. Interviewee No. 14.

57. Wolfgang and Weiner, *Criminal Violence*.

58. Interviewee No. 28.

59. Science for Peace and Security Programme, "Guidelines for Applicants."

60. Raine, Brennan, et al., *Biosocial Bases of Violence.*

61. Moffitt and Mednick, *Biological Contributions.*

62. Gabrielli and Mednick, "Urban Environment"; Rowe, "Genetic and Environmental Components"; Walters and White, "Heredity and Crime."

63. Panofsky, *Misbehaving Science,* 158–74.

64. Kevles, *In the Name,* 250.

65. Interviewee No. 1.

66. Eysenck and Gudjonsson, *Causes and Cures,* ix.

67. Gabrielli and Mednick, "Urban Environment."

68. Mednick, Gabrielli, and Hutchings, "Genetic Influences."

69. L. Baker et al., "Sex Differences."

70. Rowe, "Biometrical Genetic Models."

71. Rowe, "Genetic and Environmental Components."

72. Rollins, *Conviction,* 30.

73. Raine, *Adrian Raine Interviewed.*

74. Raine and Venables, "Classical Conditioning and Socialization."

75. Denno, *Biology and Violence.*

76. Raine, *Psychopathology of Crime.*

77. Brunner et al., "Abnormal Behavior."

78. Abi-Rached and Rose, "Historiciser les neurosciences," 51.

79. Raine, Buchsbaum, et al., "Selective Reductions."

80. Mann, "War of Words Continues," 1375.

81. Rose and Abi-Rached, *Neuro,* 181.

82. Noble, *Music of Life.*

83. R. Wright and Miller, "Taboo until Today?"

84. Brennan, "Biosocial Risk Factors"; Golden et al., "Neuropsychological Correlates"; Hillbrand and Spitz, "Cholesterol and Aggression"; Moffitt, "Neuropsychology of Juvenile Delinquency"; Moffitt, Lynam, and Silva, "Neuropsychological Tests"; Raine and Liu, "Biological Predispositions to Violence"; Rowe and Farrington, "Familial Transmission"; Siegel and Shaikh, "Neural Bases of Aggression."

85. Ellis and Walsh, "Gene-Based Evolutionary Theories"; Fishbein, "Psychobiology of Female Aggression"; Jeffery, "Biological Perspectives"; Jeffery, "Prevention of Juvenile Violence"; Walsh, "Genetic and Cytogenetic Intersex Anomalies"; Walters, "Meta-analysis."

86. Fishbein, "Psychobiology of Female Aggression," 99.

87. Ellis and Walsh, "Gene-Based Evolutionary Theories," 260.

88. Ellis and Walsh, "Gene-Based Evolutionary Theories," 260.

89. Booth and Osgood, "Influence of Testosterone."

90. Tibbetts and Piquero, "Influence of Gender."

91. Walters, "Meta-analysis."

92. Walters, "Meta-analysis," 595.

93. Booth and Osgood, "Influence of Testosterone," 93.

94. This textbook has been cited over 3,500 times according to Google Scholar metrics (accessed January 23, 2023).

95. Akers et al., "Social Learning."

96. Akers, *Criminological Theories*, 79.

97. Akers, *Criminological Theories*, 83.

98. Duster, "Lessons from History," 494.

99. Wheeler, "University of Maryland Conference."

100. Rose, *Politics of Life Itself*, 229.

101. Wasserman and Wachbroit, *Genetics and Criminal Behavior*.

102. Herrnstein and Murray, *Bell Curve*.

103. Panofsky, *Misbehaving Science*, 1–11.

104. Wilson and Herrnstein, *Crime and Human Nature*, 102.

Chapter 3

This chapter is a revised version of an article published in *Déviance et So-ciété*: Julien Larregue, "La criminologie biosociale à l'aune de la théorie du champ: Ressources et stratégies d'un courant dominé de la criminologie états-unienne," *Déviance et Société* 41, no. 2 (2017): 167–201, https://www.cairn.info/revue-deviance-et-societe-2017-2-page-167.htm.

1. Panofsky, *Misbehaving Science*, chap. 6.

2. Gilbert, "Vision of the Grail."

3. Koshland, "Rational Approach," 189.

4. Panofsky, *Misbehaving Science*, 190–92.

5. Panofsky, *Misbehaving Science*, 169–72.

6. Larregue, "'Bombe dans la discipline.'"

7. Bliss, *Social by Nature*, 53.

8. Caspi et al., "Role of Genotype," 851.

9. McDermott et al., "Monoamine Oxidase A Gene," 2218.

10. According to Google Scholar metrics (accessed January 23, 2023).

11. Byrd and Manuck, "MAOA, Childhood Maltreatment"; Kim-Cohen et al., "MAOA, Maltreatment."

12. Vassos, Collier, and Fazel, "Systematic Meta-analyses."

13. Raine, *Adrian Raine Interviewed*.

14. Dufresne, "How Does a Gene."

15. Bliss, *Social by Nature*, 40.

16. Bliss, *Social by Nature*, 58.

17. Bliss, *Social by Nature*, 49.

18. Bliss, *Social by Nature*, 45–49.

19. All results are presented as percentages to highlight the evolution of the distribution of academic and scientific capital between disciplines.

20. Norcross, Kohout, and Wicherski, "Graduate Study in Psychology."

21. Laub, "Edwin H. Sutherland"; Payne, "Expanding the Boundaries"; Steinmetz et al., "Assessing the Boundaries"; Wrede and Featherstone, "Striking Out."

22. Wood, "Knowledge Practices," 1316.

23. Raynaud, "Controverse," 747.

24. Debailly and Quet, "Passer les science & technology studies," 25.

25. Savelsberg and Sampson, "Introduction," 99–100.

26. Sampson and Laub, "Life-Course View," 40.

27. Walsh and Beaver, *Biosocial Theories of Crime*, xi.

28. J. Wright, Beaver, et al., "Lombroso's Legacy," 334.

29. Only the discipline of the first author of the articles was considered for this calculation.

30. Panofsky, "Field Analysis."

31. Rappa and Debackere, "Youth and Scientific Innovation."

32. Mulkay and Edge, "Cognitive, Technical and Social Factors."

33. Potter and Gingras, "Des 'études' médiévales."

34. Brunet and Dubois, "Cellules souches et technoscience."

35. Ben-David and Collins, "Social Factors," 454.

36. Ben-David and Collins use the term *founders* to refer to researchers who were not themselves educated in the discipline (in this case psychology) but who trained their own students (the "followers") in the discipline.

37. J. Wright and Beaver, "Do Parents Matter."

38. Panofsky, *Misbehaving Science*, 112–16.

39. Bliss, *Social by Nature*, 45–46; Panofsky, *Misbehaving Science*, 115.

40. Laub, "Life Course of Criminology," 16.

41. Morin, "Leading with His Right," C2.

42. Koehler, "Development and Fracture."

43. One exception to this trend is the Criminology Department at the University of Pennsylvania.

44. Rojas, *From Black Power to Black Studies*, 178.

45. Rojas, *From Black Power to Black Studies*, 181.

46. Abbott, "Linked Ecologies," 265.

47. Monneau and Lebaron, "Émergence de la neuroéconomie."

48. Hess, "Bourdieu and Science Studies."

49. Gingras, "Champ scientifique," 288.

50. Zuckerman, *Scientific Elite*.

51. Gingras, "Champ scientifique," 285.

52. DeLisi et al., "Copernican Criminology."

Chapter 4

1. Lebaron, *Croyance économique*, 17–18.

2. Caspi et al., "Role of Genotype."

3. Dufresne, "How Does a Gene."

4. Respondents No. 4, 9, 10, 13, 14, 17, 18.

5. Panofsky, *Misbehaving Science*.

6. Mucchielli, "Impossible constitution."

7. Lemerle, "Trois formes contemporaines," 86.

8. Interviewee No. 5.

9. Barnes, Boutwell, et al., "On the Consequences"; DeLisi et al., "Copernican Criminology"; Walsh and Ellis, *Biosocial Criminology*; J. Wright and Boisvert, "What Biosocial Criminology Offers Criminology."

10. Carrier and Walby, "Ptolemizing Lombroso."

11. DeLisi, "Revisiting Lombroso," 17.

12. Biosocial Criminology Association, "About" page, accessed January 31, 2023, https://www.biosocialcrim.org/about.

13. Interviewee No. 30.

14. Boutwell and Beaver, "Biosocial Explanation"; Ratchford and Beaver, "Neuropsychological Deficits."

15. J. Wright and Beaver, "Do Parents Matter."

16. See chapter 6.

17. DeLisi, "Revisiting Lombroso"; J. Wright, Beaver, et al., "Lombroso's Legacy."

18. Interviewee No. 31.

19. Kuhn, *Structure of Scientific Revolutions*.

20. Interviewee No. 7.

21. See chapter 7.

22. "Adrian Raine, Richard Perry University Professor, Departments of Criminology, Psychiatry, and Psychology," accessed January 31, 2023, https://crim.sas.upenn.edu/people/adrian-raine.

23. Panofsky, *Misbehaving Science*, 32.

24. Interviewee No. 6.

25. Panofsky, *Misbehaving Science*.

26. Rowe, "Genetic and Environmental Components."

27. Rodgers, Buster, and Rowe, "Genetic and Environmental Influences"; Rowe and Farrington, "Familial Transmission."

28. Rowe, *Biology and Crime*.

29. Rowe, *Limits of Family Influence*, 223.

30. Rowe, *Biology and Crime*, 1.

31. Rowe, *Biology and Crime*, 146.

32. Panofsky, "Field Analysis," 295.

33. Interviewee No. 11.

34. Panofsky, *Misbehaving Science*.

35. Interviewee No. 25.

36. Renisio and Zamith, "Proximités épistémologiques," 38.

37. Rudo-Hutt et al., "Biosocial Criminology."

38. Anderson, *Code of the Street*, 325.

39. Simons, Lei, Beach, et al., "Social Environment"; Simons, Lei, Stewart, et al., "Social Adversity."

40. Rocque, Posick, and Felix, "Role of the Brain."

41. Rocque, Posick, and Felix, "Role of the Brain," 85.

42. Rocque, Posick, and Felix, "Role of the Brain," 97.

43. Fabiani, "À quoi sert la notion," 14.

44. Burt and Simons, "Pulling Back the Curtain," 251.

45. Interviewee No. 27.

46. Burt and Simons, "Pulling Back the Curtain," 246–47.

47. DeLisi and Vaughn, *Routledge International Handbook*.

48. Cohn, Farrington, and Iratzoqui, *Most-Cited Scholars*.

49. Sampson and Laub, "Life-Course View," 40.

50. Panofsky, *Misbehaving Science*, 105.

Chapter 5

This chapter is a revised version of an article published in *Champ pénal/ Penal Field*: Julien Larregue, "Sociologie d'une spécialité scientifique : Les désaccords entre les chercheurs 'pro-génétique' et 'pro-environnement' dans la criminologie biosociale états-unienne," *Champ Pénal/Penal Field* 13 (2016), https://journals.openedition.org/champpenal/9440.

1. Burt and Simons, "Heritability Studies," 108.

2. Guillo, "Usages de la biologie," 217.

3. Panofsky, *Misbehaving Science*, chap. 5.

4. Bliss, *Social by Nature*.

5. Abbott, *Chaos of Disciplines*, 9.

6. Abbott, *Chaos of Disciplines*, 14–15.

7. Abbott, *Chaos of Disciplines*, 28.

8. Friedkin et al., "Network Science."

9. Dufresne, "How Does a Gene," 41.

10. Shapin and Schaffer, *Leviathan*.

11. Gieryn, "Boundaries of Science," 309.

12. Burt and Simons, "Pulling Back the Curtain," 249.

13. Simons, Lei, Beach, et al., "Social Environment," 883.

14. Barnes and Beaver, "Marriage," 22.

15. Walsh, "Companions in Crime," 173.

16. Keller, "Nature, Nurture," 282.

17. Morange, "Quelle place pour l'épigénétique?," 369.

18. Burt and Simons, "Pulling Back the Curtain," 244.

19. Interviewee No. 6.

20. Meloni, *Political Biology*, 31.

21. Barnes, Wright, et al., "Demonstrating the Validity," 615–16.

22. Ragouet, "Controverses scientifiques révélatrices," 65.

23. Freese and Peterson, "Emergence of Statistical Objectivity."

24. Respondent No. 7.

25. See chapter 5.

26. Beaver and Walsh, *Ashgate Research Companion*, 5.

27. Burt and Simons, "Heritability Studies," 110.

28. Griffiths et al., *Introduction to Genetic Analysis*, 745.

29. Larregue, "'C'est génétique.'"

30. Gingras, "Dynamique des controverses," 26.

31. Galton, "History of Twins."

32. Rende, Plomin, and Vandenberg, "Who Discovered the Twin Method?"

33. Bulmer, "Development of Francis Galton's Ideas," 284.

34. Degler, *In Search of Human Nature*, 185.

35. Panofsky, *Misbehaving Science*.

36. Panofsky, *Misbehaving Science*, 89.

37. Burt and Simons, "Pulling Back the Curtain."

38. Barnes, Wright, et al., "Demonstrating the Validity"; Moffitt and Beckley, "Abandon Twin Research?"; J. Wright, Barnes, et al., "Mathematical Proof."

39. Panofsky, *Misbehaving Science*.

40. This classic presentation of twin studies is somewhat misleading since humans share approximately 99.9 percent of their genes. When it is said that dizygotic twins share 50 percent of their genetic makeup, it is in fact 50 percent of that 0.1 percent that is different from one person to another.

41. Lewenstein, "From Fax to Facts."

42. Ragouet, *Eau a-t-elle une mémoire ?*

43. Ragouet, "Controverses scientifiques révélatrices," 53.

44. Pinch, "Towards an Analysis."

45. Burt and Simons, "Pulling Back the Curtain," 223.

46. Burt and Simons, "Pulling Back the Curtain," 224.

47. Turkheimer, "Three Laws."

48. Ragouet, "Controverses scientifiques révélatrices," 67.

49. Burt and Simons, "Pulling Back the Curtain," 231.

50. Burt and Simons, "Pulling Back the Curtain," 232.

51. Pinch, "Towards an Analysis."

52. Pinch, "Towards an Analysis," 25–26.

53. Barnes, Wright, et al., "Demonstrating the Validity," 591.

54. Barnes, Wright, et al., "Demonstrating the Validity," 603.

55. Burt and Simons, "Pulling Back the Curtain," 223.

56. Interviewee No. 31.

57. Moffitt and Beckley, "Abandon Twin Research?," 121.

58. Rudo-Hutt et al., "Biosocial Criminology."

59. Oreskes, "Scientific Consensus"; Oreskes and Conway, *Merchants of Doubt.*

60. J. Wright and DeLisi, *Conservative Criminology.*

61. Bourdieu, "Specificity," 19.

62. Burt and Simons, "Pulling Back the Curtain."

63. J. Wright, Barnes, et al., "Mathematical Proof," 117.

64. Interviewee No. 16.

65. Gingras, "Controverse entre sociologues," 266.

66. Friedkin et al., "Network Science."

Chapter 6

1. Raynaud, "Controverse," 721.

2. Travis, "Replicating Replication?"

3. Collins, *Gravity's Shadow.*

4. Lemieux, "À quoi sert l'analyse," 204.

5. Lajeunesse, "Identité raciale."

6. Panofsky, *Misbehaving Science,* 141.

7. Rollins, *Conviction,* 10.

8. Gieryn, "Boundary-Work"; Gieryn, *Cultural Boundaries of Science.*

9. Albert, Laberge, and Hodges, "Boundary-Work."

10. McGuire, "Cross-field Effects," 330.

11. Davie, "Born for Evil?," 27.

12. Gieryn, "Boundary-Work," 789; see also Shapin, "Phrenological Knowledge."

13. Gieryn, "Boundary-Work," 788.

14. J. J. Wright and Morgan, "Human Biodiversity," 68.

15. Walsh and Wright, "Rage against Reason," 67.

16. Walsh and Ellis, "Ideology."

17. J. Wright, Barnes, et al., "Mathematical Proof," 114.

18. Barnes, Wright, et al., "Demonstrating the Validity," 591.

19. Barnes, Wright, et al., "Demonstrating the Validity," 613.

20. Larregue and Rollins, "Biosocial Criminology," 1990.

21. J. Wright and Morgan, "Human Biodiversity," 57.

22. J. Wright, "Inconvenient Truths," 138. It is likely that the author meant to use the expression "third rail" (the electrified rail in the subway, that is, something to avoid), rather than "holy grail" (something to seek, an unattainable object with mystical powers). For instance, Social Security (mentioned in the same paragraph) is often described as the "third rail" of American politics. Comparing Social Security in the United States to the "holy grail" would probably qualify as an overstatement.

23. Boutwell, "Bermuda Triangle of Science."

24. DeLisi et al., "Copernican Criminology," 14.

25. J. Wright, Beaver, et al., "Lombroso's Legacy," 328.

26. J. Wright, Boisvert, et al., "Ghost in the Machine," 73.

27. Lloyd, *Magic, Reason, and Experience.*

28. Lombroso, *Homme criminel,* xx (our translation).

29. Ferri, "Reform of Penal Law," 180.

30. J. Wright and Morgan, "Human Biodiversity," 60.

31. Fabiani, "À quoi sert la notion," 20.

32. Walsh and Beaver, *Biosocial Criminology,* 7.

33. Walsh and Wright, "Biosocial Criminology," 132.

34. Walsh and Wright, "Biosocial Criminology," 129.

35. Walsh and Wright, "Biosocial Criminology," 129.

36. Panofsky, *Misbehaving Science,* 2014, 155.

37. Carrier and Walby, "Ptolemizing Lombroso."

38. Walsh and Wright, "Rage against Reason," 62.

39. Walsh and Wright, "Rage against Reason," 62.

40. Noiriel, *Venin dans la plume,* 65.

41. Larregue, "Conservative Apostles of Objectivity."

42. Gross, *Why Are Professors Liberal;* Gross and Simmons, *Professors and Their Politics;* Ladd and Lipset, *Divided Academy.*

43. Medvetz, "Merits of Marginality," 293.

44. Amy Binder and Wood, *Becoming Right.*

45. Platt and Takagi, "Biosocial Criminology," 7.

46. Cooper, Walsh, and Ellis, "Is Criminology Moving," 339.

47. The "social desirability" bias, in which respondents adapt their answers to satisfy the interviewer's expectations, is well known to political science researchers. See, for example, Davis and Silver, "Stereotype Threat."

48. Meloni, *Political Biology;* Nelkin and Lindee, *DNA Mystique.*

49. Rafter, "Criminology's Darkest Hour."

50. Gibson, *Born to Crime*. Lombroso himself was a member of the Italian Socialist Party.

51. J. Wright and DeLisi, *Conservative Criminology*.

52. http://www.conservativecriminology.com/who-we-are.html. While no longer active, this blog can still be consulted on Internet Archive at https://web.archive.org/web/20230000000000*/http://www.conservativecriminology.com.

53. Medvetz, "Merits of Marginality."

54. J. Wright and DeLisi, *Conservative Criminology*, 1–2.

55. Amy Binder and Wood, "'Civil' or 'Provocative'?," 175–76.

56. Panofsky, *Misbehaving Science*, 141.

57. Interviewee No. 31.

58. J. Wright and DeLisi, *Conservative Criminology*, 2.

59. Panofsky, *Misbehaving Science*, 144.

60. J. Wright and DeLisi, *Conservative Criminology*, 1–2.

61. Boutwell, "Bermuda Triangle of Science."

62. Connell, *Masculinities*, 83.

63. Connell, *Masculinities*, 55.

64. If I wanted to sound sarcastic, I would say that scientific controversies are essentially academics' bar fights.

65. J. Wright and DeLisi, *Conservative Criminology*, 9.

66. J. Wright and DeLisi, *Conservative Criminology*, 5.

67. Gibson and Rafter, "Editors' Introduction"; Wolfgang, "Pioneers in Criminology," 361.

68. Gassin, *Criminologie*, 162; Kaluszynski, "Quand est née la criminologie?"

69. Renneville, "Rationalité contextuelle," 497.

70. Gibson and Rafter, "Editors' Introduction," 8.

71. Gould, *Mismeasure of Man*.

72. Munthe and Radovic, "Return of Lombroso?"

73. Simon, "Positively Punitive."

74. Rudo-Hutt et al., "Biosocial Criminology," 22; Schug et al., "Neuroimaging and Antisocial Behavior"; Walsh and Wright, "Rage against Reason"; J. Wright, Beaver, et al., "Lombroso's Legacy"; J. Wright and Morgan, "Human Biodiversity," 68.

75. DeLisi, "Revisiting Lombroso," 6.

76. Heylen et al., "Defending Biosocial Criminology," 85.

77. J. Wright, Beaver, et al., "Lombroso's Legacy."

78. DeLisi, "Revisiting Lombroso," 5.

79. DeLisi, "Revisiting Lombroso," 6.

80. Lindesmith and Levin, "Lombrosian Myth in Criminology."

81. Walsh and Wright, "Biosocial Criminology," 125.
82. Carrier and Walby, "Ptolemizing Lombroso."
83. DeLisi, "Revisiting Lombroso," 6.
84. Beaver, Barnes, and Boutwell, "Introduction," 6.
85. Lajeunesse, "Identité raciale," 67.
86. Lajeunesse, "Identité raciale," 71.
87. Noiriel, *Venin dans la plume*.
88. Panofsky, *Misbehaving Science*, 112–16.
89. Panofsky, *Misbehaving Science*, 140.
90. Panofsky, *Misbehaving Science*, 144.
91. Panofsky, *Misbehaving Science*, 144. Another striking similarity between these controversies is the consistent use of epistemological justifications. Both Bernal and biosocial criminologists rely on Thomas Kuhn's research on scientific paradigms to provide a justification for their heterodoxy. Indeed, as with Bernal and behavior geneticists before them, the heterodox positioning of biosocial criminologists prevents them from justifying their methodological and conceptual choices according to the criteria of the normal science of their field. This requires the use of metajustifications provided by epistemology. Standing over the work of sociologists, epistemology justifies the heterodoxy of biosocial criminologists by providing a seemingly rational basis for it.
92. Lajeunesse, "Identité raciale," 95.
93. Panofsky, *Misbehaving Science*, 140.
94. Noiriel, *Venin dans la plume*, 64.
95. Ragouet, *Eau a-t-elle une mémoire ?*, 120–21.
96. Larregue, "'Bombe dans la discipline,'" 187–88.
97. Walters, "Measuring the Quantity," 2016.
98. Cole and Cole, *Social Stratification in Science*, 107–09.
99. Burt and Simons, "Pulling Back the Curtain"; Burt and Simons, "Heritability Studies."
100. Burt and Simons, "Pulling Back the Curtain," 224.
101. Albert et al., "Biomedical Scientists' Perception"; Albert, Laberge, and Hodges, "Boundary-Work."
102. Albert, Laberge, and Hodges, "Boundary-Work," 189.
103. Interviewee No. 31.
104. Interviewee No. 21.
105. Albert, Laberge, and Hodges, "Boundary-Work," 189.
106. Interviewee No. 26.
107. Interviewee No. 16.
108. Interviewee No. 16.
109. Panofsky, *Misbehaving Science*, 206.

110. T. Baker, "Evaluation of Journal Impact Factors."

111. Interviewee No. 16.

Chapter 7

This chapter is a revised version of an article published in *New Genetics and Society*: Julien Larregue, "The Long Hard Road to the Doability of Interdisciplinary Research Projects: The Case of Biosocial Criminology," *New Genetics and Society* 37, no. 1 (2018): 21–43, https://www.tandfonline.com/doi/full/10.1080/14636778.2017.1415138.

1. Knorr-Cetina, *Manufacture of Knowledge*, 34.

2. Shinn, "Formes de division," 451.

3. Frodeman, Thompson Klein, and Mitcham, *Oxford Handbook of Interdisciplinarity*.

4. Knorr-Cetina, *Manufacture of Knowledge*, 35.

5. Fujimura, "Constructing 'Do-able' Problems," 282.

6. Bachelard, *Formation de l'esprit scientifique*, 288.

7. Abend, "Love of Neuroscience"; Ehrenberg, *Mécanique des passions*, 184.

8. Barnes, Boutwell, and Beaver, "Contemporary Biosocial Criminology," 76.

9. Interviewee No. 22.

10. Duster, "Behavioral Genetics"; Duster, "Selective Arrests."

11. Rollins, *Conviction*.

12. Panofsky, *Misbehaving Science*, 154.

13. Larregue, "'Bombe dans la discipline.'"

14. Bliss, *Social by Nature*.

15. Mayrhofer and Prainsack, "Being a Member."

16. Weir and Kosloski, "Melding Theoretical Perspectives," 104.

17. Panofsky, *Misbehaving Science*, 156.

18. Harris et al., "National Longitudinal Study."

19. Mitchell, "How Much Does It Cost?" The cost of renting an MRI machine depends on the duration and power of the machine.

20. National Science Foundation, "Award Abstract # 0420794: Acquisition of an fMRI Basic Research Imaging System at the University of Southern California," accessed February 17, 2023, https://www.nsf.gov/awardsearch/showAward?AWD_ID=0420794&HistoricalAwards=false.

21. Interviewee No. 6.

22. Dubois, "Action scientifique," 108.

23. Plomin et al., *Behavioral Genetics*, 10. The growing development of epigenetics may, of course, affect the credibility of this assumption. Indeed, since epigenetics is concerned with the influence of environmental factors on gene expression, the causal chain that behavior geneticists describe might

actually be composed of intertwined, reciprocal effects. This may explain why some biosocial criminologists are wary of this line of research (see chapter 5).

24. Vaughn, Beaver, and DeLisi, "General Biosocial Paradigm," 280.

25. Vaughn, Beaver, and DeLisi, "General Biosocial Paradigm," 283.

26. Interviewee No. 31.

27. Raine, *Anatomy of Violence*, 70.

28. Panofsky, *Misbehaving Science*, 157.

29. Rowe, *Biology and Crime*.

30. Rowe, *Biology and Crime*, 146.

31. Walsh, *Biology and Criminology*, 24.

32. For an example of the use of brain imaging in neurocriminology, see Chen et al., "Abnormal White Matter Integrity."

33. Beaver, Wright, et al., "Exploring the Association"; Eme, "MAOA and Male Antisocial Behavior"; Stogner and Gibson, "Stressful Life Events."

34. A. Gibbons, "Tracking the Evolutionary History."

35. Schilling, Walsh, and Yun, "ADHD and Criminality."

36. Connolly and Beaver, "Considering."

37. Stogner, "DAT1 and Alcohol Use."

38. DeLisi and Vaughn, "Ingredients for Criminality."

39. Ioannidis et al., "Geometric Increase," 2.

40. Hirschhorn and Daly, "Genome-Wide Association Studies," 96.

41. Ioannidis, Tarone, and McLaughlin, "False-Positive to False-Negative Ratio." This problem is of course not unique to genetic research but found in all regression-type statistical analyses.

42. Ioannidis et al., "Geometric Increase," 2.

43. Ripke et al., "Mega-analysis."

44. Neale et al., "Meta-analysis," 884.

45. De Moor et al., "Meta-analysis," 9.

46. Abbott, *Chaos of Disciplines*, 130.

47. This does not mean that biosocial criminologists have developed a conscious strategy to circumvent the social control mechanisms of the scientific field.

48. Holbrook, "Peer Review," 328.

49. Bliss, *Social by Nature*.

50. Social Science Genetic Association Consortium, "Phenotypes," accessed February 17, 2023, https://www.thessgac.org/phenotypes.

51. Tort et al., *Misère de la sociobiologie*.

52. Rafter, "Criminology's Darkest Hour."

53. Herrnstein and Murray, *Bell Curve*.

54. Larregue and Rollins, "Biosocial Criminology."

55. J. Wright and DeLisi, *Conservative Criminology*.

56. Schwartz et al., "Proposing a Pedigree Risk Measurement Strategy," 773.

57. Panofsky, *Misbehaving Science*, 144–45.

58. Barnes, Boutwell, and Fox, "Effect of Gang Membership."

59. Connolly and Beaver, "Assessing the Salience."

60. Boisvert et al., "Genetic and Environmental Influences."

61. Wells et al., "Molecular Genetic Underpinnings."

62. Barnes and Beaver, "Marriage."

63. Beaver, "Effects of Genetics."

64. Connolly and Beaver, "Guns, Gangs, and Genes."

65. Barnes and Jacobs, "Genetic Risk for Violent Behavior."

66. Beaver, Barnes, et al., "Psychopathic Personality Traits."

67. Panofsky, *Misbehaving Science*, 145.

68. Interviewee No. 2.

69. Interviewee No. 2.

70. Gould, *Mismeasure of Man*, 138.

71. Rafter, "Criminology's Darkest Hour."

72. Moran, "Biomedical Research," 347.

73. Denno, "Courts' Increasing Consideration."

74. Cleveland et al., "Gene × Intervention Designs"; Gajos, Fagan, and Beaver, "Use"; Rocque, Welsh, and Raine, "Biosocial Criminology"; Vaughn, "Policy Implications."

75. Iowa State University, "Matt DeLisi, Ph.D.," curriculum vitae, accessed February 17, 2023, https://iastate.app.box.com/s/lnkju2e5vh1twcrn1c4tg7078 c9gdxje.

76. Raine, *Anatomy of Violence*, 66.

77. Raine, Buchsbaum, et al., "Selective Reductions."

Conclusion

1. Foucault, *Dits et écrits,* 1:1617.

2. Greely and Farahany, "Neuroscience."

3. Denno, "Courts' Increasing Consideration."

4. Committee on Identifying the Needs of the Forensic Sciences Community, "Strengthening Forensic Science"; President's Council of Advisors on Science and Technology, "Report to the President."

5. Meloni, *Political Biology*.

6. Rafter, "Criminology's Darkest Hour."

7. Foucault, *Surveiller et punir,* 217–27.

8. This is what proponents of neurolaw call the "G2i problem" (group to individual).

9. Castel, *Gestion des risques*, 125.

10. Abbott, *System of Professions*.

11. Rose, *Politics of Life Itself*, 226.

12. Raine, *Anatomy of Violence*.

13. It is quite conceivable that what is primarily conceived as an examination procedure by Raine could, if necessary, be transformed into an investigative tool for police investigations. For example, it would be quite easy to take DNA samples from the products or the scene of a crime in order to cross-check them with samples from the generalized biosocial file, as illustrated by the recent revelation of the FBI's access to the database of the genetic genealogy company FamilyTreeDNA.

14. Rose, *Politics of Life Itself*, 240.

15. Inserm, "Trouble des conduites."

16. Rose, *Politics of Life Itself*, 245–46.

17. Raine, *Anatomy of Violence*, 345–46.

18. Rose and Abi-Rached, *Neuro*, 180–90.

19. Cited in Rose, *Politics of Life Itself*, 247.

20. World Health Organization, "Forty-Ninth World Health Assembly," 24.

21. Krug et al., *World Report*.

22. Rollins, *Conviction*.

23. Raine, *Psychopathology of Crime*.

24. Gajos, Fagan, and Beaver, "Use," 683.

25. Rocque, Welsh, and Raine, "Biosocial Criminology," 307.

26. J. Wright and Boisvert, "What Biosocial Criminology Offers Criminology," 1237.

27. Showalter, "Misdiagnosing Medicalization."

28. Kaluszynski, "Identités professionnelles, identités politiques."

29. Harcourt, *Illusion of Free Markets*, 227–30.

30. Raoult and Harcourt, "Mirror Image," 170.

31. Richardson et al., "Society."

32. Faherty et al., "Association."

33. Groner, "Lethal Injection."

34. Bérard and Chantraine, "Carcéralisation du soin psychiatrique."

35. Monneau and Lebaron, "Émergence de la neuroéconomie."

36. Bliss, *Social by Nature*.

37. Wannyn, "Marketing du neuromarketing."

38. Larregue, "'Bombe dans la discipline.'"

39. Dartigues, "Irrésistible ascension?"; Pickersgill, "Connecting Neuroscience and Law."

40. Larregue, "'C'est génétique.'"

41. Foucault, *Abnormal*, 61.

42. Shinn and Ragouet, *Controverses sur la science*, 179–80.

43. Pykett, *Brain Culture*.

44. Center for Law, Brain and Behavior, Harvard University, "Advisory Board," accessed April 18, 2023, https://clbb.mgh.harvard.edu/advisory-board /.

45. Lemerle, *Cerveau reptilien*, 7–10.

46. Goldstone, "Why Can't We Stop."

47. Wannyn, "Cerveau 'immature.'"

48. Wannyn, "Cerveau 'immature.'"

49. Castel, *Gestion des risques*.

50. Feeley and Simon, "New Penology."

51. Harcourt, *Against Prediction*.

52. Castel, *Gestion des risques*, 104–9.

53. Rollins, *Conviction*, 16.

54. The *imaginaire* can be defined "as a coherent, dynamic system of representations of the social world, a sort of repertoire of figures and collective identities that each society endows itself with at given moments in its history." Kalifa, *Bas-fonds*.

BIBLIOGRAPHY

Abbott, Andrew. *Chaos of Disciplines*. Chicago: University of Chicago Press, 2001.

———. "Linked Ecologies: States and Universities as Environments for Professions." *Sociological Theory* 23, no. 3 (2005): 245–74.

———. *The System of Professions: An Essay on the Division of Expert Labor*. Chicago: University of Chicago Press, 1988.

Abend, Gabriel. "The Love of Neuroscience: A Sociological Account." *Sociological Theory* 36, no. 1 (2018): 88–116.

Abi-Rached, Joelle M., and Nikolas S. Rose. "Historiciser les neurosciences." In *Neurosciences et société: Enjeux des savoirs et pratiques sur le cerveau*, edited by Brigitte Chamak and Baptiste Moutaud, 51–77. Paris: Armand Colin, 2014.

Ahuja, Anjana. "The Get Out of Jail Free Gene." *The Times*, November 17, 2009.

Akers, Ronald L. *Criminological Theories: Introduction and Evaluation*. Los Angeles: Roxbury, 1994.

———. "Linking Sociology and Its Specialties: The Case of Criminology." *Social Forces* 71, no. 1 (1992): 1–16.

Akers, Ronald L., Marvin D. Krohn, Lonn Lanza-Kaduce, and Marcia Radosevich. "Social Learning and Deviant Behavior: A Specific Test of a General Theory." *American Sociological Review* 44, no. 4 (1979): 636–55.

Albert, Mathieu, Suzanne Laberge, and Brian D. Hodges. "Boundary-Work in the Health Research Field: Biomedical and Clinician Scientists' Percep-tions of Social Science Research." *Minerva* 47, no. 2 (2009): 171–94.

Albert, Mathieu, Suzanne Laberge, Brian D. Hodges, Glenn Regehr, and Lo-relei Lingard. "Biomedical Scientists' Perception of the Social Sciences in Health Research." *Social Science and Medicine* 66, no. 12 (2008): 2520–31.

Anderson, Elijah. *Code of the Street: Decency, Violence, and the Moral Life of the Inner City*. New York: W. W. Norton, 1999.

Appelbaum, Paul S. "Law and Psychiatry: Behavioral Genetics and the Pun-ishment of Crime." *Psychiatric Services* 56, no. 1 (2005): 25–27.

Bachelard, Gaston. *La formation de l'esprit scientifique*. Paris: Vrin, 2000.

Baker, Laura A., Wendy Mack, Terrie E. Moffitt, and Sarnoff Mednick. "Sex Differences in Property Crime in a Danish Adoption Cohort." *Behavior Ge-netics* 19, no. 3 (1989): 355–70.

Baker, Tom. "An Evaluation of Journal Impact Factors: A Case Study of the Top Three Journals Ranked in Criminology and Penology." *The Criminologist* 40, no. 5 (2015): 5–13.

Ball-Rokeach, Sandra J. "Values and Violence: A Test of the Subculture of Vio-lence Thesis." *American Sociological Review* 38, no. 6 (1973): 736–49.

Barnes, J. C., and Kevin M. Beaver. "Marriage and Desistance from Crime: A Consideration of Gene–Environment Correlation." *Journal of Marriage and Family* 74, no. 1 (2012): 19–33.

Barnes, J. C., Kevin M. Beaver, and Brian B. Boutwell. "Examining the Ge-netic Underpinnings to Moffitt's Developmental Taxonomy: A Behavioral Genetic Analysis." *Criminology* 49, no. 4 (2011): 923–54.

Barnes, J. C., Brian B. Boutwell, and Kevin M. Beaver. "Contemporary Bioso-cial Criminology: A Systematic Review of the Literature, 2000–2012." In *The Handbook of Criminological Theory*, edited by Alex R. Piquero, 75–99. Oxford: Wiley, 2016.

Barnes, J. C., Brian B. Boutwell, Kevin M. Beaver, Chris L. Gibson, and John P. Wright. "On the Consequences of Ignoring Genetic Influences in Crimino-logical Research." *Journal of Criminal Justice* 42, no. 6 (2014): 471–82.

Barnes, J. C., Brian B. Boutwell, and Kathleen A. Fox. "The Effect of Gang Membership on Victimization: A Behavioral Genetic Explanation." *Youth Violence and Juvenile Justice* 10, no. 3 (2012): 227–44.

Barnes, J. C., and Bruce A. Jacobs. "Genetic Risk for Violent Behavior and Environmental Exposure to Disadvantage and Violent Crime: The Case for Gene-Environment Interaction." *Journal of Interpersonal Violence* 28, no. 1 (2013): 92–120.

Barnes, J. C., John Paul Wright, Brian B. Boutwell, Joseph A. Schwartz, Eric J. Connolly, Joseph L. Nedelec, and Kevin M. Beaver. "Demonstrating the

Validity of Twin Research in Criminology." *Criminology* 52, no. 4 (2014): 588–626.

Beaver, Kevin M. "The Effects of Genetics, the Environment, and Low Self-Control on Perceived Maternal and Paternal Socialization: Results from a Longitudinal Sample of Twins." *Journal of Quantitative Criminology* 27, no. 1 (2011): 85–105.

Beaver, Kevin M., J. C. Barnes, and Brian B. Boutwell. "Introduction: Why We Need a Nature/Nurture Book in Criminology." In *The Nurture versus Biosocial Debate in Criminology: On the Origins of Criminal Behavior and Criminality,* edited by Kevin M. Beaver, J. C. Barnes, and Brian B. Boutwell, 1–8. Thousand Oaks, CA: Sage Publications, 2015.

Beaver, Kevin M., J. C. Barnes, Joshua S. May, and Joseph A. Schwartz. "Psychopathic Personality Traits, Genetic Risk, and Gene-Environment Correlations." *Criminal Justice and Behavior* 38, no. 9 (2011): 896–912.

Beaver, Kevin M., Matt DeLisi, Michael G. Vaughn, and John Paul Wright. "The Intersection of Genes and Neuropsychological Deficits in the Prediction of Adolescent Delinquency and Low Self-Control." *International Journal of Offender Therapy and Comparative Criminology* 54 (2010): 22–42.

Beaver, Kevin M., and Anthony Walsh. *The Ashgate Research Companion to Biosocial Theories of Crime.* Farnham: Ashgate, 2011.

Beaver, Kevin M., John Paul Wright, Brian B. Boutwell, J. C. Barnes, Matt DeLisi, and Michael G. Vaughn. "Exploring the Association between the 2-Repeat Allele of the MAOA Gene Promoter Polymorphism and Psychopathic Personality Traits, Arrests, Incarceration, and Lifetime Antisocial Behavior." *Personality and Individual Differences* 54, no. 2 (2013): 164–68.

Becker, Peter. "The Coming of a Neurocentric Age? Neurosciences and the New Biology of Violence: A Historian's Comment." *Medicina e Storia* 10, nos. 19–20 (2010): 101–28.

Becker, Peter, and Richard F. Wetzell, eds. *Criminals and Their Scientists: The History of Criminology in International Perspective.* Cambridge: Cambridge University Press, 2006.

Beirne, Piers. *Inventing Criminology: Essays on the Rise of "Homo Criminalis."* Albany: SUNY Press, 1993.

Ben-David, Joseph, and Randall Collins. "Social Factors in the Origins of a New Science: The Case of Psychology." *American Sociological Review* 31, no. 4 (1966): 451–65.

Bérard, Jean, and Gilles Chantraine. "La carcéralisation du soin psychiatrique." *Vacarme* 42, no. 1 (2008): 91–94.

Bernet, William, Cindy L. Vnencak-Jones, Nita Farahany, and Stephen A. Montgomery. "Bad Nature, Bad Nurture, and Testimony Regarding MAOA and SLC6A4 Genotyping at Murder Trials." *Journal of Forensic Sciences* 52, no. 6 (2007): 1362–71.

Binder, Amy J., and Kate Wood. *Becoming Right: How Campuses Shape Young Conservatives*. Princeton, NJ: Princeton University Press, 2013.

———. "'Civil' or 'Provocative'? Varieties of Conservative Student Style and Discourse in American Universities." In *Professors and Their Politics*, edited by Neil Gross and Solon Simmons, 158–87. Baltimore: Johns Hopkins University Press, 2014.

Binder, Arnold. "Criminology: Discipline or Interdiscipline?" *Issues in Integrative Studies* 5 (1987): 41–68.

Bliss, Catherine. *Social by Nature: The Promise and Peril of Sociogenomics*. Stanford, CA: Stanford University Press, 2018.

Bloor, David. *Knowledge and Social Imagery*. Chicago: University of Chicago Press, 1991.

Boisvert, Danielle, Brian B. Boutwell, J. C. Barnes, and Jamie Vaske. "Genetic and Environmental Influences Underlying the Relationship between Low Self-Control and Substance Use." *Journal of Criminal Justice* 41, no. 4 (2013): 262–72.

Bontems, Vincent, and Yves Gingras. "De la science normale à la science marginale: Analyse d'une bifurcation de trajectoire scientifique. Le cas de la théorie de la relativité d'echelle." *Social Science Information* 46, no. 4 (2007): 607–53.

Booth, Alan, and D. Wayne Osgood. "The Influence of Testosterone on Deviance in Adulthood: Assessing and Explaining the Relationship." *Criminology* 31, no. 1 (1993): 93–117.

Bourdieu, Pierre. *Homo Academicus*. Stanford, CA: Stanford University Press, 1988.

———. "L'opinion publique n'existe pas." In *Questions de sociologie*, 222–35. Paris: Editions de Minuit, 2002.

———. *Science of Science and Reflexivity*. Cambridge: Polity Press, 2004.

———. "The Specificity of the Scientific Field and the Social Conditions of the Progress of Reason." *Information* 14, no. 6 (1975): 19–47.

Bourdieu, Pierre, and Loïc Wacquant. *An Invitation to Reflexive Sociology*. Chicago: Polity Press, 1992.

Boutwell, Brian. "The Bermuda Triangle of Science." *Quillette*, March 10, 2016. https://quillette.com/2016/03/10/the-bermuda-triangle-of-science/.

Boutwell, Brian B., and Kevin M. Beaver. "A Biosocial Explanation of Delinquency Abstention." *Criminal Behaviour and Mental Health* 18, no. 1 (2008): 59–74.

Brennan, Patricia A. "Biosocial Risk Factors and Juvenile Violence." *Federal Probation* 63 (1999): 58.

Brunet, Philippe, and Michel Dubois. "Cellules souches et technoscience: Sociologie de l'émergence et de la régulation d'un domaine de recherche biomédicale en France." *Revue Française de Sociologie* 53, no. 3 (2012): 391–428.

Brunner, Han G., M. Nelen, X. O. Breakefield, H. H. Ropers, and B. A. van Oost. "Abnormal Behavior Associated with a Point Mutation in the Structural Gene for Monoamine Oxidase A." *Science* 262, no. 5133 (1993): 578–80.

Bulmer, Michael. "The Development of Francis Galton's Ideas on the Mechanism of Heredity." *Journal of the History of Biology* 32, no. 2 (1999): 263–92.

Burt, Callie H., and Ronald L. Simons. "Heritability Studies in the Postgenomic Era: The Fatal Flaw Is Conceptual." *Criminology* 53, no. 1 (2015): 103–12.

——. "Pulling Back the Curtain on Heritability Studies: Biosocial Criminology in the Postgenomic Era." *Criminology* 52, no. 2 (2014): 223–62.

Byrd, Amy L., and Stephen B. Manuck. "MAOA, Childhood Maltreatment, and Antisocial Behavior: Meta-analysis of a Gene-Environment Interaction." *Biological Psychiatry* 75, no. 1 (2014): 9–17.

Cambrosio, Alberto, and Peter Keating. "The Disciplinary Stake: The Case of Chronobiology." *Social Studies of Science* 13, no. 3 (1983): 323–53.

Carrier, Nicolas, and Kevin Walby. "Ptolemizing Lombroso: The Pseudo-revolution of Biosocial Criminology." *Journal of Theoretical and Philosophical Criminology* 6, no. 1 (2014): 1–45.

Cartuyvels, Yves. "Troubles de conduite et déviance: Des amours en eaux troubles." *Revue de Droit Pénal et de Criminologie*, no. 1 (2009): 32–62.

Caspi, Avshalom, Joseph McClay, Terrie E. Moffitt, Jonathan Mill, Judy Martin, Ian W. Craig, Alan Taylor, and Richie Poulton. "Role of Genotype in the Cycle of Violence in Maltreated Children." *Science* 297, no. 5582 (2002): 851–54.

Castel, Robert. *La gestion des risques: De l'anti-psychiatrie à l'après-psychanalyse.* Paris: Les Éditions de Minuit, 2011.

Catley, Paul, and Lisa Claydon. "The Use of Neuroscientific Evidence in the Courtroom by Those Accused of Criminal Offenses in England and Wales." *Journal of Law and the Biosciences* 2, no. 3 (2016): 510–49.

Chandler, Jennifer A. "The Use of Neuroscientific Evidence in Canadian Criminal Proceedings." *Journal of Law and the Biosciences* 2, no. 3 (2016): 550–79.

Chapoutot, Johann. *La révolution culturelle nazie.* Paris: Gallimard, 2017.

Chen, Chiao-Yun, Adrian Raine, Kun-Hsien Chou, I-Yun Chen, Daisy Hung, and Ching-Po Lin. "Abnormal White Matter Integrity in Rapists as Indicated by Diffusion Tensor Imaging." *BMC Neuroscience* 17 (2016): 1–8.

Cleveland, H. Harrington, Gabriel L. Schlomer, David J. Vandenbergh, and Richard P. Wiebe. "Gene × Intervention Designs." *Criminology and Public Policy* 15, no. 3 (2016): 711–20.

Cohen, Albert K. "Review: The Criminology of Edwin Sutherland." *Contemporary Sociology* 19, no. 1 (1990): 98–99.

Cohn, Ellen G., and David P. Farrington. "Changes in Scholarly Influence in Major American Criminology and Criminal Justice Journals between 1986 and 2000." *Journal of Criminal Justice Education* 18, no. 1 (2007): 6–34.

———. "Changes in the Most-Cited Scholars in Twenty Criminology and Criminal Justice Journals between 1990 and 1995." *Journal of Criminal Justice* 27, no. 4 (1999): 345–59.

———. "Who Are the Most-Cited Scholars in Major American Criminology and Criminal Justice Journals?" *Journal of Criminal Justice* 22, no. 6 (1994): 517–34.

Cohn, Ellen G., David P. Farrington, and Amaia Iratzoqui. *Most-Cited Scholars in Criminology and Criminal Justice, 1986–2010.* New York: Springer, 2014.

Cole, Jonathan R., and Stephen Cole. *Social Stratification in Science.* Chicago: University of Chicago Press, 1973.

Collectif Pas de zéro de conduite. *Pas de zéro de conduite pour les enfants de 3 ans!* Toulouse: Erès, 2006.

Collins, Harry. *Gravity's Shadow: The Search for Gravitational Waves.* Chicago: University of Chicago Press, 2010.

Committee on Identifying the Needs of the Forensic Sciences Community. "Strengthening Forensic Science in the United States: A Path Forward." National Research Council, report, August 2009. https://www.ojp.gov/pdffiles1/nij/grants/228091.pdf.

Connell, Raewyn W. *Masculinities.* Berkeley: University of California Press, 2005.

Connolly, Eric J., and Kevin M. Beaver. "Assessing the Salience of Gene-Environment Interplay in the Development of Anger, Family Conflict, and Physical Violence: A Biosocial Test of General Strain Theory." *Journal of Criminal Justice* 43, no. 6 (2015): 487–97.

———. "Considering the Genetic and Environmental Overlap between Bullying Victimization, Delinquency, and Symptoms of Depression/Anxiety." *Journal of Interpersonal Violence* 31, no. 7 (2016): 1230–56.

———. "Guns, Gangs, and Genes: Evidence of an Underlying Genetic Influence on Gang Involvement and Carrying a Handgun." *Youth Violence and Juvenile Justice* 13, no. 3 (2015): 228–42.

Conrad, Peter. *The Medicalization of Society: On the Transformation of Human Conditions into Treatable Disorders.* Baltimore: Johns Hopkins University Press, 2008.

Cooper, Jonathon A., Anthony Walsh, and Lee Ellis. "Is Criminology Moving toward a Paradigm Shift? Evidence from a Survey of the American Society of Criminology." *Journal of Criminal Justice Education* 21, no. 3 (2010): 332–47.

Dartigues, Laurent. "Une irrésistible ascension? Le neurodroit face à ses critiques." *Zilsel*, no. 3 (2018): 63–103.

Darwin, Charles. *On the Origin of Species by Means of Natural Selection, or the Preservation of Favoured Races in the Struggle for Life*. London: John Murray, 1859.

Davie, Neil. "Born for Evil? Biological Theories of Crime in Historical Perspective." In *International Handbook of Criminology*, edited by Shlomo Giora Shoham, Paul Knepper, and Martin Kett, 23–50. Boca Raton, LA: CRC Press, 2010.

Davis, Darren W., and Brian D. Silver. "Stereotype Threat and Race of Interviewer Effects in a Survey on Political Knowledge." *American Journal of Political Science* 47, no. 1 (2003): 33–45.

Debailly, Renaud, and Mathieu Quet. "Passer les science & technology studies en revue-s: Une cartographie du champ par ses périodiques." *Zilsel*, no. 1 (2017): 25–54.

Degler, Carl N. *In Search of Human Nature: The Decline and Revival of Darwinism in American Social Thought*. New York: Oxford University Press, 1991.

de Kogel, C. H., and E. J. M. C. Westgeest. "Neuroscientific and Behavioral Genetic Information in Criminal Cases in the Netherlands." *Journal of Law and the Biosciences* 2, no. 3 (2016): 580–605.

DeLisi, Matt. "Revisiting Lombroso." In *The Oxford Handbook of Criminological Theory*, edited by Francis T. Cullen and Pamela Wilcox, 5–21. New York: Oxford University Press, 2013.

DeLisi, Matt, and Michael G. Vaughn. "Ingredients for Criminality Require Genes, Temperament, and Psychopathic Personality." *Journal of Criminal Justice* 43, no. 4 (2015): 290–94.

———, eds. *The Routledge International Handbook of Biosocial Criminology*. New York: Routledge, 2015.

DeLisi, Matt, John Paul Wright, Michael G. Vaughn, and Kevin M. Beaver. "Copernican Criminology." *The Criminologist* 34, no. 1 (2009): 14–16.

De Moor, Marleen H. M., Paul T. Costa, Antonio Terracciano, Robert F. Krueger, Eco J. C. De Geus, Tanaka Toshiko, Brenda W. J. H. Penninx, Tanu Esko, Pamela A. F. Madden, and Jaime Derringer. "Meta-analysis of Genome-Wide Association Studies for Personality." *Molecular Psychiatry* 17, no. 3 (2012): 337.

Denno, Deborah W. *Biology and Violence: From Birth to Adulthood*. Cambridge: Cambridge University Press, 1990.

———. "Courts' Increasing Consideration of Behavioral Genetics Evidence in Criminal Cases: Results of a Longitudinal Study." *Michigan State Law Review* 2011 (2011): 967–1047.

———. "Sex Differences in Cognition and Crime: Early Developmental, Biological, and Sociological Correlates." PhD diss., University of Pennsylvania, 1982.

Desmoulin-Canselier, Sonia. "La France à 'l'ère du neurodroit'? La neuro-imagerie dans le contentieux civil français." *Droit et Société* 101, no. 1 (2019): 115–35.

Dixon, Jo, and Alan J. Lizotte. "Gun Ownership and the 'Southern Subculture of Violence.'" *American Journal of Sociology* 93, no. 2 (1987): 383–405.

Dubois, Michel. "L'action scientifique: Modèles interprétatifs et explicatifs en sociologie des sciences." *L'Année Sociologique* 55, no. 1 (2007): 103–25.

Dubois, Michel, Yves Gingras, and Claude Rosental. "Pratiques et rhétoriques de l'internationalisation des sciences." *Revue Française de Sociologie* 57, no. 3 (2016): 407–15.

Dufresne, Martin. "How Does a Gene in a Scientific Journal Affect My Future Behavior?" In *Actor-Network Theory and Crime Studies: Explorations in Science and Technology*, edited by Dominique Robert and Martin Dufresne, 37–50. New York: Routledge, 2016.

Dufresne, Martin, and Dominique Robert. "La biographie d'un gène." *Déviance et Société* 41, no. 4 (2017): 593–619.

Duster, Troy. "Behavioral Genetics and Explanations of the Link between Crime, Violence, and Race." In *Wrestling with Behavioral Genetics: Science, Ethics, and Public Conversation*, edited by Erik Parens and Audrey R. Chapman, 150–75. Baltimore: Johns Hopkins University Press, 2006.

——. "Lessons from History: Why Race and Ethnicity Have Played a Major Role in Biomedical Research." *Journal of Law, Medicine and Ethics* 34, no. 3 (2006): 487–96.

——. "Selective Arrests, an Ever-Expanding DNA Forensic Database, and the Specter of an Early-Twenty-First-Century Equivalent of Phrenology." In *Tactical Biopolitics*, edited by Beatriz da Costa and Philip Kavita, 159–76. Cambridge, MA: MIT Press, 2008.

Ehrenberg, Alain. *La mécanique des passions: Cerveau, comportement, société*. Paris: Odile Jacob, 2018.

Eichelberger, Rebecca, and J. C. Barnes. "Biosocial Criminology." In *The Encyclopedia of Crime and Punishment*, edited by Wesley Jennings, 1–8. Hoboken, NJ: Wiley, 2015.

Ellis, Lee. "Criminal Behavior and r/k Selection: An Extension of Gene-Based Evolutionary Theory." *Deviant Behavior* 8, no. 2 (1987): 149–76.

——. "Genetics and Criminal Behavior Evidence through the End of the 1970s." *Criminology* 20, no. 1 (1982): 43–66.

Ellis, Lee, Jonathon A. Cooper, and Anthony Walsh. "Criminologists' Opinions about Causes and Theories of Crime and Delinquency: A Follow-Up." *The Criminologist* 24, no. 4 (2008): 3–6.

Ellis, Lee, and Anthony Walsh. "Gene-Based Evolutionary Theories in Criminology." *Criminology* 35, no. 2 (1997): 229–76.

Eme, Robert. "MAOA and Male Antisocial Behavior: A Review." *Aggression and Violent Behavior* 18, no. 3 (2013): 395–98.

Eysenck, Hans J., and Gisli H. Gudjonsson. *The Causes and Cures of Criminality.* New York: Plenum Press, 1989.

Fabiani, Jean-Louis. "À quoi sert la notion de discipline?" In *Qu'est-ce qu'une discipline,* edited by Jean Boutier, Jean-Claude Passeron, and Jacques Revel, 11–34. Paris: Éditions de l'EHESS, 2006.

Fabianic, David. "PhD Program Prestige and Faculty Location in Criminal Justice and Sociology Programs." *Journal of Criminal Justice Education* 22, no. 4 (2011): 562–77.

Faherty, Laura J., Ashley M. Kranz, Joshua Russell-Fritch, Stephen W. Patrick, Jonathan Cantor, and Bradley D. Stein. "Association of Punitive and Reporting State Policies Related to Substance Use in Pregnancy with Rates of Neonatal Abstinence Syndrome." *JAMA Network Open* 2, no. 11 (2019): e1914078–e1914078.

Fallin, Mallory, Owen Whooley, and Kristin Kay Barker. "Criminalizing the Brain: Neurocriminology and the Production of Strategic Ignorance." *BioSocieties* 14, no. 3 (2019): 438–62.

Farahany, Nita A. "Neuroscience and Behavioral Genetics in US Criminal Law: An Empirical Analysis." *Journal of Law and the Biosciences* 2, no. 3 (2016): 485–509.

Feeley, Malcolm M., and Jonathan Simon. "The New Penology: Notes on the Emerging Strategy of Corrections and Its Implications." *Criminology* 30, no. 4 (1992): 449–74.

Feresin, Emiliano. "Lighter Sentence for Murderer with 'Bad Genes.'" *Nature,* October 30, 2009.

Ferri, Enrico. "The Reform of Penal Law in Italy." *Journal of the American Institute of Criminal Law and Criminology* 12, no. 2 (1921): 178–98.

Fishbein, Diana H. "The Contribution of Refined Carbohydrate Consumption to Maladaptive Behaviors." PhD diss., Florida State University, 1981.

———. "The Psychobiology of Female Aggression." *Criminal Justice and Behavior* 19, no. 2 (1992): 99–126.

Fligstein, Neil, and Doug McAdam. *A Theory of Fields.* Oxford: Oxford University Press, 2012.

Forzano, Francesca, Pascal Borry, Anne Cambon-Thomsen, Shirley V. Hodgson, Aad Tibben, Petrus de Vries, Carla van El, and Martina Cornel. "Italian Appeal Court: A Genetic Predisposition to Commit Murder?" *European Journal of Human Genetics* 18, no. 5 (2010): 519–21.

Foucault, Michel. *Abnormal: Lectures at the College de France, 1974–1975*. London: Verso, 2016.

——. *Dits et écrits*. Vol. 1, *1954–1975*. Paris: Gallimard, 2001.

——. *Surveiller et punir: Naissance de la prison*. Paris: Gallimard, 1975.

Fourcade, Marion. *Economists and Societies: Discipline and Profession in the United States, Britain, and France, 1890s to 1990s*. Princeton, NJ: Princeton University Press, 2009.

Freese, Jeremy, and David Peterson. "The Emergence of Statistical Objectivity: Changing Ideas of Epistemic Vice and Virtue in Science." *Sociological Theory* 36, no. 3 (2018): 289–313.

Frickel, Scott. *Chemical Consequences: Environmental Mutagens, Scientist Activism, and the Rise of Genetic Toxicology*. Piscataway, NJ: Rutgers University Press, 2004.

Frickel, Scott, Mathieu Albert, and Barbara Prainsack, eds. *Investigating Interdisciplinary Collaboration: Theory and Practice across Disciplines*. New Brunswick, NJ: Rutgers University Press, 2016.

Frickel, Scott, and Neil Gross. "A General Theory of Scientific/Intellectual Movements." *American Sociological Review* 70, no. 2 (2005): 204–32.

Friedkin, Noah E., Anton V. Proskurnikov, Roberto Tempo, and Sergey E. Parsegov. "Network Science on Belief System Dynamics under Logic Constraints." *Science* 354, no. 6310 (2016): 321–26.

Frodeman, Robert, Julie Thompson Klein, and Carl Mitcham, eds. *The Oxford Handbook of Interdisciplinarity*. Oxford: Oxford University Press, 2010.

Frost, Natasha A., and Todd R. Clear. "Doctoral Education in Criminology and Criminal Justice." *Journal of Criminal Justice Education* 18, no. 1 (2007): 35–52.

Fujimura, Joan H. "Constructing 'Do-able' Problems in Cancer Research: Articulating Alignment." *Social Studies of Science* 17, no. 2 (1987): 257–93.

Gabrielli, William F., and Sarnoff A. Mednick. "Urban Environment, Genetics, and Crime." *Criminology* 22, no. 4 (1984): 645–52.

Gajos, Jamie M., Abigail A. Fagan, and Kevin M. Beaver. "Use of Genetically Informed Evidence-Based Prevention Science to Understand and Prevent Crime and Related Behavioral Disorders." *Criminology and Public Policy* 15, no. 3 (2016): 683–701.

Galton, Francis. "The History of Twins, as a Criterion of the Relative Powers of Nature and Nurture." *Fraser's Magazine* 12, no. 71 (1875): 566–76.

Gassin, Raymond. *Criminologie*. Paris: Dalloz, 2007.

Gaylin, Willard, and Ruth Macklin. "Pitfalls in the Pursuit of Knowledge." In *Violence and the Politics of Research*, edited by Willard Gaylin, Ruth Macklin, and Tabitha M. Powledge, 3–21. New York: Plenum Press, 1981.

Gellately, Robert, and Nathan Stoltzfus. *Social Outsiders in Nazi Germany.* Princeton, NJ: Princeton University Press, 2001.

Gibbons, Ann. "Tracking the Evolutionary History of a 'Warrior' Gene." *Science* 304, no. 5672 (2004): 818–19.

Gibbons, Donald C. *Delinquent Behavior.* Englewood Cliffs, NJ: Prentice Hall, 1970.

Gibson, Mary. *Born to Crime: Cesare Lombroso and the Origins of Biological Criminology.* Westport, CT: Praeger, 2002.

———. "Cesare Lombroso and Italian Criminology: Theory and Politics." In *Criminals and Their Scientists: The History of Criminology in International Perspective,* edited by Peter Becker and Richard F. Wetzell, 137–58. Cambridge: Cambridge University Press, 2006.

———. *Nati per il crimine: Cesare Lombroso e le origini della criminologia biologica.* Milan: Mondadori Bruno, 2004.

Gibson, Mary, and Nicole Rafter. "Editors' Introduction." In *Criminal Man,* edited by Mary Gibson and Nicole Rafter, 1–36. Durham, NC: Duke University Press, 2006.

Gieryn, Thomas F. "Boundaries of Science." In *Science and the Quest for Reality,* edited by Alfred I. Tauber, 293–332. Main Trends of the Modern World. Basingstoke: Palgrave Macmillan, 1995.

———. "Boundary-Work and the Demarcation of Science from Non-science: Strains and Interests in Professional Ideologies of Scientists." *American Sociological Review* 48, no. 6 (1983): 781–95.

———. *Cultural Boundaries of Science: Credibility on the Line.* Chicago: University of Chicago Press, 1999.

Gilbert, Walter. "A Vision of the Grail." In *The Code of Codes: Scientific and Social Issues in the Human Genome Project,* edited by Daniel J. Kevles and Leroy E. Hood, 83–97. Cambridge, MA: Harvard University Press, 1992.

Gingras, Yves. "Le champ scientifique." In *Lectures de Bourdieu,* edited by Frédéric Lebaron and Gérard Mauger, 279–94. Paris: Ellipses, 2012.

———. "Une controverse entre sociologues des sciences: Pourquoi les 'constructivistes' ne se comprennent plus." In *Controverses: Accords et désaccords en sciences humaines et sociales,* edited by Yves Gingras, 245–71. Paris: Éditions CNRS, 2014.

———. "La dynamique des controverses en sciences sociales et humaines." In *Controverses. Accords et désaccords en sciences humaines et sociales,* edited by Yves Gingras, 7–33. Paris: Éditions CNRS, 2014.

———. "Les formes spécifiques de l'internationalité du champ scientifique." *Actes de la Recherche en Sciences Sociales,* nos. 141–42 (2002): 31–45.

Golden, Charles J., Michele L. Jackson, Angela Peterson-Rohne, and Samuel T.

Gontkovsky. "Neuropsychological Correlates of Violence and Aggression: A Review of the Clinical Literature." *Aggression and Violent Behavior* 1, no. 1 (1996): 3–25.

Goldstone, Eli. "Why Can't We Stop Scrolling or Eating Haribo? Blame the Lizard Brain." *The Guardian*, January 9, 2022.

Goring, Charles. *The English Convict: A Statistical Study*. London: HMSO, 1913.

Gould, Stephen Jay. *The Mismeasure of Man*. New York: W. W. Norton, 1981.

Greely, Henry T., and Nita A. Farahany. "Neuroscience and the Criminal Justice System." *Annual Review of Criminology* 2 (2019): 451–71.

Griffiths, Anthony J. F., Jeffrey H. Miller, David T. Suzuki, Richard C. Lewontin, and William M. Gelbart. *An Introduction to Genetic Analysis*. 3rd ed. New York: W. H. Freeman, 2000.

Groner, Jonathan. "Lethal Injection and the Medicalization of Capital Punishment in the United States." *Health and Human Rights* 6, no. 1 (2002): 64–79.

Gross, Neil. *Why Are Professors Liberal and Why Do Conservatives Care?* Cambridge, MA: Harvard University Press, 2013.

Gross, Neil, and Solon Simmons, eds. *Professors and Their Politics*. Baltimore: Johns Hopkins University Press, 2014.

Guillo, Dominique. "Les usages de la biologie en sciences sociales." *Revue Européenne des Sciences Sociales* 50, no. 1 (2012): 191–226.

Harcourt, Bernard E. *Against Prediction: Profiling, Policing, and Punishing in an Actuarial Age*. Chicago: University of Chicago Press, 2007.

———. *The Illusion of Free Markets: Punishment and the Myth of Natural Order*. Cambridge, MA: Harvard University Press, 2011.

Harris, Kathleen Mullan, Carolyn Tucker Halpern, Andrew Smolen, and Brett C. Haberstick. "The National Longitudinal Study of Adolescent Health (Add Health) Twin Data." *Twin Research and Human Genetics* 9, no. 6 (2006): 988–97.

Heilbron, Johan, and Yves Gingras. "La résilience des disciplines." *Actes de la Recherche en Sciences Sociales*, no. 210 (2015): 4–9.

Herrnstein, Richard J., and Charles Murray. *The Bell Curve: Intelligence and Class Structure in American Life*. New York: Simon and Schuster, 1994.

Hess, David J. "Bourdieu and Science Studies: Toward a Reflexive Sociology." *Minerva* 49, no. 3 (2011): 333–48.

Heylen, Ben, Lieven J. R. Pauwels, Kevin M. Beaver, and Marc Ruffinengo. "Defending Biosocial Criminology: On the Discursive Style of Our Critics, the Separation of Ideology and Science, and a Biologically Informed Defense of Fundamental Values." *Journal of Theoretical and Philosophical Criminology* 7, no. 1 (2015): 83–95.

Hillbrand, Marc, and Reuben T. Spitz. "Cholesterol and Aggression." *Aggression and Violent Behavior* 4, no. 3 (1999): 359–70.

Hirschhorn, Joel N., and Mark J. Daly. "Genome-Wide Association Studies for Common Diseases and Complex Traits." *Nature Reviews Genetics* 6, no. 2 (2005): 95–108.

Hirschi, Travis, and Michael J. Hindelang. "Intelligence and Delinquency: A Revisionist Review." *American Sociological Review* 42, no. 4 (1977): 571–87.

Holbrook, J. Britt. "Peer Review." In *The Oxford Handbook of Interdisciplinarity*, edited by Robert Frodeman, Julie Thompson Klein, and Carl Mitcham, 321–32. Oxford: Oxford University Press, 2010.

Indiana University Center for Postsecondary Research. *The Carnegie Classification of Institutions of Higher Education*. Bloomington: Indiana University Center for Postsecondary Research, 2010.

Inizan, Maël. "Un juge italien découvre le gène du meurtre." *Libération*, October 28, 2009.

Inserm, ed. *Trouble des conduites chez l'enfant et l'adolescent*. Expertise Collective. Paris: Institut National de la Santé et de la Recherche Médicale, 2005.

Ioannidis, John P. A., Christine Q. Chang, Tram Kim Lam, Sheri D. Schully, and Muin J. Khoury. "The Geometric Increase in Meta-analyses from China in the Genomic Era." *PLoS One* 8, no. 6 (2013): e65602.

Ioannidis, John P. A., Robert Tarone, and Joseph K. McLaughlin. "The False-Positive to False-Negative Ratio in Epidemiologic Studies." *Epidemiology* 22, no. 4 (2011): 450–56.

Jeffery, Clarence R. "Biological Perspectives." *Journal of Criminal Justice Education* 4, no. 2 (1993): 291–306.

———. *Biology and Crime*. Beverly Hills, CA: Sage Publications, 1979. https://www.ncjrs.gov/App/Publications/abstract.aspx?ID=71010.

———. *Clarence R. Jeffery Interviewed by Diana Fishbein*. Tallahassee, FL, 1996. https://www.youtube.com/watch?v=vaaCAWOWUbk.

———. *Crime Prevention through Environmental Design*. Beverly Hills, CA: Sage Publications, 1977.

———. "Criminal Behavior and Learning Theory." *Journal of Criminal Law, Criminology and Police Science* 56 (1965): 294–300.

———. "Criminology as an Interdisciplinary Behavioral Science." *Criminology* 16, no. 2 (1978): 149–69.

———. "Prevention of Juvenile Violence." *Journal of Offender Rehabilitation* 28, nos. 1–2 (1998): 1–28.

———. "The Structure of American Criminological Thinking." *Journal of Criminal Law and Criminology* 46, no. 5 (1956): 658–72.

Jeffery, Clarence R., and Diane L. Zahm. "Crime Prevention through Environmental Design, Opportunity Theory, and Rational Choice Models." In *Routine Activity and Rational Choice*, edited by R. V. G. Clarke and Marcus Felson, 323–50. Piscataway, NJ: Transaction, 1993.

Kalifa, Dominique. *Les bas-fonds: Histoire d'un imaginaire.* Paris: Le Seuil, 2013.

Kaluszynski, Martine. "Identités professionnelles, identités politiques: Médecins et juristes face au crime au tournant du XIXème et du XXème siècle." In *Histoire de la criminologie française,* edited by Laurent Mucchielli, 215–35. Paris: L'Harmattan, 1994.

——. "Quand est née la criminologie? Ou la criminologie avant les Archives..." *Criminocorpus,* 2005. https://doi.org/10.4000/criminocorpus.126.

Keller, Evelyn Fox. "Nature, Nurture, and the Human Genome Project." In *The Code of Codes: Scientific and Social Issues in the Human Genome Project,* edited by Daniel J. Kevles and Leroy E. Hood, 281–99. Cambridge, MA: Harvard University Press, 1992.

Kennedy, Raymond, and Ruby Jo Reeves Kennedy. "Sociology in American Colleges." *American Sociological Review* 7, no. 5 (1942): 661–75.

Kevles, Daniel J. *In the Name of Eugenics: Genetics and the Uses of Human Heredity.* Berkeley: University of California Press, 1985.

Kim-Cohen, Julia, Avshalom Caspi, Alan Taylor, Brenda Williams, Rhiannon Newcombe, Ian W. Craig, and Terrie E. Moffitt. "MAOA, Maltreatment, and Gene–Environment Interaction Predicting Children's Mental Health: New Evidence and a Meta-analysis." *Molecular Psychiatry* 11, no. 10 (2006): 903–13.

Knepper, Paul, and Per Ystehede. Introduction to *The Cesare Lombroso Handbook,* edited by Paul Knepper and Per Ystehede, 1–7. New York: Routledge, 2013.

Knorr-Cetina, Karin D. *The Manufacture of Knowledge: An Essay on the Constructivist and Contextual Nature of Science.* Oxford: Pergamon Press, 1981.

Kobetz, Richard W. *Law Enforcement and Criminal Justice Education, Directory 1975–76.* Gaithersburg, MD: International Association of Chiefs of Police, 1975.

Koehler, Johann. "Development and Fracture of a Discipline: Legacies of the School of Criminology at Berkeley." *Criminology* 53, no. 4 (2015): 513–44.

Koshland, Daniel E. "The Rational Approach to the Irrational." *Science* 250, no. 4978 (1990): 189–89.

Krug, Etienne G., Linda L. Dahlberg, James A. Mercy, Anthony Zwi, and Rafael Lozano-Ascencio, eds. *World Report on Violence and Health.* Geneva: World Health Organization, 2002.

Kuhn, Thomas S. *The Structure of Scientific Revolutions.* Chicago: University of Chicago Press, 1962.

Ladd, Everett Carll, and Seymour Martin Lipset. *The Divided Academy: Professors and Politics.* New York: McGraw-Hill, 1975.

Lajeunesse, Maude. "Identité raciale et guerres culturelles dans le champ intellectuel américain: La controverse autour de Black Athena." In *Contro-*

verses: Accords et désaccords en sciences humaines et sociales, edited by Yves Gingras, 65–109. Paris: Éditions CNRS, 2014.

Larregue, Julien. "'Une bombe dans la discipline': L'émergence du mouvement génopolitique en science politique." *Social Science Information* 57, no. 2 (2018): 159–95.

———. "'C'est génétique': Ce que les twin studies font dire aux sciences sociales." *Sociologie* 9, no. 3 (2018): 285–304.

———. "Conservative Apostles of Objectivity and the Myth of a 'Liberal Bias' in Science." *American Sociologist* 49, no. 2 (2018): 312–27.

———. "La nouvelle orange mécanique: La contribution des bio-criminologues à la médicalisation du contrôle social." *Zilsel*, no. 5 (2019): 57–84.

Larregue, Julien, and Oliver E. Rollins. "Biosocial Criminology and the Mismeasure of Race." *Ethnic and Racial Studies* 42, no. 12 (2019): 1990–2007.

Laub, John H. *Criminology in the Making: An Oral History*. Boston: Northeastern University Press, 1983.

———. "Edwin H. Sutherland and the Michael-Adler Report: Searching for the Soul of Criminology Seventy Years Later." *Criminology* 44, no. 2 (2006): 235–58.

———. "The Life Course of Criminology in the United States: The American Society of Criminology 2003 Presidential Address." *Criminology* 42, no. 1 (2004): 1–26.

Laub, John H., and Robert J. Sampson. "The Sutherland-Glueck Debate: On the Sociology of Criminological Knowledge." *American Journal of Sociology* 96, no. 6 (1991): 1402–40.

Lebaron, Frédéric. *La croyance économique: Les économistes entre science et politique*. Paris: Seuil, 2000.

Lemerle, Sébastien. *Le cerveau reptilien: Sur la popularité d'une erreur scientifique*. Paris: CNRS Éditions, 2021.

———. *Le singe, le gène et le neurone: Du retour du biologisme en France*. Paris: Presses Universitaires de France, 2014.

———. "Trois formes contemporaines de biologisation du social." *Socio: La Nouvelle Revue des Sciences Sociales*, no. 6 (2016): 81–95.

Lemieux, Cyril. "À quoi sert l'analyse des controverses?" *Mil Neuf Cent: Revue d'histoire Intellectuelle*, no. 25 (2007): 191–212.

Lewenstein, Bruce V. "From Fax to Facts: Communication in the Cold Fusion Saga." *Social Studies of Science* 25, no. 3 (1995): 403–36.

Lindesmith, Alfred, and Yale Levin. "The Lombrosian Myth in Criminology." *American Journal of Sociology* 42, no. 5 (1937): 653–71.

Lloyd, Geoffrey Ernest Richard. *Magic, Reason, and Experience: Studies in the Origins and Development of Greek Science*. Cambridge: Cambridge University Press, 1979.

Lombroso, Cesare. *Criminal Man*. Translated by Mary Gibson and Nicole Rafter. Durham, NC: Duke University Press, 2006.

———. *L'homme criminel*. Paris: Alcan, 1887.

———. *L'uomo bianco e l'uomo di colore: Letture sull'origine et la varieta delle razze umane*. Padua: F. Sacchetto, 1871.

Louvel, Séverine. *The Policies and Politics of Interdisciplinary Research: Nanomedicine in France and in the United States*. London: Routledge, 2020.

Mann, Charles C. "War of Words Continues in Violence Research." *Science* 263, no. 5152 (1994): 1375.

Mark, Vernon, and Frank Ervin. *Violence and the Brain*. New York: Lippincott Williams and Wilkins, 1970.

Mayrhofer, Michaela Th., and Barbara Prainsack. "Being a Member of the Club: The Transnational (Self-) Governance of Networks of Biobanks." *International Journal of Risk Assessment and Management* 12, no. 1 (2009): 64–81.

McDermott, Rose, Dustin Tingley, Jonathan Cowden, Giovanni Frazzetto, and Dominic D. P. Johnson. "Monoamine Oxidase A Gene (MAOA) Predicts Behavioral Aggression Following Provocation." *Proceedings of the National Academy of Sciences* 106, no. 7 (2009): 2118–23.

McGuire, Wendy. "Cross-field Effects of Science Policy on the Biosciences: Using Bourdieu's Relational Methodology to Understand Change." *Minerva* 54, no. 3 (2016): 325–51.

Mednick, Sarnoff A., William F. Gabrielli, and Barry Hutchings. "Genetic Influences in Criminal Convictions: Evidence from an Adoption Cohort." *Science* 224, no. 4651 (1984): 891–94.

Medvetz, Thomas. "The Merits of Marginality: Think Tanks, Conservative Intellectuals, and the Liberal Academy." In *Professors and Their Politics*, edited by Neil Gross and Solon Simmons, 291–308. Baltimore: Johns Hopkins University Press, 2014.

Meloni, Maurizio. *Political Biology: Science and Social Values in Human Heredity from Eugenics to Epigenetics*. London: Palgrave Macmillan, 2016.

Merton, Robert K. "The Matthew Effect in Science." *Science* 159, no. 3810 (1968): 56–63.

Messner, Steven F. "Regional and Racial Effects on the Urban Homicide Rate: The Subculture of Violence Revisited." *American Journal of Sociology* 88, no. 5 (1983): 997–1007.

Milicia, Maria Teresa. "La protesta 'No Lombroso' sul Web. Narrative identitarie neo-meridionaliste." *Etnografia e Ricerca Qualitativa*, no. 2 (2014): 265–86.

Mitchell, Zack. "How Much Does It Cost to Rent a Mobile MRI?" Block Imaging, July 9, 2020. https://info.blockimaging.com/how-much-does-it-cost-to-rent-a-mobile-mri.

Moffitt, Terrie E. "The Neuropsychology of Juvenile Delinquency: A Critical Review." *Crime and Justice* 12 (1990): 99–169.

Moffitt, Terrie E., and Amber Beckley. "Abandon Twin Research? Embrace Epigenetic Research? Premature Advice for Criminologists." *Criminology* 53, no. 1 (2015): 121–26.

Moffitt, Terrie E., Donald R. Lynam, and Phil A. Silva. "Neuropsychological Tests Predicting Persistent Male Delinquency." *Criminology* 32, no. 2 (1994): 277–300.

Moffitt, Terrie E., and Sarnoff A. Mednick, eds. *Biological Contributions to Crime Causation*. New York: Springer, 1988.

Monneau, Emmanuel, and Frédéric Lebaron. "L'émergence de la neuroéconomie: Genèse et structure d'un sous-champ disciplinaire." *Revue d'Histoire des Sciences Humaines*, no. 25 (2012): 203–38.

Moran, Richard. "Biomedical Research and the Politics of Crime Control: A Historical Perspective." *Contemporary Crises* 2, no. 3 (1978): 335–57.

Morange, Michel. "Quelle place pour l'épigénétique?" *Médecine/Sciences* 21, no. 4 (2005): 367–69.

Morel, Stanislas. *La médicalisation de l'échec scolaire*. Paris: La Dispute, 2014.

Morin, Richard. "Leading with His Right." *Washington Post*, February 26, 2001, C2.

Morn, Frank. *Academic Politics and the History of Criminal Justice Education*. Westport, CT: Greenwood Press, 1995.

Morris, Albert. "The American Society of Criminology: A History, 1941–1974." *Criminology* 13, no. 2 (1975): 123–67.

Morris, Aldon D. *The Origins of the Civil Rights Movement*. New York: Simon and Schuster, 1986.

——. *The Scholar Denied: W. E. B. Du Bois and the Birth of Modern Sociology*. Oakland: University of California Press, 2017.

Mucchielli, Laurent, ed. *Histoire de la criminologie française*. Paris: Editions L'Harmattan, 1994.

——. "L'impossible constitution d'une discipline criminologique en France: Cadres institutionnels, enjeux normatifs et développements de la recherche des années 1880 à nos jours." *Criminologie* 37, no. 1 (2004): 13–42.

——. "Penser le crime: Essai sur l'histoire, l'actualité et les raisons de s'émanciper de quelques représentations persistantes en criminologie." In *Histoire de la criminologie française*, edited by Laurent Mucchielli, 453–505. Paris: L'Harmattan, 1994.

Mulkay, Michael J., and David O. Edge. "Cognitive, Technical and Social Factors in the Growth of Radio Astronomy." *Social Science Information* 12, no. 6 (1973): 25–61.

Munthe, Christian, and Susanna Radovic. "The Return of Lombroso? Ethical

Aspects of (Visions of) Preventive Forensic Screening." *Public Health Ethics* 8, no. 3 (2015): 270–83.

Musumeci, Emilia. "New Natural Born Killers? The Legacy of Lombroso in Neuroscience and Law." In *The Cesare Lombroso Handbook,* edited by Paul Knepper and Per Ystehede, 131–46. New York: Routledge, 2013.

Myren, Richard A. *Education in Criminal Justice.* Washington, DC: Coordinating Council for Higher Education, 1970.

Neale, Benjamin M., Sarah E. Medland, Stephan Ripke, Philip Asherson, Barbara Franke, Klaus-Peter Lesch, Stephen V. Faraone, et al. "Meta-analysis of Genome-wide Association Studies of Attention-Deficit/Hyperactivity Disorder." *Journal of the American Academy of Child and Adolescent Psychiatry* 49, no. 9 (2010): 884–97.

Nelkin, Dorothy, and M. Susan Lindee. *The DNA Mystique: The Gene as a Cultural Icon.* New York: W. H. Freeman, 1995.

Nelkin, Dorothy, and Judith P. Swazey. "Science and Social Control: Controversies over Research on Violence." In *Violence and the Politics of Research,* edited by Willard Gaylin, Ruth Macklin, and Tabitha M. Powledge, 143–62. New York: Plenum Press, 1981.

Nelson, Alondra. *Body and Soul: The Black Panther Party and the Fight against Medical Discrimination.* Minneapolis: University of Minnesota Press, 2011.

Nemeth, Charles P. *Anderson's Directory of Criminal Justice Education, 1991: Including Criminology and Justice-Related Programs.* Cincinnati, OH: Anderson, 1991.

Noble, Denis. *The Music of Life: Biology beyond Genes.* Oxford: Oxford University Press, 2008.

Noiriel, Gérard. *Le venin dans la plume: Édouard Drumont, Éric Zemmour et la part sombre de la République.* Paris: La Découverte, 2019.

Norcross, John C., Jessica L. Kohout, and Marlene Wicherski. "Graduate Study in Psychology: 1971–2004." *American Psychologist* 60, no. 9 (2005): 959–75.

Normandeau, André. "Le Prix Nobel de Criminologie dit le Prix de Stockholm en criminologie." *Revue de Science Criminelle,* no. 4 (2008): 1007–12.

Nye, Robert A. "Heredity or Milieu: The Foundations of Modern European Criminological Theory." *Isis* 67, no. 3 (1976): 335–55.

Oreskes, Naomi. "The Scientific Consensus on Climate Change." *Science* 306, no. 5702 (2004): 1686.

Oreskes, Naomi, and Erik M. Conway. *Merchants of Doubt: How a Handful of Scientists Obscured the Truth on Issues from Tobacco Smoke to Global Warming.* Bloomsbury: Bloomsbury Press, 2010.

Panofsky, Aaron. "Field Analysis and Interdisciplinary Science: Scientific Capital Exchange in Behavior Genetics." *Minerva* 49, no. 3 (2011): 295–316.

———. *Misbehaving Science: Controversy and the Development of Behavior Genetics*. Chicago: University of Chicago Press, 2014.

Payne, Brian K. "Expanding the Boundaries of Criminal Justice: Emphasizing the 'S' in the Criminal Justice Sciences through Interdisciplinary Efforts." *Justice Quarterly* 33, no. 1 (2016): 1–20.

Petit, Carlos. "Lombroso et l'Amérique." *Revue de Science Criminelle et de Droit Pénal Comparé* 1, no. 1 (2010): 17–29.

Pickersgill, Martyn. "Connecting Neuroscience and Law: Anticipatory Discourse and the Role of Sociotechnical Imaginaries." *New Genetics and Society* 30, no. 1 (2011): 27–40.

Pinch, Trevor. "Towards an Analysis of Scientific Observation: The Externality and Evidential Significance of Observational Reports in Physics." *Social Studies of Science* 15, no. 1 (1985): 3–36.

Platt, Tony, and Paul Takagi. "Biosocial Criminology: A Critique." *Crime and Social Justice*, no. 11 (1979): 5–13.

Plomin, Robert, John C. DeFries, Ian W. Craig, and Peter McGuffin. *Behavioral Genetics in the Postgenomic Era*. Washington, DC: American Psychological Association, 2003.

Potter, Marc, and Yves Gingras. "Des 'études' médiévales à l'"histoire' médiévale: L'essor d'une spécialité dans les universités québécoises francophones." *Revue d'Histoire de l'Éducation* 18, no. 1 (2006): 27–49.

President's Commission on Law Enforcement and Administration of Justice. *The Challenge of Crime in a Free Society*. Washington, DC: U.S. Goverment Printing Office, 1967.

President's Council of Advisors on Science and Technology. "Report to the President. Forensic Science in Criminal Courts: Ensuring Scientific Validity of Feature-Comparison Methods." Executive Office of the President of the United States, 2016. https://obamawhitehouse.archives.gov/sites/default /files/microsites/ostp/PCAST/pcast_forensic_science_report_final.pdf.

Pykett, Jessica. *Brain Culture: Shaping Policy through Neuroscience*. Bristol: Policy Press, 2015.

Rafter, Nicole. *The Criminal Brain: Understanding Biological Theories of Crime*. New York: NYU Press, 2008.

———. "Criminology's Darkest Hour: Biocriminology in Nazi Germany." *Australian and New Zealand Journal of Criminology* 41, no. 2 (2008): 287–306.

Ragouet, Pascal. "Les controverses scientifiques révélatrices de la nature différenciée des sciences? Les enseignements de l'affaire Benveniste." *L'Année Sociologique* 64, no. 1 (2014): 47–78.

———. *L'eau a-t-elle une mémoire? Sociologie d'une controverse scientifique*. Paris: Liber, 2016.

Raine, Adrian. *Adrian Raine Interviewed by Brendan Dooley*. Philadelphia, 2016. https://www.youtube.com/watch?v=SmcVIBA_d7w&t=2s.

———. *The Anatomy of Violence: The Biological Roots of Crime*. New York: Pantheon Books, 2013.

———. *Psychopathology of Crime*. New York: Academic Press, 1993.

Raine, Adrian, Patricia Brennan, David P. Farrington, and Sarnoff A. Mednick, eds. *Biosocial Bases of Violence*. New York: Springer, 1997.

Raine, Adrian, Monte S. Buchsbaum, Jill Stanley, Steven Lottenberg, Leonard Abel, and Jacqueline Stoddard. "Selective Reductions in Prefrontal Glucose Metabolism in Murderers." *Biological Psychiatry* 36, no. 6 (1994): 365–73.

Raine, Adrian, and Jiang Hong Liu. "Biological Predispositions to Violence and Their Implications for Biosocial Treatment and Prevention." *Psychology, Crime and Law* 4, no. 2 (1998): 107–25.

Raine, Adrian, and Peter H. Venables. "Classical Conditioning and Socialization—A Biosocial Interaction." *Personality and Individual Differences* 2, no. 4 (1981): 273–83.

Raoult, Sacha, and Bernard E. Harcourt. "The Mirror Image of Asylums and Prisons: A Study of Institutionalization Trends in France (1850–2010)." *Punishment and Society* 19, no. 2 (2017): 155–79.

Rappa, Michael, and Koenraad Debackere. "Youth and Scientific Innovation: The Role of Young Scientists in the Development of a New Field." *Minerva* 31, no. 1 (1993): 1–20.

Ratchford, Marie, and Kevin M. Beaver. "Neuropsychological Deficits, Low Self-Control, and Delinquent Involvement: Toward a Biosocial Explanation of Delinquency." *Criminal Justice and Behavior* 36, no. 2 (2009): 147–62.

Raynaud, Dominique. "La controverse entre organicisme et vitalisme: Étude de sociologie des sciences." *Revue Française de Sociologie* 39, no. 4 (1998): 721–50.

Rende, Richard D., Robert Plomin, and Steven G. Vandenberg. "Who Discovered the Twin Method?" *Behavior Genetics* 20, no. 2 (1990): 277–85.

Renisio, Yann, and Pablo Zamith. "Proximités épistémologiques et stratégies professionnelles." *Actes de la Recherche en Sciences Sociales*, no. 210 (2015): 28–39.

Renneville, Marc. *Le langage des crânes: Histoire de la phrénologie*. Paris: La Découverte, 2020.

———. "Rationalité contextuelle et présupposé cognitif: Le cas Lombroso." *Revue de Synthèse* 118, no. 4 (1997): 495–529.

Richardson, Sarah S. *The Maternal Imprint. The Contested Science of Maternal-Fetal Effects*. Chicago: University of Chicago Press, 2021.

Richardson, Sarah S., Cynthia R. Daniels, Matthew W. Gillman, Janet Golden,

Rebecca Kukla, Christopher Kuzawa, and Janet Rich-Edwards. "Society: Don't Blame the Mothers." *Nature* 512, no. 7513 (2014): 131–32.

Ripke, Stephan, Naomi R. Wray, Cathryn M. Lewis, Steven P. Hamilton, Myrna M. Weissman, Gerome Breen, Enda M. Byrne, et al. "A Mega-analysis of Genome-wide Association Studies for Major Depressive Disorder." *Molecular Psychiatry* 18, no. 4 (2013): 497–511.

Rocque, Michael, Chad Posick, and Shanna Felix. "The Role of the Brain in Urban Violent Offending: Integrating Biology with Structural Theories of 'the Streets.'" *Criminal Justice Studies* 28, no. 1 (2015): 84–103.

Rocque, Michael, Brandon C. Welsh, and Adrian Raine. "Biosocial Criminology and Modern Crime Prevention." *Journal of Criminal Justice* 40, no. 4 (2012): 306–12.

Rodgers, Joseph Lee, Maury Buster, and David C. Rowe. "Genetic and Environmental Influences on Delinquency: DF Analysis of NLSY Kinship Data." *Journal of Quantitative Criminology* 17, no. 2 (2001): 145–68.

Rojas, Fabio. *From Black Power to Black Studies: How a Radical Social Movement Became an Academic Discipline.* Baltimore: Johns Hopkins University Press, 2007.

Rollins, Oliver. *Conviction: The Making and Unmaking of the Violent Brain.* Stanford, CA: Stanford University Press, 2021.

Rose, Nikolas. "Normality and Pathology in a Biomedical Age." *Sociological Review* 57, no. 2, suppl. (2009): 66–83.

——. *The Politics of Life Itself: Biomedicine, Power, and Subjectivity in the Twenty-First Century.* Princeton, NJ: Princeton University Press, 2009.

Rose, Nikolas S., and Joelle M. Abi-Rached. *Neuro: The New Brain Sciences and the Management of the Mind.* Princeton, NJ: Princeton University Press, 2013.

Rossiter, Margaret W. "The Matthew Matilda Effect in Science." *Social Studies of Science* 23, no. 2 (1993): 325–41.

Rowe, David C. *Biology and Crime.* Los Angeles: Roxbury, 2002.

——. "Biometrical Genetic Models of Self-Reported Delinquent Behavior: A Twin Study." *Behavior Genetics* 13, no. 5 (1983): 473–89.

——. "Genetic and Environmental Components of Antisocial Behavior: A Study of 265 Twin Pairs." *Criminology* 24, no. 3 (1986): 513–32.

——. *The Limits of Family Influence: Genes, Experience, and Behavior.* New York: Guilford Press, 1994.

Rowe, David C., and David P. Farrington. "The Familial Transmission of Criminal Convictions." *Criminology* 35, no. 1 (1997): 177–202.

Rudo-Hutt, Anna S., Jill Portnoy, Frances R. Chen, and Adrian Raine. "Biosocial Criminology as a Paradigm Shift." In *The Routledge International Hand-*

book of Biosocial Criminology, edited by Matt DeLisi and Michael G. Vaughn, 22–31. Abingdon: Routledge, 2015.

Sampson, Robert J., and John H. Laub. "A Life-Course View of the Development of Crime." *Annals of the American Academy of Political and Social Science* 602, no. 1 (2005): 12–45.

Sapiro, Gisèle. "Le champ est-il national?" *Actes de la Recherche en Sciences Sociales*, no. 200 (2014): 70–85.

Savelsberg, Joachim J., and Robert J. Sampson. "Introduction: Mutual Engagement: Criminology and Sociology?" *Crime, Law and Social Change* 37, no. 2 (2002): 99–105.

Schilling, Catrina M., Anthony Walsh, and Ilhong Yun. "ADHD and Criminality: A Primer on the Genetic, Neurobiological, Evolutionary, and Treatment Literature for Criminologists." *Journal of Criminal Justice* 39, no. 1 (2011): 3–11.

Schug, Robert A., Gianni G. Geraci, Gabriel Marmolejo, Heather L. McLernon, Leidy S. Partida, and Alexander J. Roberts. "Neuroimaging and Antisocial Behavior." In *The Routledge International Handbook of Biosocial Criminology*, edited by Matt DeLisi and Michael G. Vaughn, 205–17. New York: Routledge, 2015.

Schwartz, Joseph A., Eric J. Connolly, Kevin M. Beaver, Joseph L. Nedelec, and Michael G. Vaughn. "Proposing a Pedigree Risk Measurement Strategy: Capturing the Intergenerational Transmission of Antisocial Behavior in a Nationally Representative Sample of Adults." *Twin Research and Human Genetics* 18, no. 6 (2015): 772–84.

Science for Peace and Security Programme. "Guidelines for Applicants: Advanced Study Institute." NATO/OTAN. Accessed February 7, 2020. http://www.nato.int/science/information_for_grantees/rtf/ASIGuidelines.pdf.

Sellin, Thorsten. *Culture Conflict and Crime: A Report of the Subcommittee on Delinquency of the Committee on Personality and Culture.* New York: Social Science Research Council, 1938.

Shapin, Steven. "Phrenological Knowledge and the Social Structure of Early Nineteenth-Century Edinburgh." *Annals of Science* 32, no. 3 (1975): 219–43.

Shapin, Steven, and Simon Schaffer. *Leviathan and the Air-Pump: Hobbes, Boyle, and the Experimental Life.* Princeton, NJ: Princeton University Press, 2011.

Shinn, Terry. "Formes de division du travail scientifique et convergence intellectuelle: La recherche technico-instrumentale." *Revue Française de Sociologie* 41, no. 3 (2000): 447–73.

Shinn, Terry, and Pascal Ragouet. *Controverses sur la science: Pour une sociologie transversaliste de l'activité scientifique.* Paris: Raisons d'agir, 2005.

Short, James F., Jr., and Lorine A. Hughes. "Criminology, Criminologists, and the Sociological Enterprise." In *Sociology in America: A History*, edited by Craig Calhoun, 605-38. Chicago: University of Chicago Press, 2007.

Showalter, David. "Misdiagnosing Medicalization: Penal Psychopathy and Psychiatric Practice." *Theory and Society* 48, no. 1 (2019): 67-94.

Siegel, Allan, and Majid B. Shaikh. "The Neural Bases of Aggression and Rage in the Cat." *Aggression and Violent Behavior* 2, no. 3 (1997): 241-71.

Simon, Jonathan. "Positively Punitive: How the Inventor of Scientific Criminology Who Died at the Beginning of the Twentieth Century Continues to Haunt American Crime Control at the Beginning of the Twenty-First." *Texas Law Review* 84 (2006): 2135-72.

Simons, Ronald L., Man Kit Lei, Steven R. H. Beach, Gene H. Brody, Robert A. Philibert, and Frederick X. Gibbons. "Social Environment, Genes, and Aggression Evidence Supporting the Differential Susceptibility Perspective." *American Sociological Review* 76, no. 6 (2011): 883-912.

Simons, Ronald L., Man Kit Lei, Eric A. Stewart, Steven R. H. Beach, Gene H. Brody, Robert A. Philibert, and Frederick X. Gibbons. "Social Adversity, Genetic Variation, Street Code, and Aggression: A Genetically Informed Model of Violent Behavior." *Youth Violence and Juvenile Justice* 10, no. 1 (2012): 3-24.

Sorensen, Jonathan R., Alan G. Widmayer, and Frank R. Scarpitti. "Examining the Criminal Justice and Criminological Paradigms: An Analysis of ACJS and ASC Members." *Journal of Criminal Justice Education* 5, no. 2 (1994): 149-66.

Steinmetz, Kevin F., Brian P. Schaefer, Rolando V. del Carmen, and Craig Hemmens. "Assessing the Boundaries between Criminal Justice and Criminology." *Criminal Justice Review* 39, no. 4 (2014): 357-76.

Stogner, John M. "DAT1 and Alcohol Use: Differential Responses to Life Stress during Adolescence." *Criminal Justice Studies* 28, no. 1 (2015): 18-38.

Stogner, John M., and Chris L. Gibson. "Stressful Life Events and Adolescent Drug Use: Moderating Influences of the MAOA Gene." *Journal of Criminal Justice* 41, no. 5 (2013): 357-63.

Sutherland, Edwin H. *Principles of Criminology*. Chicago: University of Chicago Press, 1924.

Sutherland, Edwin H., and Donald R. Cressey. *Criminology*. Philadelphia: Lippincott, 1978.

TenEyck, Michael, and J. C. Barnes. "Examining the Impact of Peer Group Selection on Self-Reported Delinquency A Consideration of Active Gene-Environment Correlation." *Criminal Justice and Behavior* 42, no. 7 (2015): 741-62.

Tibbetts, Stephen G., and Alex R. Piquero. "The Influence of Gender, Low

Birth Weight, and Disadvantaged Environment in Predicting Early Onset of Offending: A Test of Moffitt's Interactional Hypothesis." *Criminology* 37, no. 4 (1999): 843–78.

Tort, Patrick, Pascal Acot, Jean-Pierre Gasc, Jacques Gervet, Jean-Michel Goux, Georges Guille-Escuret, and André Langaney. *Misère de la sociobiologie*. Paris: Presses Universitaires de France, 1985.

Travis, G. D. L. "Replicating Replication? Aspects of the Social Construction of Learning in Planarian Worms." *Social Studies of Science* 11, no. 1 (1981): 11–32.

Tsouderos, Trine. "Exploring Links between Genes, Violence, Environment." *Chicago Tribune*, February 25, 2010.

Turkheimer, Eric. "Three Laws of Behavior Genetics and What They Mean." *Current Directions in Psychological Science* 9, no. 5 (2000): 160–64.

Vassos, E., D. A. Collier, and S. Fazel. "Systematic Meta-analyses and Field Synopsis of Genetic Association Studies of Violence and Aggression." *Molecular Psychiatry* 19, no. 4 (2014): 471–77.

Vaughn, Michael G. "Policy Implications of Biosocial Criminology." *Criminology and Public Policy* 15, no. 3 (2016): 703–10.

Vaughn, Michael G., Kevin M. Beaver, and Matt DeLisi. "A General Biosocial Paradigm of Antisocial Behavior: A Preliminary Test in a Sample of Adolescents." *Youth Violence and Juvenile Justice* 7, no. 4 (2009): 279–98.

Villa, Renzo. *Il deviante e i suoi segni: Lombroso e la nascita dell'antropologia criminale*. Milan: Angeli, 1985.

Vold, George B. "Edwin Hardin Sutherland: Sociological Criminologist." *American Sociological Review* 16, no. 1 (1951): 2–9.

Walsh, Anthony. *Biology and Criminology: The Biosocial Synthesis*. New York: Routledge, 2009.

——. "Companions in Crime: A Biosocial Perspective." *Human Nature Review* 2 (2002): 169–78.

——. "Genetic and Cytogenetic Intersex Anomalies: Can They Help Us to Understand Gender Differences in Deviant Behavior?" *International Journal of Offender Therapy and Comparative Criminology* 39, no. 2 (1995): 151–66.

Walsh, Anthony, and Kevin M. Beaver. *Biosocial Criminology: New Directions in Theory and Research*. New York: Routledge, 2008.

——, eds. *Biosocial Theories of Crime*. New York: Routledge, 2017.

Walsh, Anthony, and Lee Ellis. *Biosocial Criminology: Challenging Environmentalism's Supremacy*. New York: Nova Science, 2003.

——. "Ideology: Criminology's Achilles' Heel?" *Quarterly Journal of Ideology* 27, nos. 1–2 (2004): 1–25.

——. "Political Ideology and American Criminologists' Explanations for Criminal Behavior." *The Criminologist* 24 (1999): 26–27.

Walsh, Anthony, and John Paul Wright. "Biosocial Criminology and Its Discontents: A Critical Realist Philosophical Analysis." *Criminal Justice Studies* 28, no. 1 (2015): 124–40.

———. "Rage against Reason: Addressing Critical Critics of Biosocial Research." *Journal of Theoretical and Philosophical Criminology* 7, no. 1 (2015): 61–72.

Walters, Glenn D. "Measuring the Quantity and Quality of Scholarly Productivity in Criminology and Criminal Justice: A Test of Three Integrated Models." *Scientometrics* 102, no. 3 (2015): 2011–22.

———. "A Meta-analysis of the Gene-Crime Relationship." *Criminology* 30, no. 4 (1992): 595–614.

Walters, Glenn D., and Thomas W. White. "Heredity and Crime: Bad Genes or Bad Research?" *Criminology* 27, no. 3 (1989): 455–85.

Wannyn, William. "Le cerveau 'immature': Genèse et diffusion d'un nouveau discours social sur les jeunes délinquants aux États-Unis." PhD diss., Université de Montréal, 2021.

———. "Le marketing du neuromarketing: Enjeux académiques d'un domaine de recherche controversé." *Social Science Information* 56, no. 4 (2017): 619–39.

Ward, Richard A., and Vincent J. Webb. *Quest for Quality: A Publication of the Joint Commission on Criminology and Criminal Justice Education and Standards.* New York: University Publications, 1984.

Wasserman, David, and Robert Wachbroit, eds. *Genetics and Criminal Behavior.* Cambridge: Cambridge University Press, 2001.

Weir, Henriikka, and Anna E. Kosloski. "Melding Theoretical Perspectives: A Gendered Look at Low-Resting Heart Rate and Developmental Trajectories of Antisocial Behavior." *Criminal Justice Studies* 28, no. 1 (2015): 104–23.

Wells, Jessica, Todd Armstrong, Brian Boutwell, Danielle Boisvert, Shahida Flores, Mary Symonds, and David Gangitano. "Molecular Genetic Underpinnings of Self-Control: 5-HTTLPR and Self-Control in a Sample of Inmates." *Journal of Criminal Justice* 43, no. 5 (2015): 386–96.

Wheeler, David L. "University of Maryland Conference That Critics Charge Might Foster Racism Loses NIH Support." *Chronicle of Higher Education*, September 2, 1992, A6–A8.

Wilson, James Q., and Richard J. Herrnstein. *Crime and Human Nature: The Definitive Study of the Causes of Crime.* New York: Simon and Schuster, 1985.

Wolfgang, Marvin E. "Criminology and the Criminologist." *Journal of Criminal Law, Criminology, and Police Science* 54, no. 2 (1963): 155–62.

———. Foreword to *Biology and Violence: From Birth to Adulthood*, by Deborah W. Denno, ix–x. Cambridge: Cambridge University Press, 1990.

———. "Pioneers in Criminology: Cesare Lombroso (1835–1909)." *Journal of Criminal Law, Criminology, and Police Science* 52, no. 4 (1961): 361–91.

Wolfgang, Marvin E., and Franco Ferracuti. *The Subculture of Violence: Towards an Integrated Theory in Criminology.* New York: Routledge, 2010.

Wolfgang, Marvin E., Robert M. Figlio, and Terence P. Thornberry. *Evaluating Criminology.* New York: Elsevier, 1978.

Wolfgang, Marvin E., and Neil Alan Weiner, eds. *Criminal Violence.* Beverley Hills, CA: Sage Publications, 1982.

Wood, Christine V. "Knowledge Practices, Institutional Strategies, and External Influences in the Making of an Interdisciplinary Field: Insights from the Case of Women's and Gender Studies." *American Behavioral Scientist* 56, no. 10 (2012): 1301–25.

Work, Monroe N. "Crime among the Negroes of Chicago: A Social Study." *American Journal of Sociology* 6, no. 2 (1900): 204–23.

World Health Organization. "Forty-Ninth World Health Assembly." Geneva, 1996. https://apps.who.int/iris/bitstream/handle/10665/178941/WHA49_1996-REC-1_eng.pdf.

Wrede, Clint, and Richard Featherstone. "Striking Out on Its Own: The Divergence of Criminology and Criminal Justice from Sociology." *Journal of Criminal Justice Education* 23, no. 1 (2012): 103–25.

Wright, John Paul. "Inconvenient Truths: Science, Race and Crime." In *Biosocial Criminology: New Directions in Theory and Research,* edited by Anthony Walsh and Kevin Beaver, 137–53. New York: Routledge, 2008.

Wright, John Paul, J. C. Barnes, Brian B. Boutwell, Joseph A. Schwartz, Eric J. Connolly, Joseph L. Nedelec, and Kevin M. Beaver. "Mathematical Proof Is Not Minutiae and Irreducible Complexity Is Not a Theory: A Final Response to Burt and Simons and a Call to Criminologists." *Criminology* 53, no. 1 (2015): 113–20.

Wright, John Paul, and Kevin M. Beaver. "Do Parents Matter in Creating Self-Control in Their Children? A Genetically Informed Test of Gottfredson and Hirschi's Theory of Low Self-Control." *Criminology* 43, no. 4 (2005): 1169–1202.

Wright, John Paul, Kevin M. Beaver, Matt DeLisi, Michael G. Vaughn, Danielle Boisvert, and Jamie Vaske. "Lombroso's Legacy: The Miseducation of Criminologists." *Journal of Criminal Justice Education* 19, no. 3 (2008): 325–38.

Wright, John Paul, and Danielle Boisvert. "What Biosocial Criminology Offers Criminology." *Criminal Justice and Behavior* 36, no. 11 (2009): 1228–40.

Wright, John Paul, Danielle Boisvert, Kim Dietrich, and M. Douglas Ris. "The Ghost in the Machine and Criminal Behavior: Criminology for the 21st Century." In *Biosocial Criminology: New Directions in Theory and Research,* edited by Anthony Walsh and Kevin Beaver, 73–89. New York: Routledge, 2008.

Wright, John Paul, and Matt DeLisi. *Conservative Criminology: A Call to Restore Balance to the Social Sciences.* New York: Routledge, 2015.

Wright, John Paul, and Mark Alden Morgan. "Human Biodiversity and the Egalitarian Fiction." In *The Nurture versus Biosocial Debate in Criminology: On the Origins of Criminal Behavior and Criminality,* edited by Kevin Beaver, J. C. Barnes, and Brian Boutwell, 55–74. Thousand Oaks, CA: Sage Publications, 2015.

Wright, Richard A., and J. Mitchell Miller. "Taboo until Today? The Coverage of Biological Arguments in Criminology Textbooks, 1961 to 1970 and 1987 to 1996." *Journal of Criminal Justice* 26, no. 1 (1998): 1–19.

Zuckerman, Harriet. *Scientific Elite: Nobel Laureates in the United States.* New Brunswick: Transaction Publishers, 1996.

INDEX